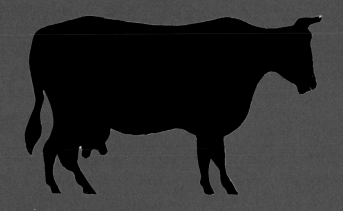

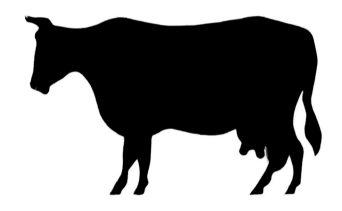

A Vision Becomes Reality

ISBN 91-630-4789-6

DISTRIBUTION: TETRA PAK INTERNATIONAL AB, CORPORATE COMMUNICATIONS, 221 86 LUND, SWEDEN

Lars Leander

Tetra Pak

A Vision Becomes Reality

A company
history with
a difference

Ruben Rausing, the man who created and inspired Tetra Pak, was born in 1895 in a village near the town of Helsingborg on the coast of southeast Sweden. This volume is dedicated to his memory in a spirit of warmth and thankfulness. Ruben Rausing was a forward-looking man, and Tetra Pak owes its existence to that quality in him – as does, indeed, the entire Tetra Laval Group.

Even so, this is neither a biography nor a conventional company history. Such projects are usually entrusted to experts recruited from the outside: economists, historians, or social scientists. We chose to proceed along different lines. The narrative is told from the inside, allowing the company to address the reader directly and as it were personally through the medium of its own employees. The responsibility for the compilation of this history-with-a-difference rested with Lars Leander, who in his turn received valuable assistance from Eric Rasmusson. Despite the extensive labours which have gone into this book, and for which we are most grateful, it has assumed the relaxed and informal tone of the narrative rather than the ponderous one of the thesis. We hope that all staff in the Tetra Laval Group will find it absorbing and worthwhile: they are its main addressees. Tetra Pak is not a company known for resting on its laurels or for lingering over the memories of past exploits. On the contrary, this was always a company determined to live in the present while looking towards the future. Hence, it may seem surprising that we decided to "look backward" at this point. However, we believe that by having the history of the company chronicled, we have done today's Tetra Laval employees a favour. After all, the past is a repository of important experiences as well as a springboard into the future – a future which opens a wide range of opportunities and possibilities for the new Group. In the days ahead, Tetra Laval will go on making significant collective contributions to solving the problems encountered in the vast project of feeding the world.

October 1995

HANS RAUSING

GAD RAUSING

A Vision Becomes Reality

Visions are like the rainbow – glistening but unattainable. Most of them remain in the realm of hope and fancy. But every once in a while, somebody manages to turn dreams into facts – a vision becomes reality.

The history of Tetra Pak is an example of such a process.

Many company histories have been written over the years. Solid, scholarly, and objective, they have often made interesting reading. This volume is, of course, only one of a large number of books about the evolution of a company. Unlike many of them, though, it does not delve into the depths of economic analysis; that sort of job is better undertaken by others. Instead, it has been informed by the desire to make events, processes, and people come alive – behind the scenes as well as on the centre of the stage.

The history of an enterprise is ultimately the story of the people who came together around a concept or an idea, and who then – as the word "enterprise" itself suggests – *took action* over this idea, making something of it. It is easy to identify the driving force behind the success of Tetra Pak. Without the audacity and powerful personal commitment of the Rausing family, the vision would not have become reality, and this tale would have remained untold. However, the present volume was never intended to be a family biography; rather, it was conceived as an unconventional narrative chronicling the birth, and the unique evolution, of a company.

Such a tale could not possibly be told without constant references to those dynamic properties which ultimately derive from the Rausing family. These properties have kept reproducing throughout the organisa-

tion, engendering echoes – and results. By the family's side, however, there were always pioneers and co-workers whose efforts were crucial to the success of the company. For obvious reasons, this publication is unable to record the names of all those who have given devoted service to the cause of Tetra Pak in the world: restrictions have been necessary. The presentation of a unique company, which so many have helped to create, has thus had to content itself with mentioning a few of the key figures involved. It would have been just as fair to include a host of other names; their labours were by no means less important, and they have all contributed to writing the exciting history of Tetra Pak.

Glimmering rainbows are all very well; but on its way towards the stars, the company has also – barely – survived sombre periods of technological failure, misfortune and disappointment, financial crisis, and the threat of bankruptcy.

We hope that this publication transmits an idea of that visionary power and determination which led to the conquest of a world market and the creation of an unparalleled industrial group in just a few decades.

We would also like to think that all those who belong to the new Tetra Laval Group today, and who read these lines, will take pride in their company and continue to defend its colours with similar power and determination.

Finally, we would be glad if "outsider" readers were to find a certain measure of enjoyment in perusing the volume, too. One of our ambitions has been to tell the story of Tetra Pak in a different way: after all, Tetra Pak *is* a company with a difference.

Lausanne, October 1995

LARS LEANDER

The Man from Raus

Raus is the name of a small parish on the west coast of Scania in southern Sweden, just south of Helsingborg. On the other side of the Sound between Sweden and Denmark stands the town of Elsinore, the outline of Kronborg Castle visible across the water. Further to the south, beyond the Isle of Hven, the Danish capital is faintly distinguishable in the warm haze of early summer.

The year is 1895 A.D.

In the fishing hamlet of Råå, August Andersson, master house-painter, and his wife Mathilda were running a small but successful business. Around midsummer that year, their first child was born, a boy named Ruben Anders.

The family was in a position to give both the eldest son and his two siblings a sound school education. Ruben went to Upper Secondary School in Helsingborg, achieving his first educational target – the certificate of education at the advanced level – in 1915.

Military service followed. By way of allusion to his origins, the young conscript was sometimes referred to as *rausingen*, "that fellow from Raus". The designation appealed to him, and at a later date he chose to adopt it as his family name. In so doing, he placed the parish of his birth on the world map of business enterprise.

With the support of his family and relatives, Ruben Rausing was able to matriculate at the Stockholm School of Economics and Business Administration in the autumn of 1916. In the spring of 1918, he graduated with First Class Honours. After a few months working for the Stockholm Enskilda Bank, he was taken on as an employee by SLT, as it then was – Sveriges Litografiska Tryckerier, "The Lithographic Printing Works of Sweden". Among 80 applicants, the company now known as Esselte picked Ruben Rausing.

Ruben Andersson,
aged about five,
in his Sunday best
for his first visit to
the photographer.

The Andersson home
at Matrosgatan, Råå.
The boy Ruben
is standing in front
of the corner of the
house and his mother
to the far right in
the photograph, taken
about 1910.

During his military
service Ruben, born
in the parish of Raus,
was often referred to as
the "rausing" lad – an
appellation which later
inspired the family name.

Class photo
from school
in Helsingborg.
The photograph
portrays the fifth
year, with Ruben
to the left in the
top row.

"I can still see Lisbeth as she was walking towards me, tall, straight, and slim. I remember the suntanned face, beautifully framed by her dark hair. She was lovely and soulful, spirit and matter at once. The impression she made was overwhelming, and I very soon realised that she was *the* woman in my life." That was how Ruben Rausing later described his wife, Elisabeth Varenius, born in 1894, from a vicar´s family in the province of Halland. Here is the smiling 24-year-old, just before their engagement.

Graduating from the venerable Helsingborg Upper Secondary School in the spring of 1915.

A photograph from the wedding in February 1921. To the right of Ruben are the parents of the bride and between them, in the background, Ruben's own father. The couple went to live in Bromma, outside Stockholm, where their eldest son Gad was born in 1922.

Family group in connection with the christening of Hans, the second son, in May 1926.

The three Rausing brothers: from right to left Gad, Hans, and Sven. The latter, the youngest son, has not worked in the company. Time: the late 1930s.

Columbia
University, New York.
Ruben is wearing the
classic mortarboard.
Spring 1920.

In an Overland
car, the two friends
Rausing and
Törnqvist went
off on a journey
of discovery along
the East Coast
of America. The
land of the future –
"God's own
country" – made
a strong impres-
sion on Ruben,
who once thought
of living there.
But fate had other
plans.

The First World War had just ended; the League of Nations had been created; the dream of perpetual peace was burgeoning; and the prospects for economic development looked bright. Hence it seemed natural to 24-year-old Ruben Rausing to utilise a School of Economics scholarship of SEK 3,000 for a trip to the United States, and in 1919 he set off for a course of advanced study at Columbia University, New York. The outcome – attained in record time – was a Master of Science degree in the field of economics, awarded in 1920. A fellow student from Sweden named Gerhard Törnqvist accompanied him on this journey, which was to prove instrumental to the future professional endeavours of both men. In due course, Törnqvist was to become Sweden's first Professor of Distribution Economics.

Ruben Rausing made use of the opportunities offered by his stay in the United States to study American big industry as well as the economic systems theories recently evolved in the States. His employer, SLT, had asked him to devote particular attention to the latest news in the field of packaging. The impressions he gained were revolutionary. They became a formative influence on those fresh approaches to industrial production which would one day transform both retailing and distribution in Sweden and abroad. Having returned to Sweden in the late summer of 1920, Ruben Rausing was rapidly promoted to Manager's Assistant and then Manager. In the late 1920s, people regarded him as an obvious candidate for the post of Managing Director. He was keen to start applying some of his recent American experiences at SLT, but his ideas failed to win support. When the new, large office complex of the group was being built in central Stockholm – a project entrusted to his management –, he wanted to streamline operations as well by introducing a number of well-advised organisational changes. The Board of Directors found some of his proposals too drastic, though. Ruben Rausing resigned from the company as an act of protest in the late autumn of 1929, not wishing to assume responsibility for an organisation and a business policy which he felt to be flawed.

During his years at SLT, Ruben Rausing had become closely acquainted with the industrialist Erik Åkerlund, and it was with the latter's help that he was able to put his ideas into practice in the early 1930s. This opportunity arose thanks to Ruben Rausing's becoming part-owner of a fairly small packing company in Malmö at that time. The company was restructured in December 1929, at which point it acquired the name Åkerlund & Rausing (Å&R). Erik Åkerlund had put up most of the capital, Ruben Rausing being in charge of company policies and management. For quite some time, the new company had to fight to survive and failed to yield any profits. After a couple of years his partner grew tired of it, and Ruben Rausing bought him off. In the spring of 1933, he was sole owner of the new company, for which he alone was responsible – at a time when the world economy was in one of the worst "troughs" it has ever known.

Now, at last, the right moment had arrived for Ruben Rausing to start turning his American impressions into Swedish industrial reality. Resolutely, he began to build up a packaging industry where innovative forces prevailed from the outset. Å&R was soon to make essential contributions to the restructuring of retailing in Sweden – a process of modernisation which would ultimately lead to self-service, supermarkets, and hypermarkets. The first target consisted in simplifying the existing patterns of distribution, replacing the sales of unpacked and unwrapped goods by selling packaged foods designed for customer convenience – flour, sugar, salt, maybe even milk one day ... A period of feverish technological development began, chiefly inspired by a legendary figure in the history of Åkerlund & Rausing, First Foreman Nils Andersson. He had started out as a typographer's apprentice, but he was a natural talent in the field of technology, and it did not take long for him to become, in practice, chief designer at Å&R. The new company flourished, though its liquidity was under strain throughout most of the 1930s. This was the soil which nourished the idea of creating a milk package. Ruben Rausing's interest had been kindled at an early stage, as is evident in his instruction to a young employee named Holger Crafoord, on the eve of a trip to the United States in 1932, to *bring samples of milk cartons manufactured in that country*".

In the meantime, Åkerlund & Rausing continued its pioneering efforts in the Swedish packaging industry. When the company required space for expansion, the City of Malmö proved less than accommodating. Ruben Rausing then decided to move operations to Lund, where the company was able to open its new plant in August 1939, on the outbreak of the Second World War. Despite the exigencies of war, "Å&R – The Packaging Company", as it came to be called, continued and steadily expanded its activities. Pre-packaged consumer units for foodstuffs helped in solving tricky distribution problems during the years of rationing. Certain manufacturing elements were modified as a result of the times of crisis, which created a need of special packs for new purposes:

Well into the 1950s, the glass bottle was the number one milk package in Sweden, entailing heavy, strenuous jobs within dairy walls as well as among distributors. When Tetra Pak came into being, a far-reaching restructuring of handling and trade ensued.

field provisions, first-aid kits, ammunition, and technical products. Research and development went on unabated. New, elegant packaging solutions were presented; so were manufacturing machines, both for materials and packages.

There was one project which was never far from Ruben Rausing's thoughts: How were "loose" milk and the glass bottle to be replaced? How could a sufficiently cheap and generally satisfactory package be created for such a vital daily food, with such small profit margins and special hygienic requirements? These questions had been put to Å&R staff on a number of occasions. The samples brought back from the United States were no good; such cartons, and the necessary packaging machinery, turned out to be far too expensive for conditions in Sweden. There must be another solution – a new, better, and cheaper one.

This publication was not conceived as a biography; but before the tale moves on to later periods, it cannot but dwell for a moment on "the man behind it all". It makes sense to try to capture something of the essential personality of Ruben Rausing, his ideas and his values, as all this came to exert a powerful influence on his life's work – first at Åkerlund & Rausing, then at Tetra Pak. This is not an easy undertaking; Ruben Rausing emerged as *the* industrial innovator in postwar Sweden at quite an early stage, and much was written about him in that capacity even during his lifetime. In other words, most of the story has been told before; but it can bear repetition – especially for readers belonging to a younger generation.

The preceding pages looked briefly at the factual, external circumstances of Ruben Rausing's youth, studies, and early work. Behind these plain and straightforward facts we catch a glimpse of a wide-ranging and singular intelligence. He was lucky in inheriting many valuable qualities from both sides of his family. Ruben Rausing's father, a devoutly religious man, worked in his chosen occupation with energy and success; he was also involved in local politics as a Liberal. His mother was a practical and resourceful housewife, hardworking and with a keen eye for economical factors – all qualities that benefited the family business.

Ruben Rausing was himself the first to recognise the importance of inherited characteristics: *"Everything is foreordained. Your genes are your destiny."* His early interest in genetics was sufficiently great for him to consider studying natural science and medicine before deciding to opt for an economic and industrial career. One might perhaps wonder how the conception of genetic "predestination" can be reconciled with that of free

Logotype from the early years of Åkerlund & Rausing. The firm, founded in 1929, soon became one of the leading packaging companies in Europe.

will, as well as with the drive and dynamic entrepreneurship which guided him throughout his life. The answer is a simple and logical one: *"The abilities of each individual are governed by his genetic make-up; but this make-up also comprises the capacity – or incapacity – to grasp random opportunities."* The active life of Ruben Rausing was to become one unbroken example of this very characteristic: perceiving possibilities and seizing them in an original, visionary manner; being able to collaborate with fate. Or, in his own words: *"You must have the instinct and the courage it takes to pick the right line of business."* As we know, he chose the packaging industry and the field of distribution, and not only because that was an undeveloped line of business in which everything remained to be done. He endeavoured to *"create something new, but something useful, too."*

At this point, a quotation from Ruben Rausing's policy statement, written in the 1930s, seems appropriate. It was originally concerned with the aims and priorities of Åkerlund & Rausing, but the ideas it contains have not aged; they are equally applicable to Tetra Pak today:

"The conception behind a company and the principles that govern its operations form the foundation on which it is constructed. From that basis, the company derives its orientation, ambition, spirit, and life; it becomes a

No great man escapes the sharp eye and pencil of the caricaturist. Picture presented by Ruben Rausing to a public collection of portraits in Lund.

21

The Swedish monarch of that time, King Gustaf VI Adolf, on a visit to Lund in the summer of 1963. Here flanked by Ruben and Hans Rausing. "Tetra Pak – Purveyor to the Royal Swedish Court!"

living organism instead of an inanimate mass. Its physical shape, buildings, machinery, and working procedures are all built according to the guidelines suggested by the basic conception. The people employed by the company are moulded by it in their work. (...) If the company is able to create a long-term need, the fundamental conception was the right one, and the company has fulfilled a function in the social fabric. The conception underlying our company is a very simple one: to rationalise the distribution of goods by way of consumer packages adapted to their purposes and by proper transport packing."

The emphasis on the company as a living organism is a significant one; it implies respect for the people concerned, indicating the importance of having highly motivated employees with a sense of joint responsibility for performing a major task. The English words "company, companion" originate in the Latin "cum" and "panis" – a group of people sharing their daily bread. Being able to pick the right "companions", to gather employees around elevated aims, and to inspire them with enthusiasm is a great talent, and Ruben Rausing had plenty of it. Many people have testified to his interested and understanding attitude to the company's employees.

"Have faith in your colleagues and co-workers – we cannot function without trust." To Ruben Rausing, freedom of action and confidence were vital concepts. He was not the sort of person who would insist on doing

22

everything himself, thereby preventing colleagues from developing towards greater maturity and competence. Quite the reverse: it was part of his basic attitude not to do things which others could do just as well or better. He expected a great deal from those who worked with him, however: they must know what they wanted, and they had to be able to present a simple, clear, and well-founded argument on all matters, great and small. A continuous testing of thoughts and ideas became a way of keeping issues moving. Some favourite expressions of his may be quoted by way of illustration: *"How do you know it won´t work? Have you really tried? I have a feeling you don´t know what you´re talking about. There´s no substance to your line of reasoning."* Ruben Rausing would offer resistance and provocation as a means of invigorating the discussion. This attitude instilled the good habit of calling matters into question in the entire organisation. It would not do to take things for granted; problems had to be turned inside out and upside down before the best possible decisions could be made.

Imagination, inventiveness, and free thinking were greatly influenced by Ruben Rausing's own conviction: *"Leading business companies are based on ideas, and it is by virtue of good ideas that a small nation can assert itself in the world."* The development of Åkerlund & Rausing and Tetra Pak as business companies has been characterised by this sparkling shower of hunches, thoughts, and ideas – some of them strokes of genius, others, naturally enough, less tenable. The important thing was to search and try out, and not to fear failure. After all, there is a saying according to which a person who never failed never tried hard enough. Where would Tetra Pak have been without this persuasion? The answer is a simple one – nowhere.

Even so, ideas are not enough; there must be funds enabling them to be put into practice, too. Ruben Rausing would always insist that an innovative company can only survive if it has a high earning potential in its own right; a slight error in percentage calculations may be decisive: *"The difference between success and failure is minute."* The time when Tetra Pak would be able to boast of healthy profits and good results was still far ahead, however. We are as yet only at the very beginning of the adventure which was to lead up to a feat of industrial entrepreneurship whose dimensions nobody could even imagine at this point – the vision which became reality.

Ruben Rausing giving a historical presentation before a large crowd of spectators during the 25th anniversary of Tetra Pak, in September 1977. He spent the last 15 years of his life abroad and died in August 1983, aged 88.

Ideas Take Shape

"A package with a shape you only ever saw in geometry classes, manufactured by a machine of whose appearance nobody had even the faintest idea, made from a material that did not exist – *and* intended for one of our most vulnerable foodstuffs, milk."

Those were said to be the original conditions in a nutshell.

Despite the international economic difficulties of the 1930s, Åkerlund & Rausing continued to develop in such a satisfactory manner that the company soon needed larger premises for its expanding operations. The new factory in Lund was opened just as a new, global political crisis began. The war affected the company in more ways than one. For instance, the increasing shortage of glass and thin sheet-metal brought forth the idea of the cylindrical paper container called Satello, which remained a major item even after the war. Alongside its normal production, Å&R also delivered to the Royal Swedish Board of War Supplies.

During the war years, Ruben Rausing felt obliged to serve the best interests of society. He was elected to leading posts on Government-administered committees and commissions of inquiry. In 1939–40, he headed the Price Department of the Industrial Commission, going on to become Chairman of the National Price Control Board in 1941–42. In addition, he chaired the Traffic Inquiry Commission of 1944. These commitments, and others too, did not prevent him from devoting much energy and interest to the development of Åkerlund & Rausing. He was assisted by a small group of highly competent supporting staff – foremost among them Holger Crafoord, employed in 1930, Deputy Managing Director from 1939, and Managing Director from 1946. For many years, Crafoord was Ruben Rausing's closest associate, and he came to play a leading role in the development both of the Å&R Group and of Tetra Pak. Other names that should be mentioned in this context are Gunnar Brime, Torsten Jeppsson, Ebbe Nihlberg, Börje Svenby, and Erik Torudd

Holger Crafoord's employment began in 1930, just after the creation of Åkerlund & Rausing. For many years he was Managing Director and part-owner of that company, and for more than three decades he was the partner and confidant of Ruben Rausing.

Detail from Satello manufacturing, the inside waxing process.

The Satello paper jar, developed during the war, was regarded as a possible model for a milk package, but these ideas were never realised.

– these men, and some others, belonged to that inner circle which ensured the rapid growth of post-war Å&R and made it into one of the the leading packaging companies in Europe.

The idea of a milk package was firmly entrenched in the company, and several of its employees had been at work on the problem for some time. However, quite a few of them were absent on military duty, and during the war years project continuity and follow-up activities left something to be desired. The man who headed the laboratory, Stig Sunner – who subsequently became Professor of Thermochemistry at Lund University – was thus away in the Armed Forces on the day in February 1944 when Ruben Rausing, paying a visit to the laboratory, gave the staff to under-

Ruben Rausing addressing words of encouragement to one of his record-milking cows at Simontorp Farm, outside Lund. Picture taken in the autumn of 1957.

stand that it was high time something tangible came out of those proposals that had been bandied about for years. *"Especially as I've just purchased a large number of cows; they're out there waiting to be milked"*, he added – by way of a jest, but not without a touch of grimness.

The recipient of this message was Erik Wallenberg, Laboratory Assistant, whom Sunner had already assigned to the matter of the milk receptacle. Up to that point, efforts had concentrated on various conventional shapes, square or rectangular. Galvanised into decisive action, Wallenberg began to think along the lines of a cylindrical shape – perhaps unconsciously influenced by the above-mentioned Satello container. What if the lid of a cylinder were to be replaced by a compressed, sealed top? And *what* if the round bottom, too, were scrapped in favour of a seal placed at right angles to the one at the top? The egg of Columbus, but in the form of a geometrical figure – the tetrahedron!

Wallenberg realised that this shape, familiar and yet unconventional, might solve the fundamental problem with which so many had struggled so hard for such a length of time. Having trimmed the shape in the laboratory and created a more equilateral tetrahedron, and encouraged by his superior Stig Sunner, Wallenberg ventured upstairs into the Managing Director's office to show Mr Rausing his new, harebrained creation. The only thing that might be said in his defence is that he was sufficiently young, new on the job, and unhampered by technological know-how to dare to suggest such a scheme. Or, as Ruben Rausing was later to put it, *"This is what you get for hiring people who have no idea of how a package is made and what it ought to look like!"*

It would be an exaggeration to say that the package was greeted with overwhelming enthusiasm. Even so, Ruben Rausing scrutinised the proposal and then determined that this was the avenue which the company was going to pursue. The degree of seriousness behind this decision is emphasised by the fact that the very first application for a patent was submitted to the Royal Swedish Patent and Registration Office only a few weeks later, on 27 March 1944. The

Erik Wallenberg, at that time an Å&R laboratory technologist, was the man behind the fundamental invention of the tetrahedron as a packaging shape.

Small picture: Stig Sunner managed the Å&R laboratory and watched the birth of the tetrahedron at close quarters.

PATENT Nº 131 599 **SVERIGE**   KLASS 81 c:27

BESKRIVNING
OFFENTLIGGJORD AV KUNGL
PATENT- OCH REGISTRERINGSVERKET

BEVILJAT DEN 8 FEBRUARI 1951
PATENTTID FRÅN DEN 27 MARS 1944
PUBLICERAT DEN 2 MAJ 1951

Ans. den ¹¹/₁, 1944, nr 2517/1944.   *Härtill en ritning.*

R. RAUSING, LUND.
Sätt att framställa en tetraederformig förpackning jämte på detta sätt framställd förpackning.
Uppfinnare: K. E. S. Wallenberg.

Föreliggande uppfinning har till ändamål att skaffa en till sin konstruktion ytterst enkel och i tillverkning billig men likväl förhållandevis formbeständig förpackning av papper eller annat lämpligt böjligt eller vikbart material. Ytterligare ett ändamål med uppfinningen är, att denna förpackning skall kunna göras av ett ämne i ett stycke, vilket från plant utbrett eller plant hopvikt tillstånd låter sig enkelt och snabbt överföra till form av den önskade förpackningen. För des-

papper eller liknande, som kan vara impregnerat eller annorlunda behandlat, t. ex. kascherat, allt efter önskan eller allt efter vad det speciella användningsändamålet kräver. Ämnet till hylsan blir då så enkelt som ett alldeles rektangulärt pappersark, som kan tillskäras ur en pappersbana utan minsta pappersspill. Den enligt uppfinningen framställda tetraederformiga förpackningen är överraskande praktisk och lämplig för många varor, däribland i synnerhet även rinnande

The first patent document concerning the new package.

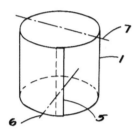

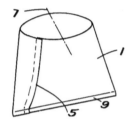

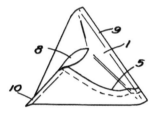

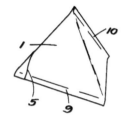

The principle of the original patent: the step-by-step shaping process, proceeding from a flat sheet of paper.

tetrahedron, a shape created by Nature herself in the crystallisation of most mineral substances, became the core – the diamond crystal, as it were – of what was to become a global business company.

With hindsight, one might speculate about who did what at this initial stage, what amounted to rational, purposeful action, and what intuitive, even fortuitous, components formed part of the creation process. A number of partial answers may be given; but the fact remains: it was Erik Wallenberg who hit on the brilliant idea of applying the tetrahedron shape to a package, *and* Ruben Rausing had the insight, courage, and determination required to pursue this original – to put it mildly – proposal. The credit for the basic invention belongs to Erik Wallenberg alone. Quite properly, he was therefore to receive the Gold Medal of the Royal Swedish Academy of Engineering Sciences from the hand of His Majesty King Carl XVI Gustaf in October 1991.

Once the decision to develop the tetrahedron system had been made, the real difficulties began. How was the package to be shaped, filled, and sealed in the course of automatic operation? What sort of paper would be good enough, and how was the receptacle to be made impermeable to liquid? The questions seemed endless. True, Å&R commanded solid expertise in the field of packing; but so far no work had been done on the packaging of liquids except at the experimental level. Nobody had any conception of what a suitable filling machine might look like, and plastic-coated paper was as yet an unknown concept. It was necessary to begin from scratch, in more ways than one.

With regard to machine design, experts both within and outside the company were appealed to for assistance. A number of solutions were discussed, among them proposals from the diligently consulted First Foreman, Nils Andersson. External staff were recruited, too, and at first everybody was working according to the idea that the machine would function in a staccato process: first, it was to make packages from paper materials, one at a time; then it would fill and finally seal them. However, the tetrahedron shape does not readily lend itself to that kind of processing. The idea that resolved the problem – one might perhaps say that it was inherent in the very shape – emerged during the next stage of development: it amounted to starting off with paper cylinders and then shaping, filling, sealing, and separating packages in a continuous process. Not until then was the conceptional basis created for that machine design which was to be Harry Järund's major contribution to the success of Tetra Pak.

As the machine was being developed, the questions surrounding the packaging material had to be solved, too: one thing presupposed the other. It had already turned out not to be so easy to pack flour, sugar, and salt; but none of these things posed anything like the challenge of milk. As time went by, a systematic research programme was evolved; but it would take long before an even half-way suitable material had emerged. In the meantime, everybody was pushing ahead in a cheerful "as-if" spirit; it was assumed that the problem of the material would be solved, although nobody knew exactly how. This approach has always been characteristic of the spirit at Tetra Pak, both with regard to technical problems and other difficulties. Not that the issues were ever ignored or put aside in the pious hope that *it'll sort itself out*. The problems were regarded with the utmost seriousness, but nobody allowed himself to become unduly depressed by dull cares along the way. From first to last, a fundamentally optimistic attitude has prevailed in the company, a factor which has provided invaluable assistance in many a bad moment.

Towards the end of the 1940s, Ruben Rausing's sons Gad (born in 1922) and Hans (born in 1926) became increasingly involved in Å&R activities. Their situation was formalised by regular employment, in 1948 for Gad Rausing and a year later for Hans Rausing. As a result, a small group came into being, a group whose intimate collaboration would lead to the unique growth of Tetra Pak. For many years, the responsibility for managing the new company was shared among the members of the family and some of their very closest associates at Å&R – particularly Holger Crafoord and Erik Torudd, both of whom made inestimable contributions during the construction phase of the new company. As the years went by, more and more of the total responsibility came to rest on the Rausing family. In 1954, Hans was appointed Managing Director of the new company, Gad becoming Deputy Managing Director that same year – at a point when official records stated that Tetra Pak only had six employees. Subsequent figures and developments in general tell a plain tale of sons taking good care of the inheritance from their father.

The Rausing family has never set store by the glaring light of publicity; a constant presence, they have been working under a veil of invisibility. Consequently, the brothers Hans and Gad Rausing are not widely known outside the company and their circle of friends. They are only names to many people in the large Tetra Pak Group, too, especially as they retired from active work in the Group a couple of years ago. At this point, it might be appropriate to supply some "background" on the two of them

First Foreman Nils Andersson, the erstwhile typographer's apprentice who became the technological genius of Å&R and the man behind countless machine designs.

Gad (left) and Hans Rausing at the time of their entry into the world of business, in 1950.

29

The Rausing
brothers posing
proudly in front
of the new Lund
office building,
erected in 1965
close by the factory
which was built in
1956.

in the form of thumb-nail sketches. They both began their careers at a very young age; they have truly grown into the company, and the company has grown along with them. Accordingly, they have had unique opportunities to gain knowledge from the inside while acquiring competent global overviews which have guided the development of the company.

Gad, the elder brother, studied chemistry and became Laboratory Manager at Åkerlund & Rausing as soon as he had completed his first academic degree in 1948. From 1949 to 1954, he was in charge of the group responsible for evolving suitable materials for the new tetrahedron package. The achievements of the group – both in the field of paper technology and in that of polymer research – are outlined in subsequent chapters. Where continued and more advanced studies were concerned, a consuming interest in archaeology gradually came to take over. Despite daily responsibilities in the business, involving many and long journeys, he found time to devote to research: *"Well, you get a fair number of left-over hours in airports and planes."* These odd moments were put to good use; they led to a Ph. D. in 1967, followed by a Readership at Lund University.

30

Alongside his commitments in an ever-growing group of companies, Gad Rausing has managed to continue to pursue his interests in the Humanities at an advanced scholarly level – no mean feat for an industrial leader. A diligent lecturer, he has amassed a varied and comprehensive list of publications. In recent years, he has given strong support to the archaeological excavations of the 10th-century Viking trading centre Birka, near Stockholm. One example of his quick repartee is supplied by his response to the concept of sponsoring, ubiquitous in the world of sport: *"Three cheers for Birka, our very own football team!"* An unusual range of knowledge has contributed to creating goodwill and making bridges in many business contexts all over the world. For instance, Gad Rausing became the member of the top management at Tetra Pak who succeeded in establishing fruitful contacts with political key figures on the other side of the Chinese wall. This, again, was a notable achievement, not least because the persons concerned were difficult to gain access to. There will be reason to return to this topic.

Many people throughout the years have testified to Gad Rausing's ability to "hold forth" in an intelligible way, capturing the interest of any audience.

A selection of pictures
from an album
of Gad Rausing's
activities: discus-
sions with scientists
and customers,
lectures, factory
openings. Here
supervising the
start-up of a new
machine in the Spanish
Tetra Pak plant.

Brother Hans' academic studies resulted in a degree in 1948. The Russian language was one of its components – an unusual choice at this time. He has continued to keep his favourite language alive, carrying Russian fiction in his briefcase on many a trip. It was hence appropriate that Hans Rausing should become the company's groundbreaker in the Russian market. At an early stage, he pointed to the importance of assisting the then Soviet Union in building up its own domestic industry: *"This ought to be a joint moral responsibility for European business managers and governments."* He has been keen to lead the way by means of the major Tetra Pak investments in, above all, Russia and the Ukraine. His efforts, which amount to a pioneering achievement in the history of Western industry, are described elsewhere in this book.

In 1954, Hans Rausing was appointed Managing Director of Tetra Pak. He was Group President for just over 30 years, winning fame as the astute and forward-looking leader of one of Sweden's most expansive industrial companies in modern times. In September 1985, he was appointed Chairman of the Board; but in connection with the acquisition of the Alfa Laval Group, he resumed the function of President of the new, greatly expanded Group. Hans Rausing's frank and straightforward way of exercising his leadership has to a great extent become a model in the business. There has been no bullying and no barking of orders: *"The only time when power is used is when you have to push something through against the will of other people. Usually the problem hasn't been sufficiently carefully analysed, which makes the whole thing a mistake. Power consists in the right*

Hans Rausing was Managing Director from 1954 to 1985 and then Chairman of the Board, a post he resigned in 1993.

Hans Rausing
was interested in
the Soviet Union
from an early point
in time. In the
large picture, he is
engaged in lively
conversation with
bacteriologists
in the laboratory
of one of the largest
Moscow dairies.
Photograph from
1976.

Awaiting the arrival of guests in front of the Tetra Pak head office in Lund. Throughout the years, Hans Rausing has acted as the host of in-numerable customer groups visiting the company.

to make the wrong decision." He has devoted his entire energy and capacity to the rapidly-growing group of companies. With never-ceasing interest, he has monitored developments throughout the field, deeply committed to the solving of technical and financial difficulties as well as of market-ing questions. *"I want to be where the problems are."* As a critical writer and lecturer, Hans Rausing has also found time to take part in the ongoing public debate, especially on economic and environmental issues. His opinions are familiar: these questions are better taken care of by respon-sible business companies than by national government agencies ("the State").

So what are the Rausing brothers *like*? This book, in its entirety, gives the best answer to a question which cannot possibly be elucidated by a few brief sentences. An attempt at a summary presentation will be made, however, though the picture will be an incomplete and unsubtle one. The brothers are different in many ways; but they have many qualities in common, too – qualities which have become crucial to the development of Tetra Pak and are hence worth dwelling on.

Both possess intellectual stature of unusual dimensions, combining analytical and technological skills with economic shrewdness in a manner which not many people can emulate. Other essential qualities should be adduced: The gift of unrestrained imagination, curiosity, and creative ability. A provocative cast of mind, able to take reasoning and argument

Illustrious visitors have been taken care of abroad as well. Here the present King of Sweden, Carl XVI Gustaf, is being welcomed by Märit and Hans Rausing during a visit to Tetra Pak in Spain.

35

beyond the pale of accepted wisdom. Passionate conviction, the force needed to swim against the tide, obstinately challenging the establishment and never surrendering. Intuitive foresight, the ability to draw conclusions on vague factual grounds which are subsequently confirmed by time and developments. A philosophical, coolly scientific attitude to problems, safeguarding an element of distance despite profound personal commitment. Vigorous leadership, exercised without arrogance or any desire to seize the limelight; instead, a quiet authority aware that constant dripping wears away a stone. Self-discipline, an unaffected manner, unpretentious simplicity. Considerateness and unfailingly generous hospitality – and in this regard, the magnificent efforts made by Hans' wife Märit and Gad's wife Birgit cannot be overestimated. Countless customers, business associates, and employees have visited their homes over the years, to be warmly received in a friendly and personal atmosphere.

For over 40 years, the company had the good fortune of growing under the influence and management of the Rausing family. From its very first day in business, the spirit and the personal involvement of the family lent the organisation its distinctive character. If one were obliged to summarise it in a single concept, it would have to be "Management by conviction". When Hans Rausing left the position of Chairman of the Board in 1993, he was able to state, smiling slightly, that *that little family business in the south of Sweden hadn't done too badly*".

Now it is time to return to the history of the company and continue the story of the various developmental stages it had to pass through before the world market lay open to the "little family business". The narrative starts out from the situation in the mid-1940s and from those initiatives that would lead up to the commercial birth and infancy of the tetrahedron system, in the first half of the 1950s.

Ruben Rausing became a widower as early as 1946. For many years afterwards, his home at Simontorp Farm and the guests he received there were in the capable hands of Gunhild Carlsson. She accompanied Ruben Rausing from 1969 to 1983, too, while he was living in Italy and Switzerland. Here she is flanked by Birgit (left) and Märit Rausing during a celebration in the Lausanne office in 1985.

Gary the cartoonist does not seem to believe that the Rausing brothers are all that fond of milk! In fact, there were no sour faces at any time; the photograph shows the two gentlemen during a merry company ceremony in the late 1980s.

37

A Chain Reaction

War and peace – shells and milk packaging – they would certainly seem to be irreconcilable opposites. And yet there is a connection; the World War initiated a peaceful and wide-ranging project, the construction of the first Tetra Pak machine.

The name of the liaison officer was Harry Järund.

"Time is money" – the adage may have occurred to the boy Harry Järund in the early 1930s, when he was obliged to select a particular line of study at the Chalmers Upper Secondary School of Technology in Gothenburg. He graduated from the school as one of the first methods engineers ("time and motion study men") in Sweden. A few years later he was among the staff of the Jonsered works, which had specialised in the manufacture of woodworking machinery. At Jonsered, he soon advanced to the post of Workshop Manager. When war broke out, his company was one of the firms commissioned to manufacture shell cases for the Swedish Armed Forces. The job of adapting the manufacturing processes was entrusted to Järund. As the authorities scrutinised and compared costs, Jonsered turned out to be able to offer the lowest prices – without any previous experience of war-materials production – in direct competition with such traditional manufacturers as Bofors.

During the first years of the war, Ruben Rausing was Chairman of the National Price Control Board, a position which made it natural for him to observe the person in charge of manufacturing at the Jonsered works. When Åkerlund & Rausing were contemplating the introduction of piece wages and needed a time and motion study man, Ruben Rausing recalled the resourceful engineer at Jonsered, whom he thought well qualified for the post. Järund came to Å&R in 1942 as the first staff member with an engineer's training, despite the fact that the company already numbered some 300 employees. In his new job, he soon saw that

The man behind the design of the classic chain-driven machine for tetrahedron packages was Harry Järund.

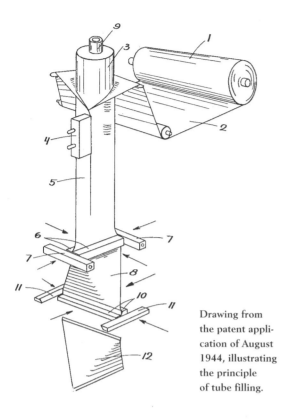

Drawing from the patent application of August 1944, illustrating the principle of tube filling.

The tetrahedron shape called for a specially designed hexagonal transport basket. The first model was made of sheet-metal.

savings could be made in the manufacturing process. Less paper wastage would result in considerably improved production economy. The employees were offered the option of sharing in these profits, and favourable results promptly ensued.

In the meantime, development work on a milk package had begun. Harry Järund studied it at close range; technologically inquisitive by nature, he was attracted by all sorts of construction problems. In the laboratory he saw various proposals which stirred his imagination; of his own accord, he spent many quiet evenings at home mulling over them. In early 1944, he thought he might have come up with a solution. Keen to secure the support of the management, he was faced with the news that Erik Wallenberg had just presented the tetrahedron and that it had been accepted as the basic principle.

It was probably Järund's spontaneous interest in the milk project that led to his being asked to devise a suitable transport box for the unconventional "triangles". He solved the problem by designing a hexagonal basket which held 18 packages, arranged according to a given pattern. This was to become his first patent, followed by many more as the years went by. The hexagonal basket is still in use on the market.

The shape of the package – the tetrahedron – was established, then; so was the transport pack. But there was no conception of what a filling and sealing machine should look like, let alone any notion of how a suitable paper material was to be composed. The initial ideas for a packaging machine had it working from pre-cut, folded sheets of paper, not unlike sealed envelopes with one short side open. Milk would pour in through the open side, which would then be closed by heat-sealing pressure shoes. In other words, each carton would be manufactured separately. The next conceptional step, the idea of shaping, filling, and sealing packages in an uninterrupted process starting from a roll of paper, has been ascribed to Ruben Rausing. With such a design, the entire process could roll on without breaks, provided the paper flow was continuously shaped into cylinders into which liquid was fed by a filling/dosing device. The great difficulty, however, was to ensure that the correct volume went into each package, as milk tends to foam during filling. Ruben Rausing himself has told us how the question was brought to its brilliantly ingenious solution:

"One day at home over lunch, I discussed the matter with my wife. Suddenly she said, 'Why don't you add milk to the tube in a continuous process ... sealing the packages right through the milk?' I replied that it would

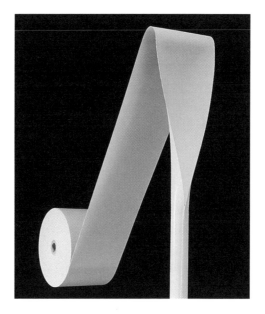

The basic idea in a nutshell – continuously shaping and filling packages issuing from a roll of paper.

be a superb idea, if only it could be applied. It would result in completely filled packages, without oxygen which has a deleterious effect on milk. But it seemed impossible, as the hot clamps used for the heat-sealing would give the milk a burnt taste. All she said was, 'Have you tried it?' – That was a typical, logical reply from this remarkable woman. I returned to my office after lunch and had a cylinder made in the laboratory, filled it with milk, and separated a number of tetrahedrons with the aid of heat-sealing clamps. Some of us tasted the milk, and we were unable to detect even the faintest burnt taste."

The idea behind the continuous filling process was thus born; but the path to its actual realisation was going to be a long and trying one. First Foreman Nils Andersson, the inventive genius of Å&R, was a man in whom Ruben Rausing placed an implicit trust, and "Foreman Nils" and Harry Järund were jointly commissioned to attempt to design a machine for the purpose. The result of their efforts was a compromise proposal: a machine intended to work from a roll and a tube; but one that would still fill packages one at a time, operating intermittently. The conception was never realised. Still, Harry Järund did not surrender the idea that shaping and filling were to take place in a running process. Feeding and sealing should be possible to implement by way of pairs of jaws, placed opposite each other at an angle and mounted on driving chains. In the early days

41

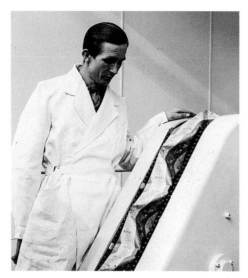

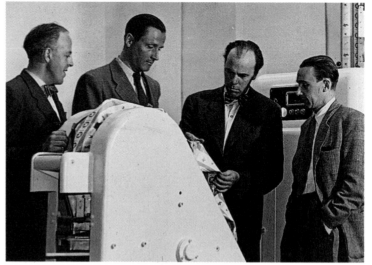

"Secrecy" Jönsson
keeping a watchful
eye on the issuing
device of the proto-
type.

The technological
quartet around
the trial machine.
From left to right,
engineers Billing,
Liljeblad, Järund,
and Lindholm.

of 1945, he was able to put forward a suggestion. The fundamental principle of chain driving seemed reasonable; but the remainder of the proposal failed to win support, and it was rejected.

A few months later, a new working team was appointed whose members delved into the problem while bringing fresh ideas to bear on it. Dieter Kunckel, a former designer of submarines in Germany, was the man in charge. He was able to rely on the assistance of three newly-employed engineers: Robert Billing, Lennart Liljeblad, and Göran Lindholm. The team also included the shrewd fitter Erik, pet-named "Secrecy Jönsson". Erik Jönsson was in a sense the key man of the entire project, in that he was in charge of the keys to the experiment room on whose door a large, formidable sign proclaimed, "Stop! Absolutely No Admittance." Kunckel concentrated on a design which did employ a continuous paper flow and jaws, but operated a complex system for paper-cylinder feeding. In the spring of 1946, he fell ill and was compelled to leave his post. At that stage, the machine was almost assembled; but nobody on the team was able to finish it. Uncertainty prevailed: would it ever work? In this precarious situation, people began to wonder whether it might be advisable to start collaborating with one of the big engineering companies in Sweden. However, such schemes never went beyond the stage of contemplation.

Instead, Harry Järund was put in charge of the continued development of the project. At this point, Ruben Rausing had evaluated several proposed machine designs. He was reluctant to dismiss Kunckel's machine out of hand, feeling that it should be possible to carry on with it. Besides, work on this machine had been going on for quite some time and entailed significant expenditure. Järund was far from convinced, though. He had continued working on his idea of a chain-driven machine, arguing that it would make the over-all design much less complicated. He held out a couple of plans, whereupon Ruben Rausing commented, with a touch of annoyance, *"I'm not an expert at assessing drawings"*. The management stuck to the view that Kunckel's project should be taken further, but Järund stood firm. In order to illustrate the mode of functioning he had in mind, he caused a simple model to be built. Its mobile parts consisted of cog-wheels and bicycle chains, to which wooden sealing jaws were attached. A few days of considerable tension followed – but the demonstration had the intended effect: *"well, Mr Järund, how much time do you need to build a prototype machine?"* Without a moment's hesitation, Järund replied: *"four months, sir."* This was in May 1946.

From that moment onwards, Järund had a free hand. However, he had to sign an undertaking to observe the time limit, despite imminent summer holidays in the workshops that would have to manufacture necessary details for the machinery. As promised, the prototype was ready in early September, which was a tremendous achievement. It had been built without access to in-house machine-tools; the components had been manufactured by small workshops which had been prevailed upon to sacrifice holiday time. Several of those firms which provided machinery parts in the summer of 1946, with varying degrees of agony, have continued to work with Tetra Pak, growing along with the company which contracted their services. The basis for the Tetra Pak sub-contractor system had been established.

The very first packaging machine, the prototype itself, was set up in an abandoned workshop at the centre of Lund, close to the railway station. Incidentally, the premises next door were those of AB Separator, the group of companies which would later be re-named Alfa-Laval. Today, a complex of shops and offices stands on the old factory ground, and the market-place in front of it is adorned by a modern sculpture called "Monument to a Street Acrobat". In view of the circumstances in which Harry Järund was obliged to work, it is no exaggeration to say that he

In order to be in a better position to illustrate his ideas, Järund caused a simple model to be built in May 1946. Today it has pride of place in the Lund Tetra Pak office.

43

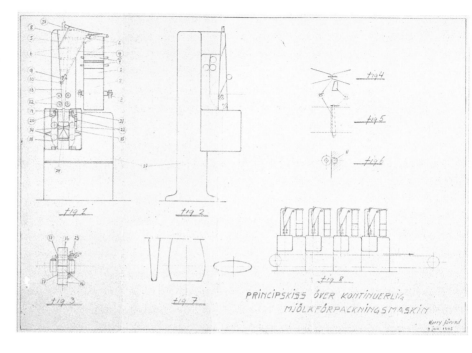

performed acrobatic marvels, too – the difference being that innumerable copies of his "monumental artefact" have travelled all over the world!

In September 1946, then, Järund was able to demonstrate a functioning machine design to his management. Its main principles were unique. The basic technical problems had been solved, although much remained to develop further. One troublesome fact caused the machine designer much concern: there was no material suitable for a trial run. His colleagues in the paper laboratory worked out a large number of proposals, but they all had their defects. In order to be able to test essential functions in the experimental machine – mechanical movement, paper-tube shaping, filling, sealing methods – Järund and his small body of men were in great need of a type of paper with consistent qualities. But nobody was able to put forward an acceptable option. Ruben Rausing was a welcome visitor in the ramshackle building, whose floor was as often as not soaked in water from all the leaking packages. His conviction that it would be possible to develop a perfectly operating machine never faltered, and he was equally sure that suitable packaging materials would emerge. His powerful commitment to the project was Järund's best source of support.

The second half of the 1940s turned out to be a time of searching, hoping, and suffering disappointment. It proved harder than the people concerned had believed to find a composition of materials which lived up to the demands made by the new machine. The elegant principle of continuous sealing "right through the milk" had major advantages, but it caused considerable difficulties as well; nothing like it had ever been attempted before. Time passed, and no results were attained. At the same time, the market began to cry out for new packaging solutions. The transition to self-service in the retail trade had begun, entailing demands for milk pre-packed for consumers. The Swedish dairy industry was facing comprehensive new investments, but was it advisable to go on investing in the glass bottle only? In America, Britain, and Germany, various forms of disposable packages had been introduced, albeit on a small scale. Stubborn rumours were rife in Sweden, too – weren't Åkerlund & Rausing in Lund up to something interesting?

The situation was coming to a head, but the Lund project still had not reached a stage where it could be presented to the public; nobody had as yet been able to attain a harmonious relationship between machine and paper. It is one of Järund's many merits that he anticipated those developments in the field of materials which would take place several years later; his design was in fact almost ten years ahead of its time. Thanks to the way in which the machine operated, it was the first construction in the world to be able to use plastic-coated paper, and its basic principles have stood the test of time. During the labours of construction, a number of technical solutions emerged which bespoke a first-class inventive talent. Järund's own comment is laconic: *"It would not have been possible to bring the work on machine development and paper experimentation to a happy conclusion anywhere but in Lund – under the wing of the Rausing family."*

After 15 years in charge of the Tetra Pak pioneering project, Harry Järund handed over the technological management of the company to others. He started running his own business instead, a business which has, on a sub-contractor basis, been delivering essential components for packaging material to Tetra Pak for years. Järund's continued activities have been characterised by abundant ingenuity and inventiveness. And he could hardly have picked a more apposite name for his firm – *Inventing!*

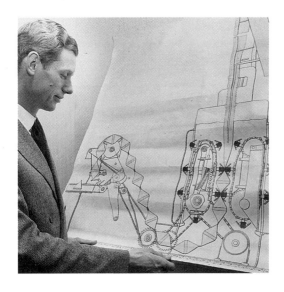

Hans Rausing studies an early sketch illustrating the functions of the chain-driven filling machine.

The packing pattern in Järund's hexagonal transport basket for the new, "triangular" packages. The sketch is from the patent document.

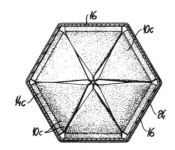

Harry Sigurd Valdemar Järund

45

'Mission Impossible'

Iron ore and forests – the two great natural assets of Sweden. Processed, they end up as steel and paper, products successfully brought to the world market by the country's industry. But nowhere have the two been so happily combined as they are at Tetra Pak. Swedish steel went into the machinery.

And – above all – Swedish kraft paper into the packaging material.

The basic invention of the tetrahedron had been made, further thought had engendered the principle of continuous filling, and an experimental machine was available in the autumn of 1946. As the machine was being developed, another group within the company was busy trying to evolve a suitable paper material. Surely that ought not to be too difficult; after all, Åkerlund & Rausing were experienced and knowledgeable in matters of packing and materials combinations, albeit in connection with solid products. Besides, valuable expertise could be derived from the technologically advanced Swedish paper industry. It looked as if everything necessary was in the company's own backyard. As it happened, though, its representatives were obliged to look far and wide for solutions – in the end, part of the materials and technological solutions were brought over from the U.S.A. and from Britain, after years of searching and experimentation.

During the early stage of the work on developing suitable materials, Gad Rausing was in charge. With a small group of co-workers, notably the engineers Alf Linderot and Karl-Erik Ekström, he made an inventory of conceivable possibilities. It was natural to start by looking at components within easy reach. Paraffin-wax was well known as a sealing medium; it was used in Å&R's own production. But ordinary solid paraffin could not be heat-sealed in the way required by the Tetra Pak machine. Cellophane-coated materials were fine for the purpose of sealing bags containing dry products, but they were useless with fluids. In

One of the "golden veins" of Sweden – timber floating on its way to being processed into pulp.

47

This small paper model of the experimental workshop "Siberia" has always sat in Gad Rausing's office.

brief, none of the tried-and-true materials was any good; no suitable material could be had for Harry Järund's machine.

In the meantime, the development of plastics had begun, both in Europe and the United States. The only material to be reasonably well known and accessible at this point was polyvinyl chloride, which was to become famous – and to a certain extent infamous – under the designation PVC. It was manufactured in Germany, among other countries; but it was being produced for entirely different purposes, and nobody had made any serious attempt to coat paper with PVC. At this stage, modern extrusion heating techniques were unknown. The method closest at hand consisted in dissolving the plastics in appropriate chemical substances and then spreading the cold fluid mixture across the paper line with the aid of rolls, thereby causing the solvent to evaporate. The procedure may not have been the perfect way out, but tested it must be. The powerful substances that had to be used – acetone and benzol – gave an unpleasant smell and taste to the sensitive material that was to go into the packages, the milk. Besides, they were health hazards, inflammable, and explosive. But what else could be done? This was as far as technology had advanced at the time.

In order to eliminate at least some of the hazards involved, a specially equipped experimental building was set up at a safe distance from the main plant in Lund. It soon acquired the name "Siberia", as it lacked both heating and indoor lighting. Light bulbs, sockets, and switches were all placed on the outside, with a view to reducing the risk of explosion in case of electric spark formation. In addition, the makeshift building was constructed in such a way that its roof and walls would collapse like a house of cards if an accident were to happen after all. And there were incidents – on one occasion Gad Rausing even had to go to hospital with acute benzol poisoning! Not until then was it generally realised how dangerous benzol actually is. Exaggerating slightly, it is hence possible to maintain that the material-development work was conducted with people's lives at stake. The problem itself was truly of vital proportions, too: everybody was waiting for an acceptable combination of materials.

Searching high and low for suitable alternatives was the number-one priority, and non-technologists were roped in as well. Erik Torudd, Manager and Head of Sales at Å&R, became intensely involved in these scouting operations. Within the company he was, along with the Rausing family and a few technicians, the only person who really believed in the potential of the tetrahedron from the outset. However, he was opposed to the proposed solvent technique, chiefly because of the matter of taste. Instead, he advocated some kind of hot-melt coating, which meant that a suitable plastic would be heated and then applied to the surface of the paper. One conceivable material was polythene, which had been developed as early as the 1930s by the large British chemical group ICI, Imperial Chemical Industries. During the war years polythene was used for military purposes, mostly for radar equipment and the insulation of electric cables. In the mid-1940s, it still had not hit the market to any great extent. Besides – as was the case with PVC –, nobody had been interested in using this material in the context of packaging. A visit was paid to ICI in the late summer of 1946; the idea was to find out more about the properties of polythene and establish whether it might be suitable for application to paper. The tetrahedron development was demonstrated, but at this point the conclusion was that polythene, as it then was, was not right for the purpose. It would take a long time before ICI joined the Tetra Pak suppliers.

As so often before, people looked towards the United States; maybe the Americans were developing something that might be useful? A small picked troop – Gad Rausing, Stig Sunner, and Erik Torudd – set out on a journey of discovery at the beginning of 1947, their brief being to study American innovations in the packaging business during and after the war. The visit lasted for four months, and a total of some 90 companies connected with the trade were investigated. It turned out to be a profitable trip as far as Åkerlund & Rausing was concerned; but it did not yield much in respect of the new milk package. The only cheering circumstance was that a new possible plastic material had been located, a polystyrene mixture known under the designation S-50. Small-scale tests were performed, both in the U.S. and at home in Lund. In due course, the results became acceptable; but not everybody was convinced. The months passed, years went by – and still there was no material good enough for the waiting Järundian machine.

The natives of the Swedish province of Småland are known for their stubbornness, and it was as a true Smålander that Erik Torudd kept looking for new plastic products and manufacturing methods during his trips to America. On one of these occasions, at the beginning of 1951, he was told that a Chicago firm called H. P. Smith had developed a technique for coating paper with polythene – a feat which nobody else had achieved at that time. The firm in question had been working on the problem for several years and arrived at a method they called extrusion,

Erik Torudd, employed by Å&R as early as 1934, became the first sales manager of Tetra Pak. His was a truly pioneering achievement in the Swedish and international markets.

49

which entailed the application of heated, semi-viscous polythene to paper. Asked whether they would be able to handle the previously-mentioned plastic S-50 as well, H. P. Smith replied in the affirmative. A roll was manufactured with all due despatch and sent off to Lund. After a trial run, Harry Järund reported that this was the best material of all the ones that had been tested.

In the autumn of 1951, Gad Rausing and Erik Torudd visited the Chicago firm together. The M.D. of H. P. Smith was somewhat concerned about the risk of industrial espionage, but agreed to demonstrate the new plant *"as the two gentlemen were ignorant of technology, one being an archaeologist and the other a salesman ..."* They were allowed to look at the idle machine from a distance; but as soon as they started asking initiated questions, the audience was abruptly terminated! Even so, a certain degree of co-operation with H. P. Smith continued; the firm tested the application of plastic to Swedish base paper, and later more regular deliveries began. At the same time, Tetra Pak's own materials-development work continued, and finally, in the autumn of 1952, the first tetrahedron machine could be installed in the Lund Dairy.

The general impression was that better times were just around the corner, and that the materials problem was on its way to being solved at last. That, however, proved not to be the case. As a result of the Korean War, the few factories capable of manufacturing the desired S-50 plastic were blocked for essential production on behalf of the American military forces. No S-50 material was being produced for civilian purposes. At the

Conditions
in the materials
factory were
primitive at first,
very far removed
from the computer-
controlled manu-
facturing of today.
Quality was uneven,
and trial runs
with the filling
machines often
resulted in paper
wastage.

The picture above is a treasure in the photo library of the company: the first Tetra Pak machine was delivered to the Lund Dairy in September 1952.

Right, the same machine installed on the dairy premises. The heat-exchanger in the background bears the sign of Alfa-Laval. Co-operation was, in practice, established as far back as the early 1950s.

beginning of 1953, Erik Torudd asked to see the Quartermaster General of the United States in an attempt to secure deliveries despite the ongoing crisis. As a visitor to Washington, however, he received the grim message: *"Mr Torudd, I want to tell you that it is much more important for us to win the Korean War than for you to get that package on the market. The answer is no."* That left no other option than looking for random quantities that might be around in the market. These efforts were successful, and the production – a small one, but of vital importance to Tetra Pak – could be kept going. Even so, the people in charge could see the day coming when all reserves would be exhausted, and the prospect filled them with dread. According to calculations, that day would be upon them in August 1953.

In the meantime, the new polythene plastic had come in for increasing attention. Laboratory trials with polythene-coated paper were conducted, and once the sealing equipment of the Tetra Pak machine had been improved, the material turned out to be serviceable. It was hence as a gift from heaven that the first delivery of polythene from ICI arrived just as the supply of S-50 was running out. Polythene was also becoming known in the United States, where the large DuPont Group had acquired a manufacturing licence from ICI. It was soon clear that this would be a major product, particularly in the packaging business. Consequently, DuPont had instructed a specialist enterprise, Frank W. Egan, to design a machine able to apply a thin coat of polythene to paper. When this so-called extruder came on the market around 1954, it was of course of the keenest interest both to Åkerlund & Rausing and to Tetra Pak.

At home in Lund, Gad Rausing's team of researchers had anticipated the American developments by presenting similar problem solutions. Experiments on a laboratory scale indicated the same principal conclusions with regard to manufacturing methods that the American experts had reached. An intensive development programme was initiated with the American firms. It resulted in the installation of a new, extremely up-to-date extruder laminator at Tetra Pak when the company's own Lund plant was completed in the late autumn of 1956. Thanks to their own efforts, Tetra Pak received a free licence for the manufacturing process, which meant that the company did not have to pay royalties for the utilisation of DuPont's extrusion technology.

When we talk about Tetra Pak paper, we think of the finished material, plastic-coated and printed. For a layman, the whole thing looks very simple indeed: nobody can imagine the full extent of those labours that led up to the process. The concept of "materials development" not only comprises the plastic coating described above; after all, the base paper itself is at the heart of the whole construction. Where the paper was concerned, a number of hitherto unforeseen difficulties cropped up. The paper had to be stiff but also malleable – conflicting properties which

The new factory in Lund, completed in 1956, soon needed to operate evening and night shifts. "Midnight oil" is being burnt one autumn night around 1960.

53

The characteristic
aeroplane tail on
the roof of the first
Tetra Pak plant,
of 1956, contains
a purification filter
as well as a heat-
exchanger absorbing
energy from the
ventilating air.
The company was
interested in en-
vironmental issues
from an early stage.

In 1954, the City of Lund sold a land area of 200,000 square metres altogether. The first factory only utilised 5,000 of them. Somewhat ironic comments ensued: "Oh, so the Rausings are going in for real estate, selling land for housing developments?" That was never necessary. The area has long been fully utilised for industrial purposes, and early foresight has paid off.

Over the years, many people have had leading positions in the development and production of packaging materials. Here are some of the pioneers: Ernst van der Pals, Karl-Erik Ekström, Sune Pettersson, and Thorsten Lindh.

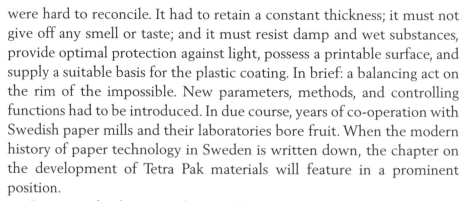

were hard to reconcile. It had to retain a constant thickness; it must not give off any smell or taste; and it must resist damp and wet substances, provide optimal protection against light, possess a printable surface, and supply a suitable basis for the plastic coating. In brief: a balancing act on the rim of the impossible. New parameters, methods, and controlling functions had to be introduced. In due course, years of co-operation with Swedish paper mills and their laboratories bore fruit. When the modern history of paper technology in Sweden is written down, the chapter on the development of Tetra Pak materials will feature in a prominent position.

Correspondingly comprehensive labours became necessary when the time came to satisfy those particular requirements as regards printing presses and paints which the decorative printing on the packages entailed. Much of this development work consisted of in-house efforts. As a result, the first generation of printing presses, under the name of "Tetra Printer", was constructed under Åkerlund & Rausing management. In addition, a special colour-coatings factory was built for the combined needs of Å&R and Tetra Pak. The last step in the processing work, the external wax impregnation of the material, also took place in machines which Å&R had caused to be constructed. In all these areas, further experiences were necessary before production could become a routine matter.

Another complication was the fact that the Tetra Pak machines work with narrow material-tolerance limits and do not accept deviations from carefully established standards. Besides, different types of machines call for dissimilar properties where paper is concerned. Finally, all the parties involved – the customer first and foremost – have a vested interest in the material being as cheap as possible while still adhering to the quality specifications. This balancing of considerations, cost versus quality, is itself a complication. How tempting it would be to buy one's way out of a sea of troubles by means of, for instance, providing the paper with a somewhat thicker plastic coat! Economically speaking, though, such a measure is an impossibility when the object of competition is a staple food with the price sensitivity of our daily milk.

A long list could be drawn up at this point – a list of problems, failures, amounts that went into development work, customer complaints. Another extremely long list would have to be compiled by anybody who wished to record the names of all those people who struggled to solve the problems connected with materials over the years. Only a few of them can be mentioned here: Karl-Erik Ekström, Ernst van der Pals, Thorsten Lindh, and Sune Pettersson. Another impressive register would be the result of an attempt to list all those customers who showed understanding, forbearance, and patience. Without their support – pioneers and latecomers –, Tetra Pak could never have developed as it did. The subject is still far from exhausted: new combinations are tried on a continuous basis; process technology is always being improved; and more and more stringent environmental demands are being met. Constant developments ensure that the chapter on packaging materials will never be closed.

As we saw, it took almost ten years from the first invention in 1944 to the point where a serviceable material could be manufactured on a large scale. At last, time and developments had begun to catch up with the Tetra Pak project. A statement once made by Ruben Rausing forms an appropriate concluding comment: *"Doing something that nobody's ever done before is in fact rather tricky."*

The first generation of machines for materials manufacturing were designed and built by Åkerlund & Rausing. Detail of a Tetra Printer.

The Starting Shot

The concept of the "starting shot" suggests competitive sport, especially perhaps a sprinters' race. For Tetra Pak, the pistol went off on Friday, 18 May 1951; at 10.15 a.m., to be exact. But what followed was no short-distance run, it was a marathon.

It took years for the finishing line to be crossed.

We have been able to follow the developmental labours at Tetra Pak up to the early 1950s, both with regard to machinery and carton materials. There had been a couple of experimental machines for quite some time, but no large-scale production of satisfactory paper had taken place – the number of leaking packages was embarrassingly high. The situation did improve; but nobody was in a position to say with any certainty when the problem would be solved once and for all.

However, the Tetra Pak project had become known outside the company too. In the late 1940s, contacts with several Swedish industries were established. A search was on for a suitable financer and partner in the metal-trade sector, for the future manufacturing of the packaging machines. Discussions were conducted with such well-known companies as Bofors, Electrolux, and Separator – later Alfa-Laval. The last-mentioned company was even offered a partnership, but the offer was turned down in view of the risks involved. The question was raised with Axel Wenner-Gren of Electrolux as well, but again no results were attained. Foreign interested parties, partly alerted by way of letters patent, announced their interest. At an early point in time, the biggest dairy federation in Sweden – *Mjölkcentralen* (MC), now the Arla Group – had been informed about the project; after all, it was essential to receive reactions from the intended customers. A new decade had begun;

but still no saleable system existed, and the people involved in the project were far from the goal of their dreams. Even so, the curiosity of the outside world had been roused.

In the meantime, intense activity had developed over the patent issue. Since the submission, in 1944, of the application for the original patent, a large number of new patents had been reported. Another important event took place during a Board Meeting in 1950, over a discussion of the question what the company should be called. It was Erik Torudd, the Åkerlund & Rausing Manager responsible for the co-ordination of the new project, who presented the logical as well as brilliant proposal that the company be named *Tetra Pak*. The word "tetra" is, of course, associated with the tetrahedron – a plane figure with four sides whose name originates in the Greek numeral which simply means *four*. At the end of the year, on 20 December 1950, Aktiebolaget (the Limited Company) Tetra Pak was registered.

The early organisation was not a very big one. On one occasion, the then Planning Manager at Å&R, Lars Hallberg, described it in the following succinct and humorous terms: *"The organisation at Tetra Pak consisted of four engineers and a technician. Once they'd got a machine together, three managers were appointed, and I was taken on as salesman."* The engineers/technician were the men mentioned before: Harry Järund, Robert Billing, Lennart Liljeblad, Göran Lindholm, and the fitter Erik ("Secrecy") Jönsson. The managers were Hans and Gad Rausing as well as Erik Torudd. The statement is a little exaggerated, of course; there were a few more people around. However, the team that was to face the world market, and the customers, certainly was not large.

External expectations were growing. In view of the loans that had been granted for the purpose, bankers were especially keen to hear news. The long-discussed official presentation would have to be made soon, and it was finally scheduled for 18 May 1951. A secondary intention behind this public demonstration was to inspire the company's own forces to make even more vigorous efforts, if that was at all possible. The same method has been employed on subsequent occasions. It has been unusual for new designs to be allowed to mature at leisure; machines have been shown and installed, often long before they were thoroughly tested and in reasonably good working order. This has in fact been a necessity. It is impossible to simulate reality in a laboratory: only proper field-work supplies the necessary experience. At times, risk-taking has bordered on the "indecent"; the stresses and strains inflicted on the

All Tetra Pak
machinery carries
a sign proclaiming
its origin – here,
a fairly venerable
model.

All Tetra Pak
machinery carries
a sign proclaiming
its origin – here,
a fairly venerable
model.

18 May 1951 was
a historical date.
At last the curtain
would rise and the
world behold those de-
velopments about
which whispers had
been rife for so long.
At the press demon-
stration, Ruben
Rausing delivered
the opening address
himself. The large pic-
ture shows him being
questioned by eager
reporters.

company's own organisation – and on customers – have called for both courage and generosity of spirit.

Everybody recognised the importance of this initial presentation. A carefully elaborated plan was concealed behind the modest official programme. Nothing was allowed to be left to chance – there were quite enough uncertain factors as it was. It may be of interest to reproduce some of the details of the internal programme, as this first press demonstration set the pattern for the way in which presentations came to be handled at Tetra Pak, both in front of customers and in official contexts. All practical details carefully planned; clear division of responsibility; high-quality demonstration materials – and good food to follow! The abbreviations used in the ensuing schedule stand for: RR Ruben Rausing, HR Hans Rausing, GR Gad Rausing, HC Holger Crafoord, ET Erik Torudd, HJ Harry Järund.

Harry Järund demonstrating the functioning of the machine – how shaping, filling, and sealing take place in an unbroken process.

9.45 a.m.
Cars call for all participants at the Grand Hotel in Lund. 12 cars necessary. Guests are deposited outside the main entrance to the office, where HR welcomes them and takes them through to the film-showing room. GR introduces the journalists to Mr Crafoord, who in his turn introduces them to Mr Rausing. All participants from Å&R wear badges with their names on them, attached to their lapels.

Equipment in the film room: On a table to the left of the entrance are spiral writing-pads and pencils. At the very front, beside the screen, are a table and a chair for the speaker. Rows of chairs for the audience.

10.15 a.m.
RR calls for attention and delivers a 10-minute speech. The film is shown; HR then goes to the speaker's table for a 5-minute address.

11.15 a.m.
Assembly in the demonstration room. Preliminary work: 200 non-leaking tetrahedrons are selected at 10 a.m. They are packed in boxes at 11.30. In

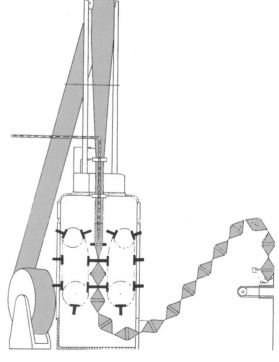

the packing room, 2 girls and 1 engineer check the tetrahedrons. If they leak, they are opened. A number of leak-free tetrahedrons are packed into the transport containers for demonstration. 10 pairs of scissors are lying on a table to the left of the entrance. On the wall above the table is a large block-letter description of how the tetrahedrons are to be opened.

11.30 a.m.
ET has been put in charge of the demonstration. He asks participants to come and stand around the machine and gives the sign to start it. HJ starts the machine, which runs for 4 minutes. ET gives the sign to stop. HJ ascends the rostrum (a box), placed next to the entrance. HJ speaks for 5 minutes.

ET announces that the interior of the machine will now be shown. One side is removed, whereupon the machine runs for another 4 minutes.

12.00 noon
ET gives the signal for boxes of tetrahedrons to be carried into the room and placed on the table beside the entrance. HJ demonstrates the tetrahedrons and the opening technique, whereupon he invites participants to try opening and drinking from them.

12.30
RR leaves the floor to anyone who wishes to ask questions, whereupon he welcomes everybody to lunch.

1.30 p.m.
HC speaks for 15 minutes; this is followed by a tour of the plant. Each guide holds up a placard bearing the names of the guests he will be conducting. After the tour, participants are shown to the film room where they receive memoranda and photographs. They are then conducted straight through to the waiting cars.

6 p.m.
Assembly in the Grand Hotel for dinner.

NB – the following items/procedures must not be shown:
   1) The regulating devices of the machine
   2) It is absolutely forbidden to describe the automatic packing
   3) Handles and openers for the tetrahedrons.

An impressive schedule, resembling that of a military plan of attack – but then this was the prelude to a struggle for the world market. And yet the forces had to be redeployed time and again; not everything went according to plan. Thus, for instance, a visit to the demonstration room immediately before the press show led to the statement that *"this place stinks like hell"*. Bearing obvious traces of previous trial runs, burnt milk residues sticking to its sealing jaws, the demonstration machine spread a less than delightful odour all over the premises. It was abundantly sprinkled with 96-per-cent alcohol, thus receiving a much-needed purifying bath. The same operation anaesthetised the olfactory nerves of the journalists to some degree.

The representatives of the press were only permitted to see the filling machine itself, not the automatic packing device which placed individual packages into custom-designed hexagonal metallic cases. With reference to the circumstance that the letters patent pertaining to the automatic packer were not yet ready, this engineering detail had been prudently screened from view. Visitors could see the packages disappearing via a conveyor belt through a hole in the wall, and on the other side of the specially constructed double wall packed cases then emerged for general inspection. The journalists hence saw the result of the automatic packing procedure without having the design and operating mode of the machine revealed to them. With this everyone was content.

The true story was completely different. There was no operational automatic packer in existence. The cubby-hole which supposedly housed this machine actually contained two helpers. One took care of the incoming, usually leaky packages, which were placed into special receptacles – the minimal floor space was covered in sawdust, just in case. The other man placed duly filled cases on the outgoing belt at regular intervals. These cases had been hand-packed earlier in the morning and placed in the cubby-hole, each package having been carefully examined. None of the guests had any inkling of the true state of affairs; everyone was exhilarated over the novelty, the first of its kind in the world, that had just been presented before their very eyes. Accordingly, press reactions were highly favourable: *"After nearly 20 years of research and secret experimental work the iron curtain lifts, and a machine is presented for which the dairy industry all over the world has been waiting. Those who hoped for a sensation will not be disappointed. This is more than a good package; it is a process which bears the stamp of genius."* Some people might wonder why there is so little in the way of photographic documentation from this first demonstration. The explanation is a simple one; the in-house photographer Stig Andersson was one of the two men who shifted packages in the secret hole!

Even though the Tetra-Pak developments at Åkerlund & Rausing had been known to a limited number of people for some time, the press demonstration became a confirmation as well as a promise for the future. Now the die was cast, and psychological pressure increased – it was simply necessary to get out into the market as quickly as possible. And yet another 18 months would pass before the official start. Technical progress in the meantime had not been impressive; leakage was the overriding problem, and everyone in the company knew it. When, on an autumn day in 1952 in the Å&R canteen, Hans Rausing announced that the première of Tetra Pak in Lund was imminent at last, one of his colleagues hence uttered the swift rejoinder, *"Then I'll go into the laundry business!"* More than anybody else, the people who worked for Tetra Pak received daily object lessons in the art of not crying over spilt milk – and they became masters in the art of comforting tear-stained dairymen, too.

The problem of leaky packages was to hang on stubbornly for years. Much later, at an internal conference in the early 1970s, it caused Ruben Rausing to deliver an address expressively entitled *"My leaking life"*.

Every machine was tested in the factory before delivery. Such trial runs would sometimes consume sizeable quantities of material.

A Swedish Prophecy

We have it on the highest authority that "a prophet is not without honour, save in his own country". For Tetra Pak, though, it was absolutely vital to be the exception proving the rule. A platform was necessary if a subsequent conquest of the world market was to be possible.

Sweden just had to become a point of reference.

"Curtain up" – after numerous rehearsals, the day when the new package was to have its world première had finally come. It was December 1952, the stage was the humble little dairy of Lund, and the housewives of the city were sitting in the front stalls. Borrowing theatrical terms is hardly far-fetched – the tetrahedron has always been the focal point of drama. Its shape is spectacular; it invites discussion; nobody remains indifferent to it. Feelings have often run high around the package, and much of the emotion can be summed up in the expression "love-hatred relationship".

The very first Tetra Pak customer was the manager Hilding Borstam of the Lund Dairy Association. A machine for one-decilitre packages had been installed on his premises since September, and the autumn months had been spent adjusting the system. Now, in the weeks before the Christmas of 1952, the commercial start was due. This point in time had been chosen with some care *"in the hope that consumers and journalists would be in a good mood – in case they had trouble handling the package"*. In other words, the special Christmas parcel for shops and housewives from Tetra Pak and the dairy was the new cream package, available in

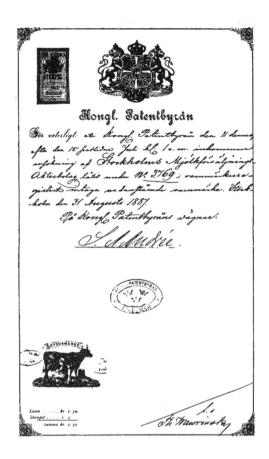

The largest dairy company in Sweden has a distinguished ancestry. The letter of registration from 1887 pertains to the Stockholm Mjölkförsäljning ("Milk Sales") Aktiebolag, precursor of what was to become Mjölkcentralen, the Milk Centre. In 1975 the company acquired its present name, Arla.

food shops just in time for the holiday season. At first production was modest, but it slowly rose up to 10,000 packages a day. It was essential to gather experiences from shopkeepers and consumers by way of preparation for continued introductions elsewhere in the country. Next in line was *Mjölkcentralen* (the MC, "Milk Centre") of Stockholm, the biggest dairy company in Sweden, which had been keeping an eye on the development of the project for a long time.

A few years previously, the MC had appointed a new manager, Gösta Winberg. Before his time, the general view had been that anyone who wanted to advance to senior posts in this line of business had to have a dairyman's training. Gösta Winberg, however, was a Master of Engineering and had been recruited from the manufacturing industry. He started his new life by going to the U.S.A. in order to take a close look at the trade which would be his for the remainder of a long, active life. America was considered to be a model for the rest of the world where consumer milk was concerned, and Winberg came home with many new ideas. One thing which had drawn his particular interest was those disposable packages which he had seen put to practical uses during his trip. In his opinion, the MC ought to be testing cartons; but the Board received the suggestion with scepticism. Such new-fangled notions would make people's daily milk more expensive. The slightest price rise was immediately noticed; a popular Swedish song dating back to this time was called *"The Milk's Gone Up a Farthing"*. No savings on distribution were included in calculations at this point; the time was not yet ripe.

During the years immediately after World War II, much of the milk sold for drinking purposes was distributed "loose", unpacked. As such, it must not be sold together with other products, except for bread, cheese, and eggs. In the late 40s, there were still about 2,000 small "round-the-corner" shops in Greater Stockholm whose main article was milk. Their daily volume might be as small as 20 litres. The customer would bring his or her own receptacle to carry the milk home in. Around 1950, a readjustment in shopping patterns took place in the direction of self-service and supermarkets, the new kind of shop presupposing consumer-packed products. It did not take long for most groceries to be pre-packaged. This was a modernisation process to which general packing developments at Åkerlund & Rausing made powerful contributions. As a result, handling became less costly, and the public could be offered lower prices. Milk remained the great stumbling-block for retailers, though, putting a brake on rationalisation in the trade.

LOM, the dairy
association of
Lund, introduced
its one-decilitre
cream package
in December 1952,
as the first cus-
tomer in the world.

LOM, the dairy
association of
Lund, introduced
its one-decilitre
cream package
in December 1952,
as the first cus-
tomer in the world.

"Loose" milk
was around for
quite some time,
alongside the
glass bottle whose
Swedish sales
passed their peak
in the mid-1950s.

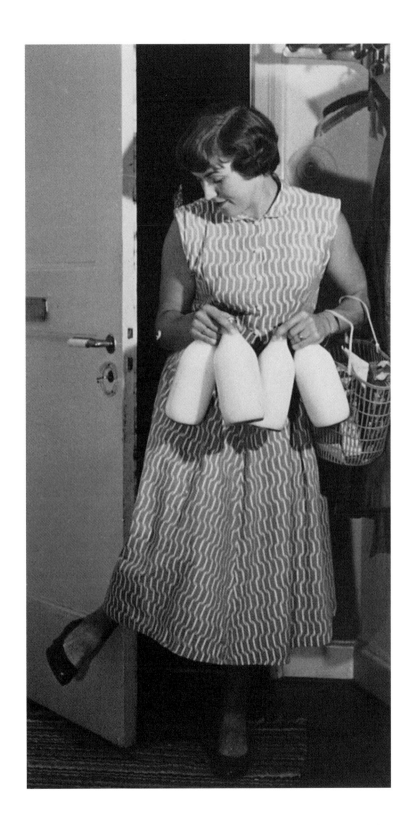

Gösta Winberg,
M.D. of the Milk
Centre from 1946
to 1969, supported
Tetra Pak through
thick and thin dur-
ing many critical
stages in the devel-
opment of the com-
pany. This fruitful
co-operation has
continued through-
out the years.

The only alternative to loose milk was the glass bottle. To be sure, its ancestry in the dairy industry went back as far as the last decades of the nineteenth century; but economic considerations had precluded its general use. Louis Pasteur's achievements in bacteriological research in France, and his discovery that tuberculosis, the great scourge of his time, could spread by way of infected milk, accelerated developments, and fighting the illness became an urgent priority in Sweden as well. A safe alternative began to be provided in the form of so-called controlled milk from farms operating under the inspection of the public health authorities. In order not to be mistaken for ordinary, uncontrolled loose milk, it was filled into glass bottles. The Audhumbla Milk Company in Stockholm was the first to offer milk of this type, which came with a hygiene guarantee. The name of the company might seem mysterious: in Old Norse mythology, Audhumbla was the cow whose milk invigorated the gods of the heathen and Viking ages. Consequently, the slogan *"Milk – a drink fit for the gods"* rests on old traditions. This "health milk" came expensive, though, and remained a product for the few.

Pasteurisation and refrigeration soon came into general use, and milk in "loose" quantities would long remain an acceptable alternative where large volumes were concerned. At the same time, the glass bottle gained ground, partly as a guarantor for hygiene but mostly because it offered a consumer-packed transport unit which was reasonably easy to buy, bring home, and use. Still, more and more people thought it inconvenient, especially at a time when so many other goods were beginning to appear in shops in packages which were easy to handle and generally consumer-friendly. The dairy industry had to keep up with developments. Consequently, Gösta Winberg became extremely interested when he first heard of the milk-packing experiments at Åkerlund & Rausing around 1947. He instantly realised that the tetrahedron, which entailed a minimum of waste, would be a genuine alternative for such a tightly price-controlled food as people's daily milk: *"There probably isn't a more brilliant and material-saving type of package in existence."* Besides, it was a Swedish idea; it would help the national industry, not only milk producers but those farmers who owned woodland, too.

In order to allow market and consumers to become accustomed to the unconventional shape, the MC adhered to the example set by the première in southern Sweden: cream in one-decilitre packages was introduced in Stockholm, but not until November 1953. Winberg's comment was: *"You people promised to deliver within six months, but it took*

A distribution lorry bearing the familiar "Arla cow" in front of the group´s head office in the city centre of Stockholm. The then MC ran several manufacturing premises in the Swedish capital. Right, an interior view from the Bromma dairy, around 1960.

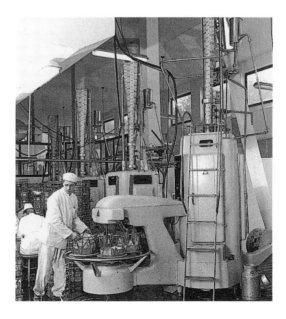

six years!" Experiences derived from Lund, the city of learning, were put to good uses. In order to maximise the impact of the new departure, the MC and Tetra Pak arranged a magnificent "revivalist meeting" for Stockholm retailers on the day before the introduction. In addition to lectures and general information, performances by top-class artists were inserted as a means of attracting visitors. There were so many of them that three performances had to be arranged. The introduction went smoothly, and consumers learned to handle the new, original object relatively quickly. Now the MC was eagerly awaiting machines for larger packages; after all, milk was the crucial article, and this was where the large profits would arise as a result of cheaper handling. The predominant volume was, of course, one litre; but the MC understood that Tetra Pak had to move forward one step at a time and was happy to contemplate introducing the half-litre package while waiting for the big one.

In Lund, Harry Järund's team of engineers had had a machine completed for the half litre for quite some time, but the composition of the paper had caused problems. Not until the spring of 1954 was it possible to start selling the new package. In the market, interest had increased; machines were installed simultaneously in several different places, and the introductions were supported by advertising campaigns as well as by various measures geared to informing consumers. As there was no one-litre carton to be had, the important thing was to convince milk buyers that purchasing two half-litre packages instead was an extremely rational step. The management of Tetra Pak were cherishing a secret hope that no one-litre machine would have to be constructed, at least not for a long time. They sensed that this size would create problems, both in respect of technology and handling. However, consumer habit is a powerful force, and the attempts to sell "two for one" were not particularly successful. The market was not going to be happy with half measures – in the literal sense of the word –; a litre pack was demanded. Investigations showed that nearly 85 per cent of all consumer milk was sold by the litre. In other words, the Lund engineers had no choice; they were obliged to tackle the enlargement process. Using the so-called T500 machine as a basis, it must be possible to create a T1000 model, too. Gösta Winberg of the MC urged Tetra Pak to forge ahead with the project; he needed this size of package as well, and as quickly as possible, if he was going to be able to rationalise operations in the MC dairies in a decisive manner. In the city of Linköping, with old, cramped dairy premises right in the city centre, there was a choice: either new installations for glass bottles, or a compact plant for disposable packages. Space problems and progressive thinking settled the matter, and the Linköping dairy became the first to rearrange its entire production of consumer milk according to the Tetra Pak system. The one-litre pack began to be sold there in March 1957. The installation was soon followed by others in various places all over the country.

Linköping, the city where the advanced SAAB aeroplane manufacturing is located, became the place where another technological "high flyer" took off as the first Tetra Pak one-litre machine went into operation in 1957.

73

Dairies and retailers agreed: the new package entailed great advantages in comparison with the heavy glass bottle. Everything was done – by Tetra Pak, too – to support sales: advertisements, publicity materials, demonstrations in shops, advisers who gave lectures. Linköping was enough of a success for many other towns and cities in Sweden to venture to follow its example and launch the one-litre package. Throughout the years that followed, the dairy of Helsingborg, managed by the faithful ally Rolf Holmstedt, became one of Tetra Pak's most important objects of demonstration: a newly built, modern dairy in the vicinity of Lund, with plenty of space to accommodate large groups of visitors.

Hälsingborgs Mjölkcentral, HMC, with its Manager Rolf Holmstedt, was always happy to receive groups of customers from far and near.

Machine check-up on one of the HMC machines after completed production.

74

In its early years, Tetra Pak would often arrange information meetings for retailers and housewives. On such occasions, trial tasting and a generous distribution of free samples were the rule.

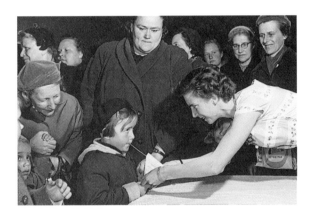

Helsingborg, gateway to Europe. This is the narrowest point of the Sound, and ferries run constantly.

75

Thore Larsson
shouldered and
coped with the
thankless task
of planning and
implementing the
Gothenburg intro-
duction.

Gothenburg, the second-biggest city in Sweden, also planned the construction of a new, large dairy in the late 1950s. It had been intended for glass bottles only, but at the last moment a decision was made to introduce the one-litre Tetra Pak carton. The introduction was attended by unfortunate circumstances. During the run-in of the new plant, problems with the taste of the milk cropped up; they were instantly, and unfairly, blamed on the package: *"This milk tastes like paper!"* The dairy also took this opportunity of introducing so-called homogenisation, which entails the atomisation of butterfat and makes it impossible to skim the cream off the top of the milk, the way people were used to doing. *"It has to be the package that's at fault!"* The large, awkward shape was not easy to handle. Enthusiasm among housewives and consumers was not overwhelming. And, finally, the glassworks of Surte, the main supplier to the Swedish dairy industry, was situated close to Gothenburg. Public opinion was turning against the package. In the early days, a newspaper was able to joke about a storm in a milk-glass; but the gale soon increased to a hurricane. The press wallowed in letters from the public fulminating against the wretched package. One of the newspapers organised a voting procedure which attracted 60,000 voters, less than two per cent of whom voted for Tetra Pak. These few persons were immediately contacted by telephone; maybe they could yield juicy titbits to feed to the public during the continued campaign. One of the interviewees is said to have replied: *"I like Tetra Pak because they've given my son a job."*

Another newspaper wrote a leader containing the following attack: *"Psychologically speaking, and without claiming to possess profound insights into the implications of glass versus Tetra in the context of the Swedish economy, we find it a complete mystery that this type of package, which nobody has greeted with joy and which is also considerably more expensive than glass, continues its – well, there is no other word for it than 'triumphal march' all over the country. We are reluctantly compelled to salute the gentlemen at Tetra for having succeeded so well in introducing such an expensive and detested package. The ever-increasing presence of the splashy triangles in various places in Sweden must, after all, be due to purposeful sales activities."* The person who did more than anybody else to deserve a salute was the Tetra Pak Sales Manager Thore Larsson, who was chiefly responsible for the introduction. During the tempestuous days in Gothenburg, he and a small group of advisers and women demonstrators gathered valuable insights into those special tricks that were required in the marketing efforts. Thorough information had to be given to all the

Gothenburg, home of Volvo, proved a recalcitrant market for Tetra Pak. It took several tough rounds before the match was finally won.

The Lantbrukarnas Mjölkcentral (Farmers' Milk Centre), the LMC, became an impressive plant. Among the machines shown in the picture is a "Steel Mate" for the automatic transfer of baskets from filling machine to conveyor belt. The design implies that the robot age is on its way.

The imposing height of the machinery often called for special arrangements to be made in the roof of the filling hall.

categories involved: dairy staff, shop assistants, and households. It takes a comprehensive planning endeavour to break up a consumer habit. One day, in spite of everything, the storm had blown over. The one-sided newspaper campaign became tedious, and in the middle of the brouhaha another news item hit the headlines, knocking readers out flat: Ingemar "Ingo" Johansson, a Gothenburg man, became World Champion of heavyweight boxing in June 1959.

The ice was broken, the points of reference multiplied, and the Tetra Pak system gained an increasingly firm footing, even in the northern parts of the country. A new problem arose in one of the dairies in the North. With the construction of the one-litre machine, the Lund engineers had established a record in terms of height, too: the machine was 5.2 metres (approx. 17 feet) high, of pole-vaulter dimensions. The dairy in question did not possess sufficient height in its filling hall; about half a metre was missing. The dairy manager's own office was right on top of the hall. What was to be done? An intrepid Tetra Pak salesman is never at a loss: *"Make an opening for the top of the machine and put glass all round it, and then you'll be able to monitor operations in the production hall without leaving your office."* To start with, the manager regarded the proposal as a typical example of Lundian burlesque humour, but he gradually warmed to the idea. Despite this unique arrangement, he was never one to look down on Tetra Pak – on the contrary, he became one of the company's keen supporters.

In the late 1950s, Sweden had turned into that reference market which the company so sorely needed, though the process had been a painful one at times. The one-litre package had been the final, difficult piece in the puzzle. Countless foreign customer groups went on pilgrimages to Swedish dairies which proudly showed off their model installations. The social-welfare policies of the country – the so-called "Swedish model" – brought many advantages, but it also entailed high salaries, high taxes, and high costs. Consequently, demands for the modernisation of the retail trade kept increasing, and cost-effective distribution systems were urgently required. The tetrahedron system was an initial answer to these demands, but it was, as we shall see, only a partial one. For the time being, the market was content with the spectacular triangular object, especially as there was no alternative within reach.

Despite the initial statement of this chapter, the Swedish prophecy had come true: Tetra Pak had managed to obtain recognition in its own country. But times would change. The Biblical passage is often quoted with something of a difference: *"A prophet is not without honour, save in his own city."* That version was to prove more apposite. It did not take many years for the Lund dairy where it all started to be absorbed by another, larger dairy company, whereupon it was closed down. This, in its turn, meant that a competing package began to be sold in Tetra Pak's own city, even in the company canteen. Long live competition!

"Now milk comes both in mama and in paper", was the witticism accompanying this cartoon.

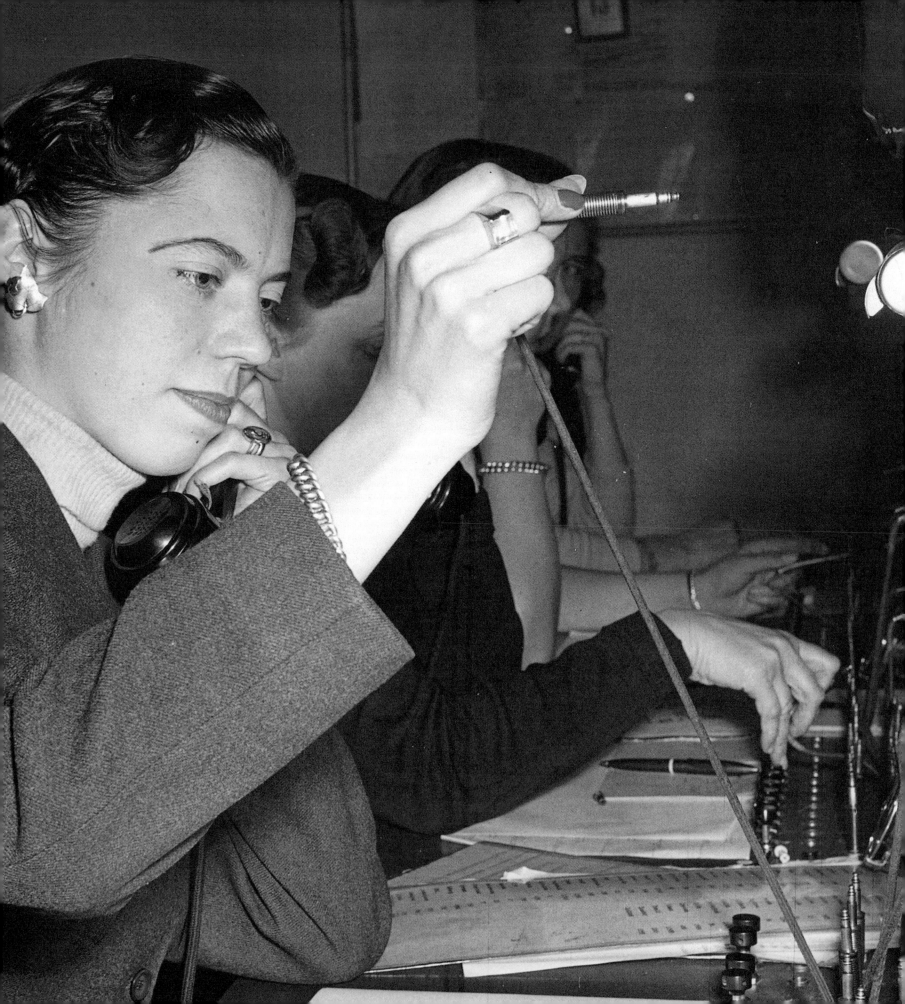

Open Sesame

The magic formula from "The Arabian Nights" was badly needed; now, at last, the world market was to open. There was no time to lose: everybody had been waiting – not only the nights involved could be counted by the thousands, but the days as well. A flying carpet would have been very useful indeed.

It was time for the message to spread at the speed of the wind.

The early 1950s determined the future fortunes of Tetra Pak. The company had been registered in December 1950, and from the very beginning Ruben Rausing had declared that it was going to operate all over the world. Concrete proof of the dynamic plans is contained in the minutes of a Board Meeting in January 1951 – the first ever of the company: *"It was decided that the trademark Tetra Pak would be registered in 57 countries."* In June the same year, the press conference described in a previous chapter took place, and preparations were made for the installation of the first machine in the Lund Dairy. However, things did not get off to a flying start. For technical reasons the première was delayed, and as we have seen it did not ensue until December 1952.

In the meantime, the members of the company management were conducting another discussion of vital significance to the business strategy of the future: under what forms was the Tetra Pak system to be offered to customers and market? The summer of 1951 witnessed the launching of the idea – obviously influenced by American thinking – that the machines were not to be sold, but leased. The issue often featured on the agenda during the next 18 months. Some of the people involved felt that an ordinary sales contract would be enough and that a leasing agreement ought not to be necessary: *"Tetra Pak must always make sure that its packing material is sold at the lowest conceivable price, and that will safeguard our deliveries to the filling machines."* After protracted debates, however, it was decided that the company would assume total responsibility for the system and that the leasing principle was to be applied. Åkerlund & Rausing's senior legal adviser Carl Borgström was instru-

The decision to lease machines rather than sell them outright was crucial to the Tetra Pak business concept. When drafting the texts in contracts, the company relied on the legal expertise of Carl Borgström.

mental in formulating an agreement proposal. There will be reason to return to the matter of the leasing contract and its design later on.

The company aimed to make its own country a fixed point for future sales. At the same time, it would not do to delay the leap into the export market for too long. Preparatory work outside the country began, and was conducted, alongside those efforts that were made on Swedish soil. In the late spring of 1953, Tetra Pak took part in its first official exhibition, in the Dutch city of Utrecht. It was imperative to pass the word about the new tetrahedron system as rapidly as possible and to put out feelers for interest among dairies. Besides, it was essential to establish contacts with suitable people or businesses that might represent the company in the international market. For the global conquest ahead, the "own" troops would not suffice; it was time to recruit mercenaries.

The new developments had acquired an independent status as a result of the creation of the new company, separated from Åkerlund & Rausing. The responsibility for sales rested on Erik Torudd, who had been strongly committed to the project throughout its period of development. Now that the time had come to set up a sales network, this crucial task was entrusted to him. The smoothest, quickest, and cheapest way would seem to be the tried-and-true approach, namely hunting out and roping in local sales agents. That way, it was hoped, the milk gospel could be disseminated on a wide front, the company acquiring valuable knowledge of the various markets along the way. There were two paths that could be followed: Tetra Pak could join forces either with agents who were established in the general packaging sector, or with agents who worked with the dairy industry on a regular basis, selling process equipment, tanks, pumps, or other dairy paraphernalia. Contacts were established with people who knew the business and who became Tetra Pak representatives on a commission basis. In Europe, the situation was a mixed bag; some countries were taken in hand by sales agents, whereas others had their own company from the outset.

Where the material was concerned – that which was generally known as "Tetra paper" in those days –, the company did everything it could to retain the new Lund plant as the point of delivery. This was an advantageous arrangement, as the Swedish raw material was inexpensive and of the right quality. Besides, it was important to create volume for production in Sweden and to make full use of the capacity of the new plant. Very soon, however, demands for locally-produced paper were raised in various quarters. Customers in Europe had no wish to be dependent on long-haul transport and on set times of delivery, not to mention the danger of strikes and other hazards. Cows are milked twice a day; milk is perishable; and it must be possible to deliver products on a daily basis – no "milk engorgement" could be allowed to happen. Dairies felt more secure with manufacturing within reach, in their own country. At this time, in the mid-1950s, Tetra Pak did not possess the necessary funds for building its own factories; the solution would have to consist in appointing licensees. In swift succession, co-operation agreements were signed with firms in Britain, Finland, France, the Netherlands, Norway, Germany, and Austria.

BRITAIN

Express Dairy was one of the first Tetra Pak customers. The sale of milk by way of vending machines was a novelty tested in London.

The first grand exhibition in Britain took place in 1955, during a dairy show in the Olympic Hall, London. Here, the advantages of Tetra Pak are being demonstrated to no less a person than HM the Queen Mother.

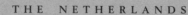

FINLAND

NORWAY

In the mid-1950s,
licence agreements
for the local manu-
facture of the special
Tetra Pak material
were signed with
several West Euro-
pean countries.
Soon the package
was a familiar sight
in European outdoor
scenes.

FRANCE

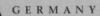

GERMANY

AUSTRIA

85

Carl-Axel Althin was in charge of European sales during the second half of the 1950s.

The "Council of Europe" numbered Erik Sandberg, Harald Strander, Lars Leander, and several others among its members.

Once operations had been reasonably satisfactorily established in Europe, the leap into the remainder of the world market had to follow quickly. *"The Board decided to commission Mr Torudd to visit and work up overseas markets where Tetra Pak has not been introduced, such as Brazil, the Argentine, the remainder of South and Central America, India, Australia, New Zealand and further countries."* The quotation comes from Board minutes of early 1957. At this time, Dr Carl-Axel Althin had taken over responsibility for operations in Europe. His small team of salesmen came to include Harald Strander, Erik Sandberg, Lars Leander, and a few more staff members. Over the next ten years, it was Erik Torudd's job to build up, reinforce, and manage activities in all those countries outside Europe which had not as yet been subjected to serious penetration. In some of them, agents joined in the efforts; in others sales companies took over some of the work, and there were countries where licensees handled the manufacturing of materials. The company head office was far away, business activities took time, and political as well as economic circumstances were difficult. These organisations often led dull lives characterised by very little movement and meagre, if any, results.

Torudd was keen to get things going on the spot, and he became a globetrotter in the true sense of the word. His visiting schedules – planned in detail, and with very small margins for changes or delays – took him on constant journeys all around the globe; how many times he is hardly able to say himself. On one occasion only, in 1961, he met a man who surpassed him where long-distance travel was concerned. His diary reveals: *"Touchdown in Dakar, Senegal. Needed swift access to my hotel room, but the staff had not managed to extract the previous guest from it. Waited for an hour or so in the lobby, but then got tired of the whole thing and hammered on the door of the room I'd been promised. Who should open the door – slightly drowsy – if not Yury Gagarin, the Russian cosmonaut who became the first man in space. A friendly, unassuming fellow. No wonder a space-traveller's diurnal rhythm had gone haywire on earth!"*

During his innumerable trips, Torudd frequently visited Swedish embassies, legations, and trading houses, meeting fellow countrymen in faraway places who had gathered years of experience of various foreign markets. Some of these people were connected to the company as local sales agents; others came to hold more central posts in the organisation. The latter, for instance, applied to Jan Rimberth, who was previously employed in one of the major Swedish trading houses and had worked in East Africa, among other places. For a long time, Rimberth held a key position at the overseas sales department in Lund, where he was in charge of contacts with many of the local sales representatives and subsidiaries outside Europe.

The words "agent" and "act" are both derived from the Latin verb *agere*, meaning "to do", and consequently imply resourcefulness and enterprise. Even so, the degree of success obtained by way of sales through the agent network turned out – with a few exceptions – to be rather moderate. One main reason for the difficulties involved was the commercial system which Tetra Pak had adopted, namely the leasing procedure which was crucial to the entire construction of the company. A brief description of the sales strategy that was established and applied from the outset might hence be in order at this point. According to the American pattern, it had been decided that the machines were to be hired out, not sold, and that payment should be made by stages. Income from machines was divided into three components: a so-called basic rent, a quarterly rent, and a production rent, often called royalty. The design of the contract was an unusual one in those days, containing clauses that tied down both parties in an uncompromising manner. Tetra Pak undertook responsibility for the system as a whole, which entailed far-reaching consequences in respect of deliveries, warranties, and service. The obligations were mutual, however, and the customer was expected to co-operate in a spirit of loyalty, buying paper, distribution equipment, and spare parts from the company, employing its technical services, and so on. What the agreement amounted to, in fact, was a commercial marriage entered into without a premarital settlement – a pretty unconditional business on both sides. As the market has developed over the years, the contract design has successively been modified and adapted to modern conditions; but many of the guarantee undertakings have remained, in the best interests of the customer.

In those days, local agents were not used to dealing with situations of the kind outlined above, nor did they possess adequate resources for doing so. When a machine was taken under contract, that was by no means the end of the deal – actually, that was the point at which it began. The agents involved might have been used to supplying "after-sales service" to a certain extent; but they had no experience of the sort of all-out commitment that Tetra Pak pursued. Hence, agents were simply incapable of living up to those demands that were made on them both by the contract obligations and by the relevant technology. While this did not exactly come as a revelation to the Lund management, their compa-

For years, Jan Rimberth and Bertil Paulson held vital positions in what was then called the Overseas Division. One of their functions was to make sure that work on essential and difficult export markets was properly coordinated.

Kenya Cooperative
Creameries, KCC,
was a pioneering
customer in Africa.
Interior view from
the dairy in Nairobi.

ny was an impecunious one and salesmen on commission were, after all, the cheapest solution. Usually, selling agents would not be paid until a deal had been concluded; by contrast, an "own" local organisation would cost money from the word go. However, there was an ambition to encourage "own" forces to take over operations in every country as soon as possible, thereby attaining a guarantee for swift and good results. As the business volume grew, the company gradually phased out the sales-agents system in favour of its own companies. Kenya, the first market outside Europe, may serve as a good example of this development.

Conversely to what many people believe, milk is a greatly appreciated product in many African countries, and Kenya is no exception. In the early years of the twentieth century, the availability of pasture up in the so-called highlands in the western parts of the country persuaded European settlers to breed cows and start producing milk. As time went by, small local dairy firms amalgamated, forming the Kenya Cooperative Creameries – the KCC – in the 1930s. The fast-growing capital, Nairobi, became an attractive market. In order to be able to cope with distribution in the prevailing climate – Nairobi is almost on the equator – the milk had to be packaged, and the glass bottle was the only reasonable option. An unforeseen problem emerged, however, and gradually assumed grave proportions. Ingenious milk- and middlemen developed remarkable skills when it came to removing bottle tops unnoticeably, pouring off some of the milk, replacing it with whitish chalk water, and putting the top back in place again. The stolen milk was sold "on the side" at a considerable profit, whereas consumers of KCC bottled milk often fell ill; the added water was usually polluted and dangerous to people's health.

By way of a Danish trading house which had been appointed as the Tetra Pak agent, the new package was brought to the attention of the KCC. Now this was something that could not be manipulated; here was the solution of the watered-down milk! A contract was signed, machines were delivered, and in 1957 Kenya became the first market outside the boundaries of Europe. Volumes grew fast; but the expansion was not without friction. Despite the great efforts that were invested in training the technicians working in the dairy, frequent disruptions occurred in production. The Danish agent did not have the resources needed to remedy the shortcomings, and expeditions from Lund became more and more common. The service engineer who went on the largest number of these trips was "Kenya Svensson", with the Christian name Lennart. As

soon as he returned to Sweden, chaos erupted in the KCC. Kenya Svensson had to be stationed in Nairobi, but at the expense of Tetra Pak. This was to be the first step towards a permanent organisation in the country. In the end, looking after a big and growing customer became too much for the local agent. Tetra Pak (Kenya) Ltd was formed in 1969; competent Tetra Pak staff were in place, and commercial as well as technical involvement increased. A service workshop was established, a Tetra Pak training centre was set up for the customers' technicians, and after another ten years or so the decision was made to start a factory in the country, for the manufacturing of packaging materials. As in many other places, Tetra Pak activities have contributed to creating employment for the local population.

It would be possible to adduce a number of examples similar to that of Kenya. Most of them have adhered to the same pattern. After a modest start, either initiated directly from Lund or achieved by way of the work-up efforts of agents, markets have emerged, gradually becoming capable of bearing the costs of their own sales organisations. Today, Tetra Pak has almost 60 marketing companies which, under the direction of four regional head offices, are in charge of commercial operations in 125 countries (in 1995). Nowadays sales agents are few and far between.

In Kenya, the distribution of protein to the young is a national concern of such importance that the country's Central Bank was inspired to put a picture of milk-drinking school-children on one of its notes.

The local M.D. of Tetra Pak, Torbjörn Nilsson, demonstrating the advantages of the packaging system.

89

For more than
20 years, in the
capacity of Deputy
Managing Director
working with the
group executive board,
Ragnar Mandersson
was in charge of such
projects as the con-
struction of Tetra Pak
materials factories
all over the world.

Step by step, the licensees for materials manufacturing who predominated during the early expansion have been replaced by "own", modern
plants, as soon as the volumes of the respective markets were able to
justify local manufacture. Apart from the costs of technological development, investments in materials factories have been the most weighty
item of expenditure over the years. The first of Tetra Pak's own manufacturing units outside Sweden was built in Italy, and the engineer Ragnar
Mandersson was put in charge of it. Mandersson, who originally came
from the textile industry, had been employed at Åkerlund & Rausing in
1958. According to Ruben Rausing, the textile trade was an excellent
background: *"That line of business has been wrestling with problems of
profitability for years, so it's a useful school for forward-looking technologists.
There, tutored by scarcity, they have had to learn rational methods of
production."* At Å&R, Mandersson came into contact with Tetra Pak
production technology, and for some time he assisted the company's
licensees, in Finland among other countries. After a couple of years with
another employer, he returned to Lund and Tetra Pak in 1963.
Mandersson faced his first major challenge in 1965, as Managing Director
of the Italian plant. There was much at stake; this, after all, was the first
time that Tetra Pak paper was going to be produced under its own steam,
as it were, outside the boundaries of Sweden – and for a market which
had had time to grow to sizeable proportions.

Thanks to the first-class results which Ragnar Mandersson achieved
during five instructive years in Italy, he was summoned back to the Lund
headquarters in 1970. There, Mandersson was appointed Technical
Manager and entrusted with global responsibility for factories and the
manufacture of materials. Later, he was also put in charge of research and
development, as well as of the production of machinery. Mandersson
keenly supported the exportation of Swedish technology: young
engineers were given intensive training in Swedish plants and then sent
abroad as production managers, frequently under demanding circumstances. Technical departments were strengthened and became im-
mensely helpful to the international marketing organisation. When
Ragnar Mandersson retired in 1989, he was able to count the factory flags
on the world map with justifiable pride. By now, there were quite a
number of them – approximately 30, in fact. Despite countless problems
along the way, he was also able to state: *"All these years, I've gone off to
work every morning with a feeling of happy anticipation – Tetra Pak really
gets into your blood, you know!"*

As developments continued, the company had often entered into alliances with various partners, sales agents, and licensees, especially during start-up phases. In many cases difficulties jointly tackled bred a spirit of unity, and years of trusting collaboration ensued. However, the company's ambition has always been to be independent and stand on its own two feet as soon as possible. Like so many others, Tetra Pak has had reason to learn the truth of the contention that *"if you want anything done, you had better go and do it yourself"*.

The Rubiera plant in Italy was the first Tetra Pak factory outside Sweden. The small picture shows Ragnar Mandersson talking with the M.D. of Tetra Pak in Italy, Danilo Severi.

Right, Hans Rausing pressing the start-up button when the factory went into operation in the spring of 1965.

Long Live Milk

Daughter, Tochter, dotter – all three of them are derived from the Greek word θυγατερ, which means just that, "daughter". The word is said to have a secondary meaning, too: "female milker". It was the job of the woman of the family to milk the cow, sheep, or goat – domestic animals in the literal sense of those words: they were close by and belonged to the household, and they were able to deliver their perishable produce every day, at any hour. There were no distances in time and space of the kind we are familiar with today; durability was not to become a problem until much later, when animals and people were increasingly far apart and the thirsty person would be miles from the source.

In our modern society, this problem has been brought to an extreme.

If all things went according to Nature's intentions, everybody would drink his or her first milk at the maternal breast. It is no coincidence that we see a connection between the Latin *mamma, mamilla* ("breast") and the word which most of us learn to pronounce before any other. Soon enough, however, we have to become used to other, animal milk products which have accompanied humanity through the millennia. In agrarian society, milk was easily accessible. The difficulties arrived when larger communities were formed and milk could no longer be consumed directly "at source". It became necessary to make this vulnerable product more durable. Some early solutions to this problem are found in sour milk, cheese, and butter.

After the breakthrough of industrialism, during the latter half of the nineteenth century, heat treatment began to be applied, and milk was sterilised at high temperatures. The outcome was increased durability, but also a dead product, far removed from the invigorating natural milk. A boiled taste, often caramelised, made it more suitable as an addition to coffee and tea, or as an ingredient in cooking, than as a drink on its own. In spite of this, sterile milk became widely accepted in some countries, although it was an expensive, complicated alternative.

By far the most elegant solution was the one that followed on Louis Pasteur's discovery – made around 1870 – that pathogenic bacteria could be made harmless by means of brief heating up to approx. 75 degrees centigrade. At first, Pasteur had been interested in beverages rather closer to French hearts – wine and beer –; but soon the method came to be applied to milk, too. Suddenly people found that there was a product which had not been boiled beyond recognition, tasted better, and was more nutritious as well. If pasteurisation was combined with cold storage, and preferably with some sort of packaging that protected it from the action of airborne bacteria, milk could remain fresh for a couple of days and be prevented from turning sour. Alongside sale as a "loose" commodity, small quantities of milk began to be filled into glass bottles, primitive devices covering their apertures. This was the situation during the first half of the twentieth century. As time went by, methods of processing and filling became increasingly refined. In the United States, too, the 1930s witnessed the slow appearance of the first cartons in the market.

The dream of eternal life is peculiar to mankind: now that it had been possible to preserve milk for several days thanks to pasteurisation and packaging, perhaps there might be a way of prolonging durability without adopting too drastic measures? The ingenious closed-circuit filling system invented by Tetra Pak afforded glimpses of hope in this respect. Conditions were favourable: the milk never came into contact with the ambient air nor with any part of the machinery, and shaping and sealing took place from the outside. Only the filling pipe was inside the paper tube. The packaging material was uncomplicated in that the process started out from a smoothly unrolling line of paper; there were no folds, corners, or nooks and crannies. Finally, the finished package did not contain any air, as sealing was performed from below, beneath the surface of the liquid. In other words, the tetrahedron system had built-in advantages which were waiting to be explored. The Rausing family and the Tetra Pak engineers working on developments continued to ponder ways of extending durability. *"Time is money"* – here the old saying was more than apposite. Fancy making milk last for longer periods, maybe a week or even longer, and without refrigeration – what benefits that would create, both in terms of storage and distribution!

On Ruben Rausing's initiative, a number of efforts geared to sterilising the packaging material were set in motion as early as 1953-54. One of the approaches that were tried consisted in sterilising the paper surface by means of a flame, but this method of burning damaged the interior plastic film. Attempts were also made to sterilise the paper, enclosed in cassettes, by means of gas. This method worked; but it was a complex one and deemed to be infeasible in the dairy. Another idea was to conduct the flow of paper through a kind of steam cabinet, but this thought had to be abandoned, too. Besides, it was of course essential to improve the sealing quality – how was the company going to be able to guarantee a bacteriologically sealed package, if the receptacle was not even one-hundred-per-cent tight?

New methods had to be tried by which bacteria could be effectively removed from the inside of the package. It was well known that hydrogen peroxide kills bacteria – in the olden days, many people had had to submit to having the cuts and grazes of childhood disinfected by peroxide. Actually, this kind of sterilisation was discussed as early as the mid-1940s, at which point Erik Wallenberg, inventor of the tetrahedron, had raised the issue. Not until ten years later were purposeful investigations initiated, proceeding from the existing standard machine. In the early days, the engineer Alex Tuma, an immigrant from Czechoslovakia, had been in charge of the project. He was employed as a service engineer in 1955; but somewhat later he received a proposal from the top management: *"We heard that you only spent a couple of weeks at home last year, so would you perhaps be interested in a job that involves somewhat less travel?"* Tuma experimented widely with chemical sterilisation, finding that in order to achieve results it was necessary to combine peroxide with heat. For this purpose, he constructed a special machine which was installed in the Centre for Experimental Dairy Development at the agricultural college of Alnarp outside Lund. The technique did work; but it turned out to be too complicated in practice and was abandoned when simpler applications had been evolved.

During the years in question, Ruben Rausing conducted another project which came in for a good deal of attention and is related to the matter in hand. On his farm Simontorp outside Lund, he had kept a large dairy herd for a number of years. Now, he had the cow-house and cattle-tending arranged in such a manner that the best possible hygienic conditions were created. Stringent directives were observed during milking. The result was milk with an extremely low incidence of bacteria, a

The Simontorp AAA milk was produced under extremely hygienic conditions. As it contained so few bacteria, it could be sold without having been subjected to heat treatment.

95

Experts at
the Alnarp Dairy
Centre, Professors
Swartling (left)
and Thomé,
sampling Simontorp
milk with Ruben
Rausing. Picture
taken around 1960.

virtually sterile natural product. It was instantly chilled and then immediately packaged in a Tetra Pak machine, installed in a closed, air-filtered room beside the byre. In this way, untreated fresh milk was obtained in half-litre tetrahedron packages, a kind of milk which would keep for a considerably longer period – if refrigerated – than ordinary pasteurised milk. Besides, the package made it possible to deep-freeze the product. Manufacturing was expensive, of course, and the outlet was very small. For example, Simontorp AAA Milk was sold to the vessels "Kungsholm" and "Gripsholm" of the Swedish American Line which sailed from Gothenburg to New York. Passengers could hence enjoy fresh Swedish milk at their breakfast tables after eight to ten days at sea, watching the Statue of Liberty emerge out of the morning mist. The Simontorp milk became an episode, but it was an important one, and the experiment paved the way for what was to become a revolution on the same scale as Pasteur's discovery: the development of the aseptic, entirely bacteria-free filling process, applied in combination with careful sterilisation of the milk.

In order to push matters ahead as quickly as possible, outside experts were also called in to help. At an early stage, contacts were established with a Swiss industrial group, Ursina. During a Meeting in November

1954, Hans Rausing reported to the Board of AB Tetra Pak that *"negotiations have been initiated regarding co-operation aimed at establishing, by way of experiments, a method for the packaging of sterile milk in Tetra packages."* Ursina had evolved interesting specialist competence in the milk sector, and the group had created a new type of process equipment called the Uperisator. By means of steam injection, Ursina had managed to attain swift and cautious sterilisation of milk – taste and nutritional values were almost comparable with those of pasteurised products. Several other companies were working on the problem; but Ursina, with its research-and-development company Alpura, was ahead of the rest. The new technique called for the product to be packaged at once in a bacteria-free environment, so as to prevent reinfection. The solution thitherto adopted by the Ursina Group consisted in filling into sterile tins, according to an American method. Practical experience was available, as Ursina sold milk-based puddings and some other products filled in tins of the relevant sort. These fairly expensive goods could live with an expensive package; but for ordinary milk a tin would be too costly. Consequently, Ursina was anxious to find another kind of package.

The German subsidiary of Ursina offered to help with the developmental work, and a Tetra Pak machine was sent off to Munich for certain experiments which actually resulted in a patent application. But the technique turned out to be beset by problems, and the project was dropped. Ursina was interested in continuing to collaborate with Tetra Pak and suggested that a filling machine be installed in the Alpura experimental workshop outside Berne. The German results had generated other ideas which were held to be worth trying. At Tetra Pak, people were somewhat reluctant to place a machine for developmental purposes with a foreign company, without having a watertight guarantee to the effect that all inventions which belonged to the Tetra Pak method would duly become Tetra Pak property. This difficulty had in fact arisen before, during the German trials. Complicated negotiations were being conducted regarding a basic comprehensive contract which would also regulate the terms of compensation in relation to Ursina/Alpura. Finally, an agreement was reached at the beginning of 1957. A machine was delivered to Switzerland, and concrete co-operation could start.

At this early stage, neither side had any idea of the hardships ahead – nor of the colossal market success that this joint endeavour would entail. The years 1957–61 were characterised by the search for a sufficiently simple and safe method, preferably integrated in the filling machine, for the sterilisation of the packaging material. The answer was provided by a fusion of old and new ideas. The flow of material passes through a peroxide bath and a couple of wipe-off rollers on its way from paper roll to tube formation. A heating device is placed on the filling pipe inside the paper tube, just above the liquid surface. The device vaporises any small peroxide residues which might linger on the inside of the paper. Simultaneously, an upward-flowing stream of hot sterile air is created, preventing airborne bacteria from entering the paper tube. A simple, practical solution to a tricky problem was the tangible outcome of these joint efforts. In a modified form, the same method is used in the Tetra Pak machines of today. Results from tests kept growing better and better, and co-operative work was pursued in a spirit of relative harmony. At times, the Swedes would grumble that the Swiss were being unnecessarily pernickety, but this was probably just as well. Bacteriology is not the sort of thing you handle carelessly; the spreading of contaminated milk could have had disastrous effects.

In the middle of 1961, things had proceeded to the point where a decision was made to arrange an international press demonstration. It took place at the beginning of September that year outside Berne. In front of journalists and scientists, representatives from Alpura and Tetra Pak described the results that had been obtained so far. They emphasised all the advantages of the new method, and it was during this press conference that "aseptic milk" came into being as an officially recognised phenomenon. There had been some doubt as to what the product should be called. There was no denying that "aseptic" smacked of the pharmaceutical laboratory. At the same time, it was important to distinguish the new product from the kind of milk that existed already – sterile and pasteurised. For this reason, people were unwilling to launch the term "ultra-pasteurised", which had also been considered. Tetra Pak attempted to introduce the concept of *teperised* milk, by way of allusion to the bacteria-free *TP method* used during packaging. A short time after this decision had been made, and even discussed on the Board, a German-speaking colleague pointed out that the expression was uncomfortably close to the slightly vulgar German dialectal word *Tepp* or *Depp*, which means "fool", "nincompoop". The proposed name was buried right away, never to reappear!

For lack of better things, "aseptic milk" hence became the basic designation. A description of the process was contained in the expression "UHT-treated" milk, which was also adopted. The abbreviation stands

Hans Rausing in a position to establish that the small, original cream package is far less weighty than the half-litre package – the latter size was introduced for aseptic, long-life milk.

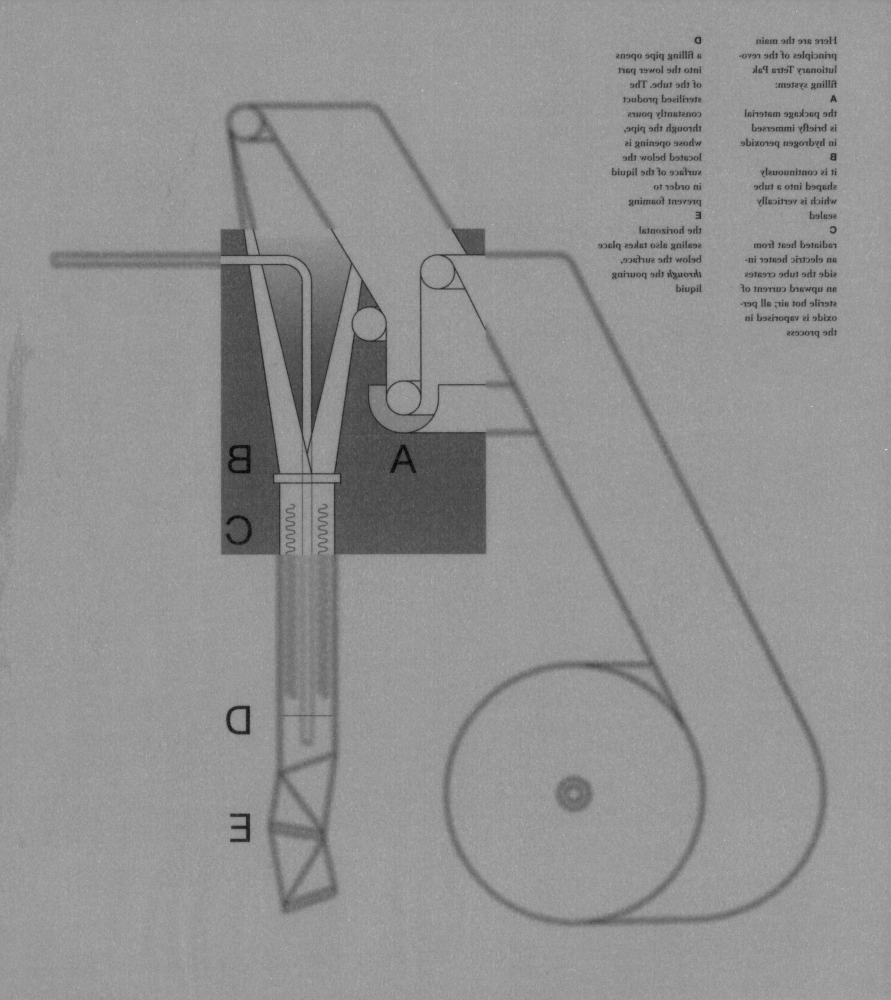

Here are the main
principles of the revo-
lutionary Tetra Pak
filling system:

A

the package material
is briefly immersed
in hydrogen peroxide

B

it is continuously
shaped into a tube
which is vertically
sealed

C

radiated heat from
an electric heater in-
side the tube creates
an upward current of
sterile hot air; all per-
oxide is vaporised in
the process

D

a filling pipe opens
into the lower part
of the tube. The
sterilised product
constantly pours
through the pipe,
whose opening is
located below the
surface of the liquid
in order to
prevent foaming

E

the horizontal
sealing also takes place
below the surface,
through the pouring
liquid

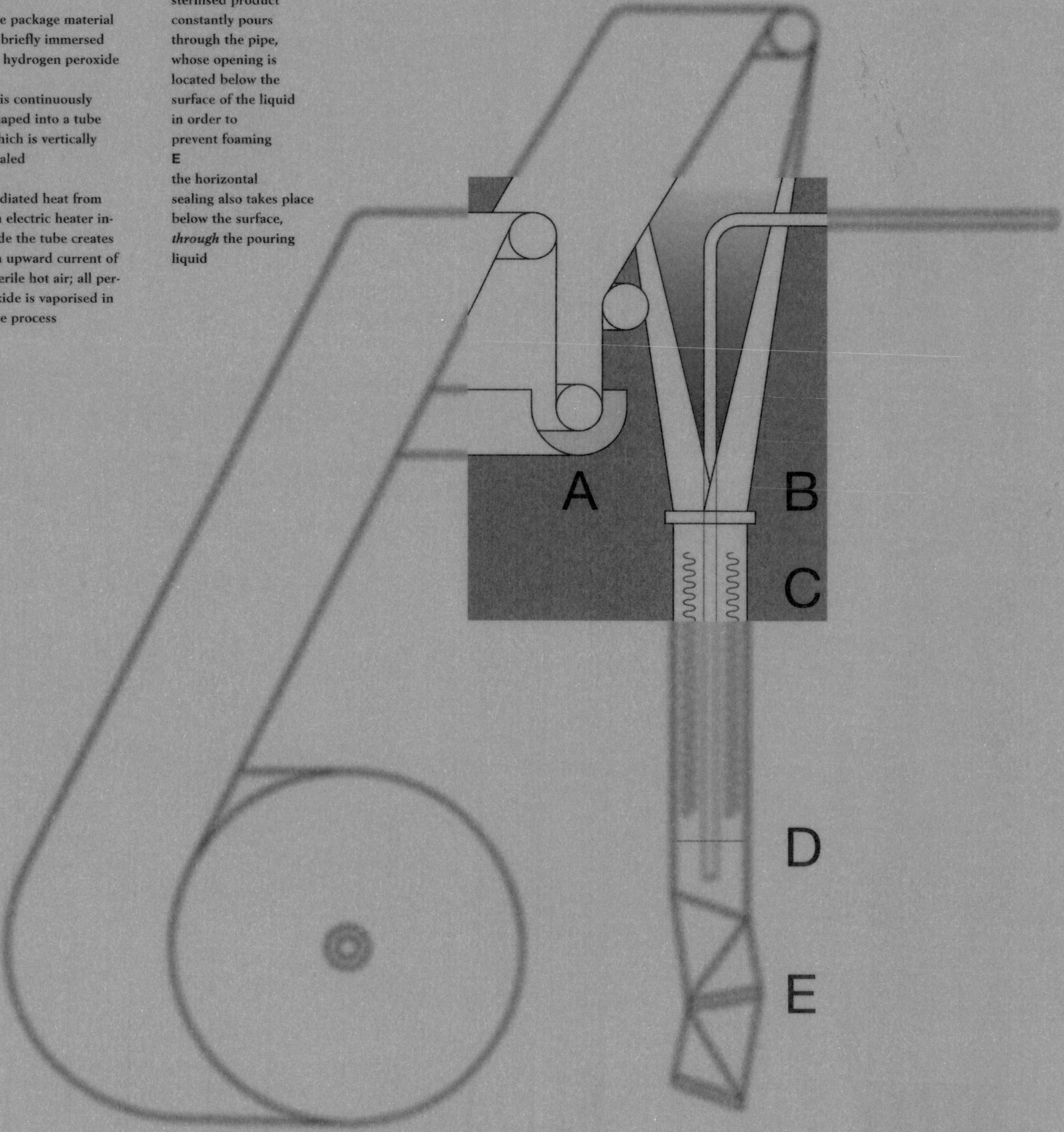

A

B

C

D

E

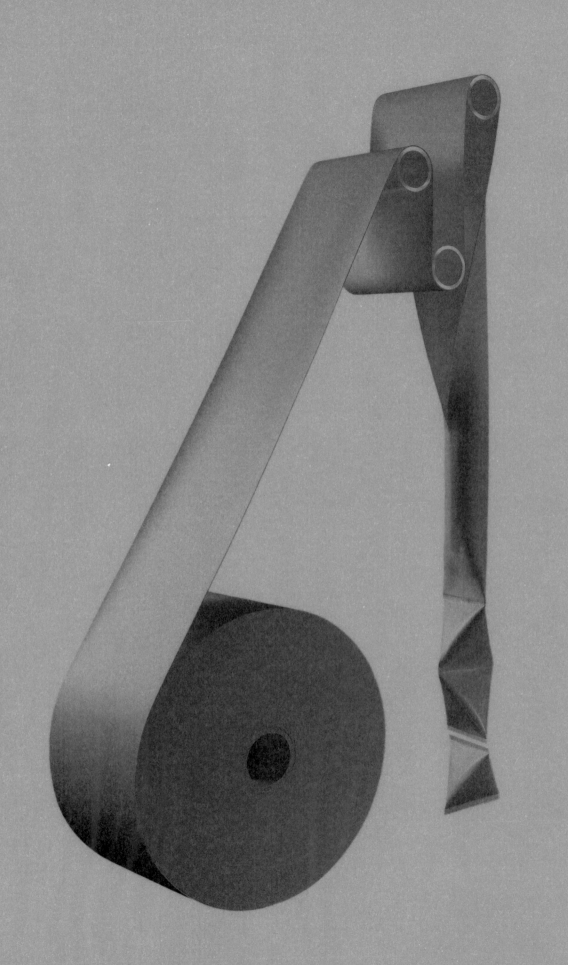

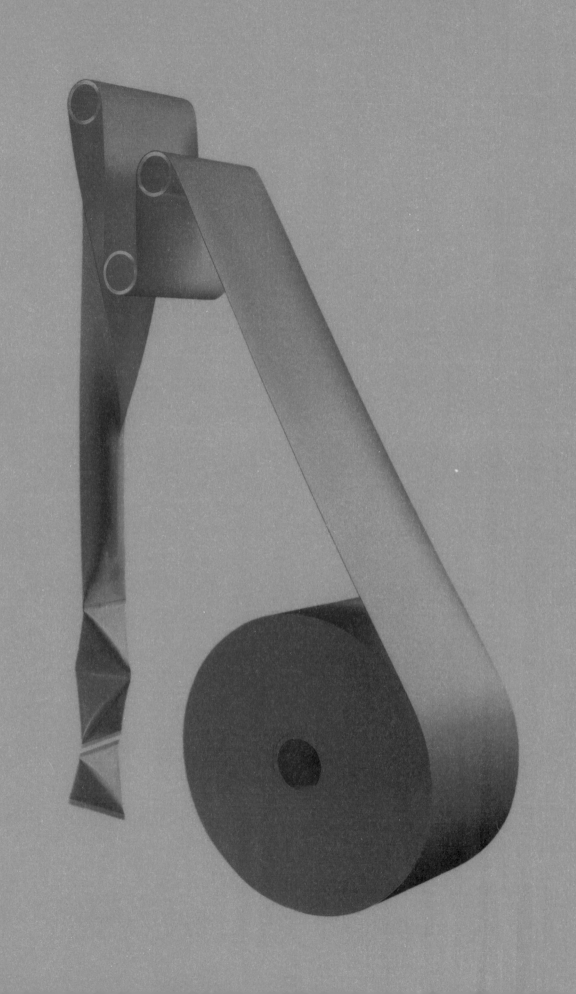

In consequence of Tetra Pak collaboration with Ursina/Alpura, the announcement that there was now such a thing as long-life milk was first made in Switzerland. There was a press conference in 1961, attended by scientists as well as by representatives from publications in the field.

for Ultra High Temperature, that is, rapid heating to a considerably higher temperature than the one used during pasteurisation. In due course, aseptic milk would acquire a number of different commercial appellations. In Scandinavia and in German-speaking countries, the designation H-milk was introduced, H being short for *hållbar*, *haltbar*. English-language markets tend to favour the term *long-life*, whereas Latin nations adopt paraphrases: *longue conservation* (French), *lunga durata* (Italian), *larga vida* (Spanish), and so on. Cherished pets have many names, and this milk was a truly appreciated novelty. Here at last was a durable product which preserved much of the character of the original milk with regard to taste, vitamins, and nutritional value.

After the press conference in 1961, the experimental machine was used at Alpura for limited market trials. By way of a contract with the dairy of Berne, minor quantities were sold in the Swiss capital. By and large, the product was favourably received by consumers. In June 1962, the dairy received a machine of its own, and the new "H milk" began to

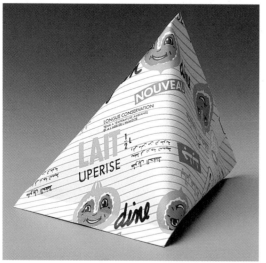

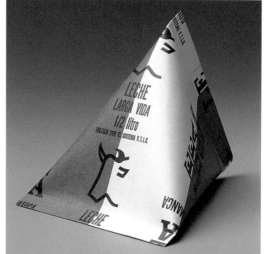

The new Ultra Heat Treated milk, which keeps without refrigeration, was soon found all over Europe.

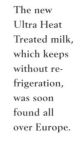

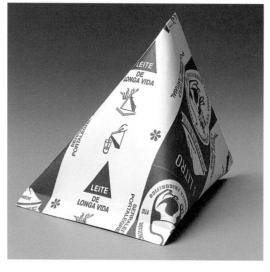

be sold on a continuous basis. As a result, work on international marketing could begin. However, "more haste, less speed" was still a watchword; the technique was not yet perfectly developed. The installations that were made frequently produced milk that turned out not to keep for as long as people had hoped. In such a complicated plant, it was also hard to prove just where unsterility originated – in the steriliser, the homogeniser, the pumps, the couplings, the pipes, the filling machine, the packaging material, or in poor cleaning and care of the machine itself? There were many sources of error, and the hazards involved in the distribution of unsterile products were apparent. This, after all, was an entirely new product which did not go sour in the only-too-familiar way. It might be harmful to the health of humans, and the consumer still would not be able to avert danger by instantly reacting to smell and taste. Now that aseptic technology has conquered the world market, it is hard to comprehend what a perilous venture the parties concerned entered into, suppliers as well as dairy customers. Faith and a sense of conviction far beyond the ordinary were required from everyone involved.

At the same time, the advantages were obvious, and interested parties were not difficult to find. After the experimental period in Switzerland, the system was held to have come far enough for cautious introduction in countries such as France, Italy, and Germany, beginning in the autumn of 1962. For security reasons, it was thought best to restrict the initial moves to Europe. Although asepsis as an idea spread like wildfire during the next few years, with pilot installations in many countries, considerable efforts were required to make the system work. Not until a few years later was the technological aspect satisfactorily taken care of: a decision was made to utilise paper with a thin aluminium-foil coat on the inside. As a result, the sealing technique could be improved, and the method became safer. Besides, the foil provided perfect protection against the effects of light and air.

For Tetra Pak it was essential not to abandon sales opportunities unnecessarily, but the company also had to be selective when picking its partners in the field of asepsis. The worst thing that could possibly happen was for aseptic filling machines to be connected to inadequate sterilisers, which would jeopardise the entire new technology. In view of this, rigorous agreements were drawn up with new manufacturers of sterilisers. No connections were allowed in the market unless careful preliminary tests had been performed according to a detailed schedule. When all bacteriological results were acceptable, the steriliser in ques-

The ground-
breaking aseptic
filling method
called for com-
prehensive staff
training. Here
Jack Berggren,
an engineer
at Tetra Pak, is
teaching a course
for dairy tech-
nicians.

tion was approved for sale together with Tetra Pak machines. These dictates may seem tough; but at that time they were necessary: a completely new system was being introduced, and the market was not accustomed to handling it. Customers had to be persuaded to adopt super-hygienic standards and a mode of bacteriological thinking which had never been necessary before. Dirty hands, careless washing, or other sins of omission might bring the whole thing down. A comprehensive training programme was initiated; dairy engineers and technicians as well as dairy-machine operators were offered a period of "education" at Tetra Pak. Today, it might seem difficult to understand that such demands could be articulated; but the fact that the system constituted such a great advance at the time made it possible to impose stringent terms. As standards rose in the dairy industry, they gradually became less mandatory.

The entire concept – UHT sterilisation and aseptic packaging – was a novelty of a kind never seen before. In comparison with pasteurised milk, the new product was of course more expensive. Still, clever Tetra Pak salespeople did their utmost to persuade the market that the additional expense was offset by rational distribution without refrigeration. The arguments were plausible, although calculations after the event some-times showed that the truth was rather a different story. As early as the second half of the 1960s, long-life milk products gained ground quickly, in spite of the costs involved; it was impossible to resist the temptation of breaking through established zones of distribution and expanding beyond familiar boundaries – even national ones. The aseptic "triangle" began its triumphant progress all over the world, laying the foundations for an entirely new way of handling, storing, and distributing milk, juice, and other liquid foods. When, at a later date, the system was supplemented by the more distribution-friendly Tetra Brik package, the conquest of the world market continued at an even faster rate. It is hardly an exaggeration to claim that UHT products, aseptically packaged and distributed outside the refrigeration chain, constituted *"the greatest innovation since Pasteur"*. These days, long-life milk goes everywhere. Distances in time and space, challenging conditions for distribution, and unsuitable climates no longer pose obstacles. Tasty, nourishing products are not the privileges of the few who are fortunate enough to live in well-developed societies. Today they are available to everybody, not least to the hungry and thirsty inhabitants of the Third World.

To anyone who considers the birth pangs which the system, the organisation, and the market had to go through in order to achieve this comprehensive presence in the market, a word of wisdom from the top management seems a fitting recapitulation: *"Remember that every complaint is the gateway to a new order!"* There were certainly complaints in plenty in the early days; but then the number of orders has gone on to assume incalculable proportions, too.

A Square Deal

It is a fine autumn day in 1958, and the telephone rings: "Hello, Åke here, can I see you this afternoon for a short while? I'll come by your office at 2.25 p.m., but I'll have to leave at 2.40." He was as good as his word, arriving right on the dot and hurrying off a quarter of an hour later.

But that time had sufficed for the discussion of essential matters.

That is the picture which most people have of Åke Gustafson, the live wire who headed technological developments at Tetra Pak during some eventful years from the late 1950s onwards. Those were the years when the tetrahedron system was consolidated and the first results with the aseptic method were achieved. And, above all, those were the years that witnessed the birth of the Tetra Brik – the product which was to become the flagship of the company.

Throughout the 1950s, the idea of conquering the world with the technology supplied by the "triangle" permeated the company. After a slow start during the first few years, market gains picked up speed towards the end of the decade – the product was becoming well established, new package sizes were created, the list of customers grew. But expansion was not without friction. The most cumbersome development project was that of the one-litre carton, which Swedish dairies began to introduce in the spring of 1957. Like every new model, the 1-litre machine turned out to be marred by shortcomings – an unusually large number in this case. They were proportional to the size of the package; people felt that this was the limit of what the tetrahedron shape was capable of. Great efforts were called for; in the beginning there were daily disruptions in production, as well as persistent leakages; and customer patience suffered hard trials. In addition, the "triangular litre" was hard to handle for the end consumer – in the shopping bag, in the refrigerator, and on the breakfast table. The ironic slogan *"Buy Tetra Pak,*

For many years Tage Norberg, originally a patent engineer at Å&R, was responsible for technological matters in the Tetra Pak management.

Karl-Erik Sahlberg laid the foundations for the effective international service organisation at Tetra Pak.

Olle Stark and Kjell Mårtensson were members of the group of design engineers around Åke Gustafson.

and there'll always be milk on your table" acquired proverbial status; after all, not everybody was able to handle and pour from the package.

In spite of the problems, the management's faith in the superiority of the system was unbroken. However, it was felt to be necessary to add reinforcements to the small group who had been in charge of technological matters from the start. At this point, it was essential to consolidate the machine programme, but also to forge ahead with the aseptic, bacteria-free filling system which was being developed. Some suitable person or persons should be hand-picked for these jobs. Besides, the Board had already begun to extend and rejuvenate the technical cadres. It was no longer possible to rely virtually exclusively on staff who had learnt on the job and moved up through the ranks; technologists with up-to-date and advanced educational qualifications were recruited, too. Karl-Erik Sahlberg, Ernst van der Pals, and Tage Norberg – all Masters of Engineering – already held important technological posts in the group: Sahlberg was in charge of international services, van der Pals was responsible for materials development and manufacturing, and Norberg headed the joint patents division of Å&R and Tetra Pak.

Now, however, towards the end of 1957, the management was looking around for someone to manage the design division, which consisted of some 20 men – among them Kjell Mårtensson, Olle Stark, and Harald Swede. By way of Curt Nicolin, then Managing Director of the ASEA Group of whose board Ruben Rausing was a member, the name Åke Gustafson came up. A marine engineer from the Stockholm School of Technology – where he had come to know Nicolin –, Gustafson was at this time working for De Laval Steam Turbines close to Stockholm. Dairies, milk, and packaging machines were matters of total indifference to him. However, the young and enthusiastic Managing Director of Tetra Pak, Hans Rausing, managed to persuade Gustafson to join the company after a visit to Lund, and he took up his post in June 1958. The company's expectations were high; there was a lot to be done. In preceding years, the development division had been working under great pressure. Documentation, follow-up measures, and monitoring had been deficient and unsystematic; in short, it was necessary to set the house in order. As an initial measure, Åke Gustafson formed the Technical Committee, a forum for all matters of technology. Routines were created for the systematic reporting of field experiences; drawings and sketches were registered in readily comprehensible ways; and minutes were kept during every meeting.

One high-priority move at this early stage consisted in trying to prevent customers from returning their one-litre machines. During the early autumn of 1958, the MC in Stockholm delivered the following grim ultimatum: *"Either packages are tight before the end of the year, or the machines get thrown out of our dairies."* Forceful measures were adopted and the situation was brought under control, good personal contacts contributing significantly to the happy outcome. In the beginning of 1959, deliveries of tetrahedron machines were well under way. There were installations in some 30 countries, and the company was fast approaching a volume of a thousand million packages per annum. True, there was often milk on the dairy floors; but the problems did not seem too daunting, and by dint of applying systematic measures leakages and disruptions would soon be a distant memory. The sun was shining from a fairly cloudless sky. The one-litre system was gaining ground internationally, too, despite the awkwardness of the package. The advantages of the tetrahedron – technical, hygienic, and economic – were so great that nobody questioned its form; it was felt to be the best there was. And then, the next step in the development was waiting – the aseptic method which would make it possible to keep milk, that most vulnerable of foodstuffs, for a longer period of time. The Lund management harboured no serious thoughts of a new system of any kind. At this time, no decisions concerning the development of alternative projects were on record anywhere.

The notions which, in the early months of 1959, swam into the minds of Åke Gustafson and a small development team that worked with him were hence akin to blasphemy, verging on a taboo. Was the tetrahedron really the one and only solution, or might there be an "afterlife"? Without making a song and dance about it, Gustafson started a systematic evaluation of the pertinent circumstances and conditions; there are well-documented reports from this time in the company files. First, a thorough inventory was set up of the milk packages available in the market: Perga, Satona, Pure Pak, Seal King, and so on. Next, mathematical calculations were made with a view to attaining theoretical optimisations of the available alternatives. Compared to the process which resulted in the creation of the tetrahedron, these efforts took place according to a different, more scientific, approach. But – and this is a crucial point – the already-established system cast a healthy shadow over the new development team. It was logical to go on working on the principle of continuously shaping, filling, and sealing packages on the

Åke Gustafson was in charge of technological developments for some crucial years in the company history, from 1958 to 1964.

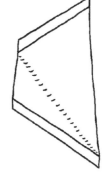

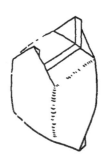

Would the company dare to move away from the brilliant tetrahedron shape? From time to time, technicians attempted some simple "transformation exercises".

107

It was
Eric Rasmusson
who christened
the new package
the "Tetra Brik".
Naturally enough,
it became his
"baby" and re-
mained so for
the 20 years
during which he
was responsible
for the Swedish
market.

Up to now,
the standard
European pallet
had not been
used in the dis-
tribution of milk.
By way of the
Tetra Brik,
it became
a fundamental
component in
transportation.

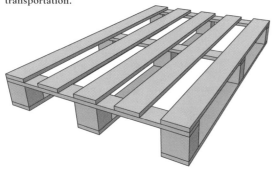

roll-and-paper-tube basis. Every now and again, someone had amused himself folding in the "ears" of tetrahedron packages, thereby approaching a squarish shape: as in painting, there was something of a Cubist movement at Tetra Pak. But these attempts had not gone beyond the experimental stage.

That was when it happened – once again the usefulness of competition was proved. At the rather low-key Vienna Spring Fair in May 1959, a new German milk package called Zupack was exhibited for the first time. It is best described as rectangular paper bag, with thin walls and corners standing up, manufactured from plastic-coated, wholly-bleached paper. The technology behind it was not yet perfectly developed, but the package served a psychological purpose: it implied that there might be cheaper solutions than previously-known variants, and that made it a threat to the Tetra Pak system. Now everybody realised that there had to be a "square" development programme, geared towards the one-litre volume, and that it had better move along fast. Previous musings and studies formed its point of departure, and a rectangular, brick-like package began to take shape. When, in due course, the system was to be christened, it was natural to call it "Tetra Brik". It was Eric Rasmusson, Sales Manager for the Swedish market, who came up with the ingenious name for the new package. At this stage, nobody had any idea that this new development would engender countless "tons of bricks", laying the foundation for an edifice whose building history would extend over decades.

The autumn of that year was a decisive period. During a meeting in December 1959, despite internal resistance from several quarters, Gustafson persuaded the management to adopt the decision to go ahead with the development of a new system along lines that had already been drawn up. On this occasion, too, packages wrapped in paper were demonstrated; such wrappings would make transport cases redundant – a relatively bold idea at the time. After long discussions, the decision was made; a mandate was issued to start work on the project, and as a result the Manager of Engineering Design, Åke Gustafson, came to play a central role in the history of Tetra Pak's development. Not everybody invents; they also serve who innovate, and sometimes the distinction can be a very subtle one. It was Gustafson who systematised research on a new packaging system. He was the man who forced through one of the major decisions in the history of the company. Of course, it is possible to maintain that one thing will normally lead to another and that this was the logical continuation of a path along which people were already proceeding. While there is some truth in that, we must remember that there were several possible options and that it was imperative to make the right choice and make it quickly. The temporal aspect was vital: the development of the Tetra Brik turned out to be a race against time and against various forms of competition.

Once the decision to develop a new type of package had been made, a careful evaluation of possible solutions began. A number of development teams were appointed and given the task of looking into certain key issues: format variants, shaping problems, sealing alternatives, materials specifications. Gustafson himself devoted all his time to processing incoming proposals and results, always looking towards the optimum for the whole system as well as for its parts. Among other things, he emphasised the importance of ensuring that the dimensions of the package base would fit the standardised loading pallet that was just being introduced in the retail business.

The next few years saw a pooling of forces around the project known under the provisional title "System 2". The shape and format of the actual package were established, and several different proposals were put forward as regards the packaging machine. Two different lines of development soon crystallised, and they were conducted alongside each other – this project could not be allowed to fail; there was neither time nor money enough. One of the two projects, headed by Herwig Pupp, M. Eng., proceeded from a machine which ran intermittently, by stages; it only had one pair of jaws, and its capacity was low. The other variant adhered more closely to the tetrahedron principle and ran continuously, with two pairs of jaws. This made the machine faster, but it became more complicated as well. Harald Swede, M. Eng., was in charge of the latter project.

Although fundamental experiences were readily available, this development work took much longer than expected. Besides, the scant resources that funded it were frequently fragmented as staff members were temporarily "borrowed" for other jobs in the company; at this time, from 1960 to 1963, several extensive development projects were in progress, particularly the aseptic business, and they all required skilled staff. In addition, Tetra Pak constructed a small, fast-running machine for tetrahedron packages holding one portion each. This machine was nicknamed "Åke's Bag of Tricks" and contained technological part-solutions which could be directly applied to the Tetra Brik system. Besides, the

Harald Swede and Herwig Pupp (left) were in charge of two separate development projects which they pursued in a spirit of friendly competition.

"Åke's Bag of Tricks", in certain respects a technical predecessor of the Tetra Brik machine.

ordinary tetrahedron machines very often required staff to dash off to help at short notice. The market was impatient, and so was the company's own sales organisation; both made unreasonable demands regarding staff efforts and times of delivery. All these things put staff at the development division under severe strain; the technicians were forever feeling the whip on their backs.

In mid-1962, the problematic situation came to a head. The Norwegian firm Elopak had acquired the European licence for the American gable-top package Pure Pak. Times had changed; the carton which had been felt to be far too expensive for the European market only a few years before was actually becoming an alternative worth considering. An intense campaign of persuasion targeting Swedish dairies had begun; and by way of the media, public opinion was marshalled against the clumsy tetrahedron which was so difficult to handle. It was high time Tetra Pak produced its "brick". Development work was far from finished; but there was no choice: the prototype had to be launched in the field. Close co-operation with the Milk Centre made it natural to deliver the first machine to a dairy belonging to the MC group. On 12 March 1963, the town of Motala in Central Sweden was able to announce a world première – milk in the Tetra Brik. The start-up phase was far from painless; according to the dairy manager, it entailed the shedding of quantities of *"blood, sweat, and milk, but never tears!"* Other sacrifices were called for, too: the superb Tetra Pak fitter Helge Andersson, nicknamed Tarzan, who spent days and nights literally climbing the machine, later claimed to have done 220 overtime hours in the course of one month in connection with the Motala business! By the late summer of that year, the package had reached Stockholm; but it was still manufactured by prototype machines suffering from teething troubles. Now, the development division – which was already working under considerable strain and stress – was given a certain degree of responsibility for field production as well, and its staff were obliged to continue their systems development under extremely realistic conditions on the dairy floor. The patience and co-operativeness shown by the MC during these years were truly admirable.

Norwegian Elopak, which had set up office premises in Helsingborg, were carefully watching the laborious birth of the Tetra Brik, making use of every opportunity to advertise their own Pure Pak. This package was not free from leakages either; but its shape was more conventional and hence acceptable, especially in comparison with the "triangular litre". A vehement public debate flared up, culminating in a number of dubious statements on television. The MC group stood firm, however, remaining loyal to Tetra Pak. Simultaneously, market pressure increased in the rest of the country; polemics continued in the press and on television, and soon all of "dairy Sweden" was divided into two camps. After all, Tetra Pak held a solid position in the market and was able to draw on excellent personal contacts – without them, the foundations would have given way to a much greater extent than they ultimately did.

Even so, the pressure on the technicians and engineers was inhuman, the machines that were out in the field functioned poorly, promised remedial action was delayed, set times of delivery for new machines could not be honoured, and the packaging material was still not out of the development phase – in short, conditions were infernal. The fact that the credit situation was also strained did not help at all. The Board and management incessantly demanded new confirmations and guarantees from the development division. In the end, the whole thing became too much for Åke Gustafson, who established that he *was not compatible with the way in which this business [was] run"* and was not prepared to continue working under such stressful conditions. He handed in his resignation in the early autumn of 1963, but promised to remain in his position up to the end of 1964, at which point there was every reason to expect that the Tetra Brik system would be properly evaluated. Gustafson felt a strong commitment to rowing the boat ashore, and it is possible that his decision to leave the company led to his doubling his efforts during the remaining period. One often hears the contention that *"it is best to leave at once, as soon as the decision has been made"*; but in this case it certainly did not apply. When Gustafson left his post in December 1964, he was able to hand over a functioning technology for those machine systems of which he had been in charge.

In the spring of 1965 Gustafson moved to Switzerland, where he set up a team of researchers which was diligently consulted by Tetra Pak in the following years. Besides, he was personally summoned as an expert and top executive consultant on subsequent occasions when technical crises arose and methodical analyses entailing forceful measures became necessary. More recently, Åke Gustafson has established his own successful industrial operations in the field of high technology. Never a man who courted the limelight, he has continued to accomplish major feats on the basis of that innovative power, curiosity, and Smålander stubbornness that are so characteristic of him.

Hans Rausing, full of anticipation – and he does hold the future in his hand.

A Brick Becomes a Corner-Stone

"Construct", "construction" — the words carry overtones of creativity and communal efforts, of the kind put to use in the erection of a building. The Tetra Brik became the constructive unit, the corner-stone, in a construction project which would span the world: the automatised handling of liquid foods.

Once again, a Swedish example set the standards.

During the latter half of the 1950s, the crucial initial step had been taken towards the rationalisation of the distribution of milk for drinking purposes in Sweden. At this point in time, the "milk pyramid", as the tetrahedron was frequently called, served a vital function, namely that of offering a cheap, disposable alternative to the glass bottle. Where the Swedish people's daily milk was concerned, costs and prices were under constant pressure; this package, which entailed a minimal waste of material, was the only option, or so it seemed – other cartons appeared too expensive. But the system had its limitations, and for all its pyramidic shape the package never became a "succès pyramidale". The competitiveness of the system was marred by the external casing, which caused extra costs as well as creating difficult situations during transport and sales operations. When demands for more rational, automatised handling of the heavy daily milk increased, the triangle was just not good enough. Due to a number of fortunate circumstances, however, helpful influences had made themselves felt in company in the meantime. Thanks to them, the next step in the development could go ahead quickly, in tune with the altered conditions. The Tetra Brik was going to be the convincing answer to a number of questions.

Even during the Åkerlund & Rausing years, Ruben Rausing had established that *"we are surfing on the wave of change that's sweeping through the retail trade"*. The important thing for Tetra Pak was not to lose speed, to make sure the company stayed on the crest of the wave. The surf-board was the standardised loading pallet which had come into general use in the 1960s, serving as the new basis for the storage and transportation of large staple commodities in retailing. The "brick" would turn out to be the perfect corner-stone in an entirely new, revolutionary handling system for milk, a system whose foundation was the pallet.

When Åke Gustafson tried to optimise the measures of this new, rectangular package, he was applying several starting-points at once. To begin with, it had to waste as little in the way of materials as possible. The relationship between volume and material consumption was determined by certain optimal figures which could be calculated without much difficulty. The next step consisted in satisfying the requirements of distribution. The "vital statistics" of the package, its technical ideal shape, had to be modified, but only slightly. With minor adjustments, the bottom space of the "brick" came to fit the pallet standard which a burgeoning European market had adopted, with the basic measurements 80 centimetres by 120. It is true that Sweden was at this point outside the integrated market of today; but that did not prevent the so-called EUR pallet from becoming the norm in this country, too. It was necessary to look, and be, ahead. As manufacturers, wholesalers, and retailers were endeavouring to agree on the rational handling of goods, it was essential for the components, the individual packages, to fit in with the standard European pallet. Much hard work on harmonising conditions was performed by a group comprising representatives from all the parties involved. This "experience group", in which Tetra Pak took very active part, aimed to improve and simplify the flow of a fast-growing assortment of goods. High wages and salaries, as well as high costs generally, accelerated developments: it was becoming increasingly important for manual handling to be replaced by automatised processes. Today, in our robotised world of electronics and computers, conceptions of this kind may seem childishly simple. However, the stand of technology in those days offered no self-evident solutions. The compact Tetra Brik package, which lent itself so easily to stacking, became the key to a new way of thinking, a basic component in entirely novel flow constructions.

As was mentioned before, the long-awaited introduction of the Tetra Brik took place in a rural dairy – the one at Motala – in March 1963; local tradesmen were full of the "world première". The general public, accustomed to glass bottles and triangular packages, greeted the new object with enthusiasm. The first practical experiences of small-scale production were collected and processed. A few months later it was

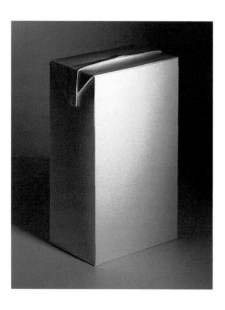

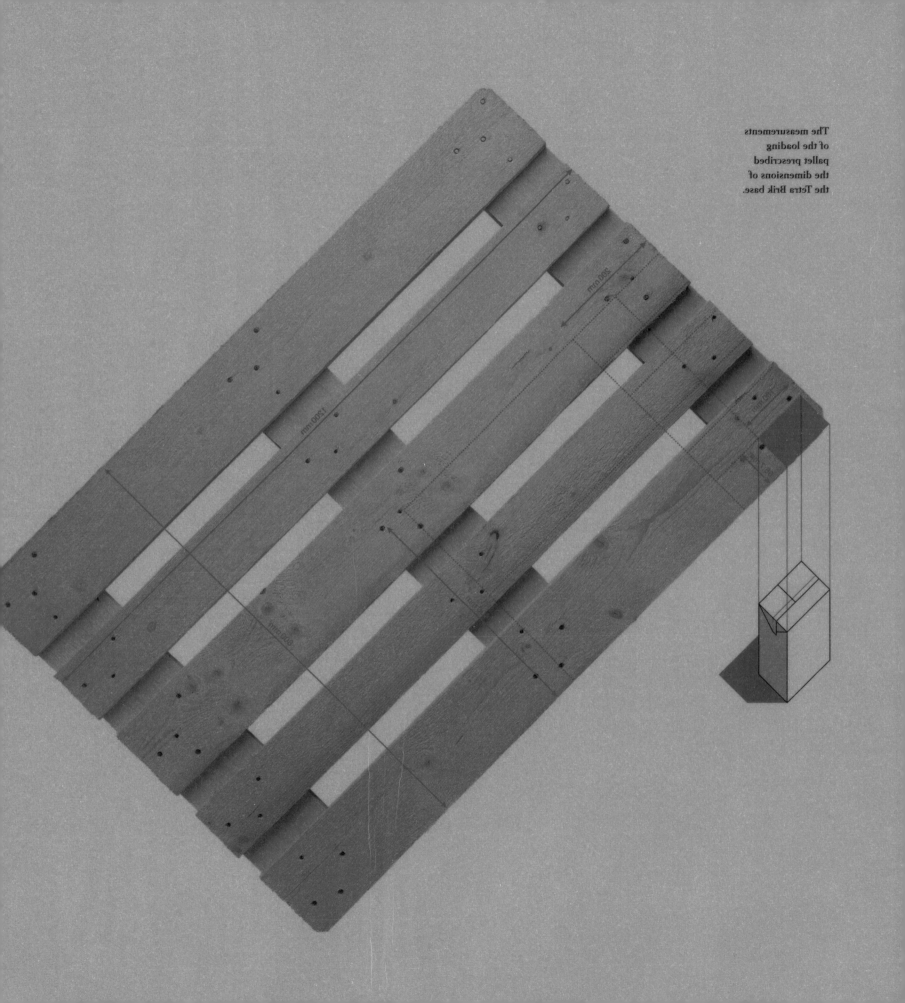

The measurements
of the loading
pallet prescribed
the dimensions of
the Tetra Brik base.

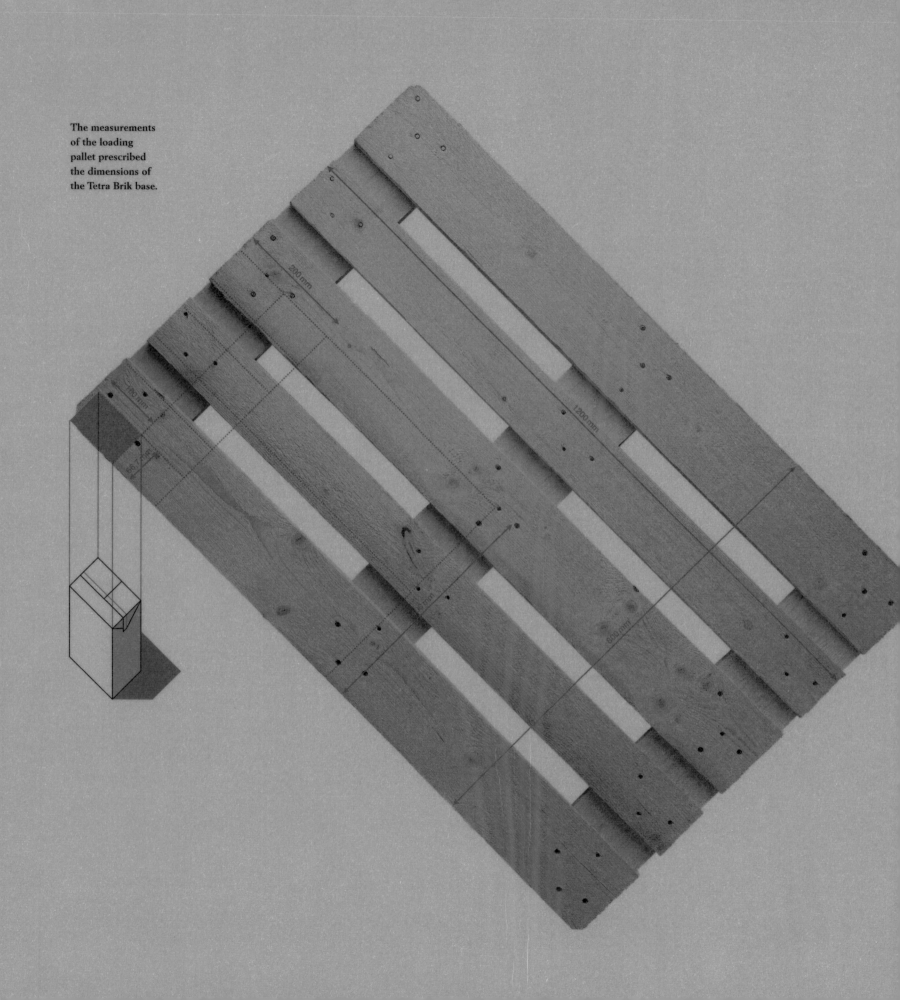

The measurements
of the loading
pallet prescribed
the dimensions of
the Tetra Brik base.

Stockholm's turn, and this was where the true baptism of fire took place. At last, a package which looked the way a package should look, a package which was easy to buy, carry home, and store in your refrigerator. Opening and pouring? Well, yes, of course you needed a pair of scissors for that, and naturally you wanted to be careful pouring; but compared to what you were used to, why, it was heaven!

For many years, some of them critical ones, Evert Lindahl was in charge of the Stockholm service station.

Housewives and others were blissfully unaware of what was going on behind the scenes. The new type of machine caused problems even for seasoned Tetra Pak technicians. Heroic efforts were made, and in this context special mention should be made of Evert Lindahl. For many years, he was the man in charge of the service station in the Stockholm area. Everyone realised and accepted that the machines would need daily service inspections at first. However, the fact that nights had to be sacrificed as well came as something of a surprise. To quite a few people, the idea of being "on call" acquired a significance it had not possessed before. Night was transformed into day; it was only during the hours of the night, when the machines were idle, that engineers and fitters were able to exchange spare parts and perform reconstructions. The machines had to be ready and waiting for the dairy staff when they arrived around four in the morning to start production; this was when their working day would normally begin. When the Milk Centre decided to adopt a new name some years ago, they chose a peculiarly fitting one in christening themselves "Arla" – an old Swedish word meaning "early".

The difficulties came to a head when a number of shops did not receive their morning milk until well into the day for several days running. Customers were furious and shopkeepers helpless. The patience of the MC technical management wore thin, and there was open talk of changing to another package. In order to lend extra weight to its displeasure, the Milk Centre stopped paying all Tetra Pak bills. After three weeks, the amount due was SEK 800,000 – enough for the salaries department in Lund to despair of finding the means with which to discharge its monthly payments. A settlement was reached at the last moment, and people received their wage packets and salary envelopes as usual. The incident shows how small margins actually were: even in the mid-1960s there was nothing to fall back on in case of economic emergencies; the company did not have any financial reserves at all.

When the MC spoke of turning to another system, they were not making idle threats. As was pointed out before, the Norwegian company Elopak had started operations in Sweden with the American package

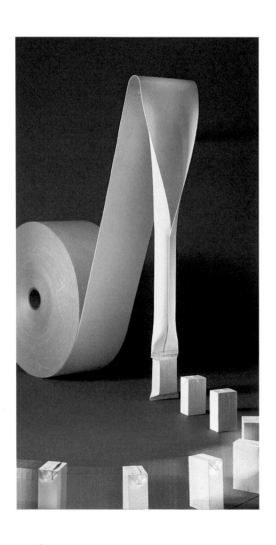

Pure Pak, and they had acquired some customers, albeit outside the Milk Centre area. It was indeed fortunate for Tetra Pak that the machines on offer were not the most recent models. In the U.S.A., the transition to plastic-coated materials was under way; but the machines placed in Europe and Sweden would still be of the type that produced cartons impregnated with solid paraffin. This was a fly in the ointment from the Pure Pak point of view. But the "paper bottle" had other advantages, and the dairy industry was not insensitive to them. The capacity of the machine and its ability to produce different sizes were attractive, as were the consumer-friendly aspects of the package itself. In the background there was also a wholly Swedish package which was being developed by a company owned by Swedish Match (or Svenska Tändsticks AB, as it then was). A large, complicated prototype machine, intended for two-litre packages into the bargain, was installed in one of the Stockholm dairies. It never came past the experimental stage, though. In spite of the difficulties, Tetra Pak managed to hold the fort; but disaster was just around the corner. A revealing quotation from Board minutes of this time sheds light on the grim realities: *The market situation in Sweden and the rest of Scandinavia is exceedingly unstable. However, it was to a great extent possible to postpone the threatening collapse of the market in favour of competing packages, partly thanks to the introduction of the Tetra Brik and to the policy according to which tetrahedron machines are being placed in dairies as loans pending the delivery of Tetra Brik machines.* In other words, the pistol was placed right against the head of Tetra Pak; but it was imperative to put a good face on things and make sure the technology was operational as quickly as possible, with a minimum of fuss.

Naturally enough, curious dairy colleagues from other places in Sweden went on pilgrimages to the few demonstration machines that were available in the early days. The Tetra Pak management was also keen to display the new model in operation. Among these early groups of visitors was a dairy board from the north of Sweden, and there was a special background to their interest. Due to the long, cold winters up north, it was not rare for glass bottles to freeze until they burst, either on lorry platforms or in the early hours of the morning outside the doors of shops. The people afflicted by these problems were eager to try a "cold-proof" alternative, and Tetra Pak was apparently in a position to provide one. The decision had, in principle, already been made; only a study visit remained, to see the machine in production. But just as the customers were to leave the filling hall, there was a minor fire in the filling machine.

"The Dairy
of Tomorrow",
built on the basis
of the Tetra Brik –
streamlined,
automatised,
lean-staffed –
began to emerge
on the drawing-
board as far back
as the mid-1960s.

117

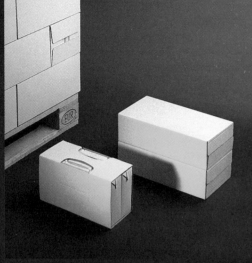

TETRA WRAPAROUND

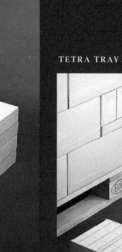

TETRA TRAY

TETRA MULTI SHRINK

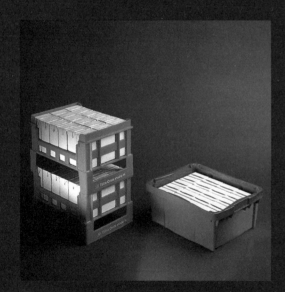

TETRA CRATE

TETRA MINI PALLET

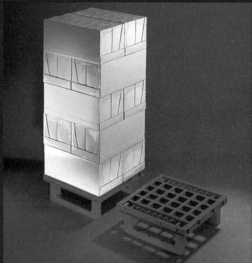

TETRA ROLL CONTAINER

In his mind's eye, the wretched Tetra Pak salesman saw the whole deal vanish in smoke, and he was hence pleasantly surprised when the dairy board announced that they regarded the incident as a good omen. The smell of fire in his nostrils, their chairman asked for a pen to sign the contract with! The Northerners, so used to being in a cold climate, had clearly been impressed by the warmth of their reception.

The greatest advantages of the new package are found in the areas of storage and distribution. This was where the Tetra Brik was able to prove its superiority. Adapted to the European pallet from the start, compact, completely filled and easy to stack, it offers virtually unlimited possibilities in the way of transport solutions. When the very first installations were made, returnable baskets were employed, sometimes inherited from the glass bottles. As time went by, though, all the elegant alternatives we are familiar with today evolved: rolling pallets, paper troughs, shrink film, multipacks or other custom-made variants, all according to the wishes of customers. Rationalisation gains arise at an early point in the handling procedure, in the filling hall and cooling premises of the dairy. An automatised, computer-supervised system of so-called Tetra Carriers – self-operating trucks – delivers convenient quantities to the cold-storage premises and then on to the loading facilities outside. Compact rolling pallets have literally put milk on wheels: it can be rolled on board distribution lorries, and it is rolled into shops and supermarkets – right into the refrigerated display cabinet.

In the 1960s, demands for ergonomic solutions were growing both within the walls of the dairies themselves and in the chain of distribution; that is to say, more and more people insisted that the working environment should be better adapted to the physical capabilities of human beings. Thus, for instance, Swedish trade unions for employees in the private wholesale and retail business pushed through regulations regarding maximum-weight limits for goods that needed lifting and manual handling. In addition, employees insisted on reasonable temperature limits in their working environment. In both cases, the number 16 became the magic limit – no more than 16 kilogrammes for lifting, and not less than 16 degrees centigrade on working premises. The transport solutions of the Tetra Brik system easily satisfied these demands. The primary role of the package, to protect its contents, has been extended; it now also includes protecting those who handle it from unnecessary strain. Gone is the heavy lifting, gone are the aching backs; gone, too, are the uncomfortable conditions that used to prevail in cold-storage rooms.

The opposite page: The Tetra Brik, easy to handle and distributor-friendly, inspired a number of new packaging solutions for transport purposes: troughs made of corrugated cardboard, shrink-film with handles, plastic baskets, rolling pallets, and so on.

Eric Rasmusson's Tetragrams became a greatly appreciated channel of information for Swedish clients.

Swedes consume large quantities of milk; consequently, dairy products form the biggest category of goods in the retail trade. It was thus particularly important to raise the efficiency of distribution where these products were concerned. Besides, it was natural to think of the juice market, and indeed the Tetra Brik has come to play an equally prominent role there. The solutions evolved by Tetra Pak frequently came to set the standards for other lines of trade in products that were heavy to handle. As a matter of curiosity, it might be pointed out that the Swedish Sugar Corporation chose the identical bottom size for their cartons of lump sugar. This, in its turn, meant that the size of the individual lump of sugar was modified: a bijou revolution. Similar rationalisation measures have been carried out with regard to most other kinds of goods – all with a view to improving distribution flows and keeping consumer prices at a minimum.

Sweden became the experimental workshop of these new developments in the realm of transport economics. The chief spokesman for the new ideas was Eric Rasmusson, who was Managing Director of Tetra Pak's Swedish marketing company for many years. With never-failing enthusiasm, he argued in favour of – and implemented – those innovative, rational solutions which the "brick" permitted. Year after year, he issued his monthly *Tetragram*. Its name affords a clue to the nature of its message: brief, essential information, mostly focusing on problems of distribution. This, too, was a subject often brought up during those *Tetra Days* which were arranged in Lund on an annual basis for over two decades. During these conference days, Nordic experts gathered to gain information on trends in the business, but also to familiarise themselves with general political and economic issues, both from Swedish and international points of view. Eric Rasmusson's purposeful, streamlined techniques for disseminating information went straight for the important aspects: the European pallet and modules of it – that is, smaller units of its basic measurements – became the common factor for producers, distributors, and retailers. In the last 25 years, a flow of goods has been created in Sweden the efficiency of which is probably hard to match anywhere in the world. The key word is "logistics" – the science of material flows. The Tetra Brik paved the way, and now the winding transport paths between producer and consumer have been widened as well as straightened – these days, "the Milky Way" is an ultra-modern motorway.

The Tetra Days gradually grew into a forum for information and discussion on the topmost level. Programmes would usually feature key figures from the worlds of business and politics. In front of a stylised image of the Lund Cathedral stands Gunnar Sträng, Chancellor of the Swedish Exchequer, talking to the conference host. Dr Marcus Wallenberg is at the lectern. Prime Minister Olof Palme is sitting beside Hans Rausing. All these pictures were taken in the 1970s.

A House of Want

Genesis 41 tells us the story of Pharaoh's dream of the seven well favoured, fatfleshed kine and the seven ill favoured, leanfleshed ones – symbols of prosperity contrasted with famine and want. The Biblical tale was set in ancient Egypt; but the parable applies to Tetra Pak, too.

Only the lean cows came first, and they were far more numerous.

There was no need to be an expert interpreter of dreams to grasp the meaning of the Biblical story: after seven years of ease and plenty, Egypt would suffer crop failure and grievous famine; consequently, everyone had to lay up corn in their storehouses while there was still time, in readiness for the bad times ahead. But no such opportunity was open to Tetra Pak. It was a "house of want" from the start; there were no supplies to draw on. The lean years were not just a nightmare: for a considerable period of time, they were only-too-tangible reality.

Today's employees can have no idea – and outsiders still less – of the financial difficulties that beset the company from its inception and for a number of years thereafter. Coping with the perpetual headaches of funding called for skill as well as imagination. However, need is, as we all know, the mother of invention, and by resorting to various expedients the company managed to make its way through a couple of severe crises. Investment in technological development was always the most pressing issue. Anyone asked to summarise the main problem of the company in the 1950s and 60s might be tempted to turn the proverb back to front and establish that *"invention became the mother of need"*. There would be some truth in that claim. All the delayed projects – the tetrahedron system, asepsis, the Tetra Brik, and others too – demanded large sums and took far longer to begin generating profits than everyone had hoped.

While head of financial operations at Tetra Pak, Boris Carlsson would often be "seeing red". Technological development and investment called for capital, and the financial situation was strained.

As early as 1950, Tetra Pak was registered as an independent company, and as such it was obliged to draw up its own annual accounts. The figures were not impressive. The position of Financial Manager during the rigours of the pioneering years was far from enviable. When Tetra Pak prepared to move away from Åkerlund & Rausing and to establish its own accounts department, the company advertised that it was looking for "The Financial Manager of Tomorrow". The post was filled by Boris Carlsson, B.Sc. (Econ.) – but during his years at Tetra Pak, 1956–1964, he found himself waiting in vain for tomorrow's rosy dawn. This was not only due to the initial location of the office premises in the new factory, where they had no windows. In order to lend a cheering note to the drab environment, someone hit on the idea of decorating the walls: "blind" windows with curtains and pot plants were painted in suitable places. For Boris Carlsson, everyday work was dark, but hardly colourless; bright red was the prevailing shade. *"The figures became redder every year – the Financial Manager's nightmare. In the annual accounts for 1958, I was able, after much hard work, to present a loss amounting to SEK 3 million – a*

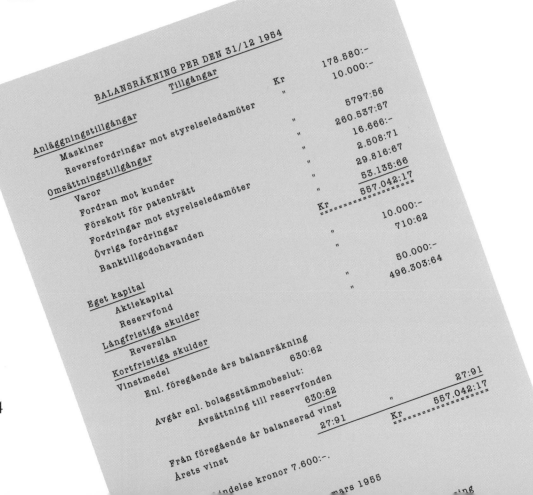

The profit of 1954, 27 Swedish crowns and 91 öre, would yield to virtually astronomical losses for several years ahead.

124

mind-boggling amount in those days. Hans Rausing's comment wasn't long in coming, but it wasn't what I'd feared. 'This doesn't look bad at all. Next year, when our volumes increase, it'll turn around, you'll see.' That's the reaction of a true entrepreneur, and we know he was proved right."

In the course of these years, Boris Carlsson had to endure many difficult moments before the turnaround really happened. Suppliers were queuing to have their invoices paid, and those who were particularly hard up themselves fell into the habit of turning up in person on Friday mornings to try to make the "Lottery Draw of the Week". Britta Hansson, Chief Assistant in Accounts, spun the tombola wheel, feeling like the Goddess of Fortune when she was able to tell the odd supplier that his lottery ticket had won a prize.

Another person in the Tetra Pak management who came to shoulder a considerable burden in respect of finances was Ingvar Wenehed. A law graduate, he was employed in the capacity of Assistant Company Lawyer at Åkerlund & Rausing in the autumn of 1959. Ruben Rausing himself interviewed the young District Court Clerk, paying special attention to the fact that he had managed to support himself throughout his studies without resorting to loans, the usual means of subsistence for students. It did not take long for Wenehed to assume wider responsibilities at Å&R. As the right-hand man of the Chief Company Lawyer, Carl Borgström, he undertook various tasks which meant that his contacts with the Rausing family kept growing. Several development projects conducted outside the packaging sector proper called for both legal and general managerial efforts, and in this context Wenehed's competence was especially useful. The objects of his endeavours varied widely: machines for counting coins; credit-card systems for banks and filling (petrol) stations, water-purification technology; a process for the tempering of glass; and so on.

At Å&R itself, advanced plans for export and expansion abroad were rife at this time. One factory was completed in Germany in the late 1960s, built with an eye on the fledgeling Common Market. A few years after joining the company, Wenehed was appointed Export Manager in Lund, where one of his tasks would consist in creating a suitable organisation for working on the large markets in Europe. It turned out not to be a long-term assignment; discussions about selling Åkerlund & Rausing had started, and he soon found himself very much involved in these proceedings. The plans were realised in September 1965, when Å&R was sold to Svenska Tändsticks AB – a transaction greeted with

From 1965 to 1974, Ingvar Wenehed was the "strong man" in charge of Tetra Pak finances.

125

A spirit of community, optimism, and enthusiasm were always characteristic of conditions within the company. During a meeting in the factory, Hans Rausing thanks the staff for their sterling efforts and proposes a toast to the future.

much surprise. *"Surely the Rausings have made the most tremendous mistake this time? Fancy selling such a fine company as Åkerlund & Rausing just to be able to put more resources into Tetra Pak!"* Wenehed was not "part of the deal"; that same year he went over to Tetra Pak, where he was appointed Deputy Managing Director with special responsibility for finance, administration, and legal affairs. In due course, too, he became Hans Rausing's deputy.

Now a number of measures were implemented within the organisation, all with a view to improving cost and capital structure. Such things are never popular; but the plans were carried out with a firm hand. The outcome was surprisingly favourable and gave people much to think about: although the staff had been reduced, efficiency in the Swedish organisation rose rather than fell. Within the group management, Wenehed also became directly responsible for the financing and administration of costly expansion projects; the plants in Italy and Japan form examples. Besides, he was the prime mover of negotiations for a new manufacturing unit in Forshaga in Central Sweden. The decade which Ingvar Wenehed spent at Tetra Pak, and during which he – with the full backing of the Rausing family – restructured the group, became the period in the company history which finally saw the wind shift. Before

leaving the company in the autumn of 1974, he was in a position to sound a loud all-clear. He went on to other prominent posts in Swedish business, but does not hesitate to say, *"Everything has been fun and exciting – but nothing beats those years at Tetra Pak. We were all caught up in a marvellous spirit of youthful enthusiasm."*

Thanks to a combination of helpful forces, the financial difficulties could be overcome, although the situation sometimes looked hopeless. No account of the financial ups and downs of Tetra Pak could possibly omit the names of the people who came to the rescue from outside. At least some of these good geniuses must be mentioned by name; in this way, Tetra Pak also has an opportunity to express its gratitude – although late in the day – to some of those outside the company who believed in its basic concept, showed patience, and dared to give their support when times were uncertain.

First in line, of course, is the parent company Åkerlund & Rausing – particularly the paper mill Östanå Pappersbruk, situated some 60 English miles to the north of Lund, which formed part of the group. During the war years, bankrupt Östanå was purchased by Ruben Rausing, who wanted to use it as a means of breaking the Swedish kraft-paper cartel, which duly happened. The company was put on its feet and given unique technology, and in Rausing hands it became a profitable concern, coming to specialise in a kind of photosensitive paper for blueprints. Managed by Ebbe Nihlberg for many years, Östanå was able to assist Tetra Pak with loans even up to the mid-1960s. In Swedish currency, these loans finally amounted to almost SEK 20 million, which was quite a sum in those days. Later, the mill passed to new owners, and it has now been closed down.

The Å&R group and the management of Tetra Pak itself were not alone in being inspired by optimism; it was shared by many suppliers and customers who had a variety of reasons for being anxious that the Lund venture would succeed. The Swedish mills of Uddeholm and Billerud were among the first suppliers of paper, and they were keen to see volumes expand. Their standard terms prescribed payment within 30 days; but the Tetra Pak account was to be a conspicuous exception. They were often obliged to wait for months, sometimes up to a whole year, and it was not unusual for invoiced amounts due to be transformed into short-term loans, at low interest rates. In this way, the Lund company occasionally found itself in possession of a working capital amounting, in practice, to several million Swedish crowns. Even so, the patience of the

The Östanå Paper Mill, a member of the Åkerlund & Rausing group, was the chief granter of internal loans.

During the difficult years, its manager Ebbe Nihlberg often found himself having to pay the bills of Tetra Pak's suppliers.

Aktiebolaget Armerad Betong

paper suppliers paid off in the long run. The total annual requirement of the group comes close to 1.5 million tons (1995), and Tetra Pak is the biggest single customer of the Swedish paper industry.

British ICI, one of the world leaders in the field of petrochemistry, adopted a similarly long-term-orientated attitude. ICI became the first Tetra Pak supplier of polythene; but purchases were modest for most of the 1950s – a couple of hundred tons, no more. However, the British company evinced an unshakeable belief in the development potential of their Swedish customer. In 1962, they stood surety for a loan amounting to SEK 15 million – eleven to Å&R and four to Tetra Pak. The loan had a lifetime of twenty years, the first ten of which would be exempted from amortisation. Nor did this supplier speculate in vain; these days Tetra Pak consumes over 300,000 tons of polythene a year (1995).

By rights, a number of other suppliers should be mentioned as well; but it is impossible – a few individual names will have to suffice. Thus, for instance, Armerad Betong ("Reinforced Concrete") were most helpful, granting far-reaching credits when Tetra Pak built one plant and office building after another in Sweden. Many suppliers of machine components were long-suffering in waiting for payments. The Wahlquist works in Linköping is one of the best examples; and here, too, endurance turned out to be good business. From having had approximately ten employees around 1955, this company employs a couple of hundred people today, and half of their output goes to Tetra Pak.

It is not, after all, so very surprising to find suppliers helping out with loans; but it is a pretty rare thing for customers to do. As previous chapters described, the Tetra Pak project had the support of Swedish dairies as the years went by, above all the "Milk Centre", Mjölkcentralen. To be sure, it was essential that the new milk package be allowed to develop into a finished product; but customer patience would often be strained to breaking point. Therefore, the granting of a loan for SEK one million from MC to Tetra Pak at a time when the latter was in particularly dire straits must be termed a handsome act. It is to be hoped that Arla, the successor of MC, has since found the gesture a profitable one. Co-operation with the Swedish dairy and foodstuffs industries has remained good over the years. The range of packaging systems supplied by the company has always been at hand to assist these industries in the modernisation and product-development efforts which are still going on.

As was suggested before, a list of all those who assisted in keeping the company afloat would be a very long one; it would run all the way from A to the last letter of the Swedish alphabet, Ö – from Armerad Betong to Östanå! However, by far the most important name is that of what was then the Stockholm Enskilda Bank, with its key personages Jacob and Marcus Wallenberg. Both had been friends of Ruben Rausing's since their student days and had solid confidence in his abilities as an entrepreneur, though there were times when they found him rather too fanciful. Thus, for example, Messrs Wallenberg did not approve of Ruben Rausing offering the then Managing Director of Alfa-Laval, Harry Faulkner Sr, the option of acquiring a fifty-per-cent share in Tetra Pak for one million Swedish crowns in 1950. The Wallenbergs found such an investment too risky, and there would be no lack of future occasions when they felt that the whole project was something of a hazard, too. Even so, the Enskilda Bank continued to give Tetra Pak its unbroken and unreserved support. Had it not been for that support, the company could not have survived its many cash-flow crises. At times, credit commitments were stretched way beyond the bounds of reason. The Wallenbergs themselves were not the only people at the Enskilda Bank who took a keen interest in Tetra Pak. One of the others was Göte Engfors, who served in a "controlling capacity" on the Tetra Pak Board for ten years. These days the ownership

There were times when the Stockholm Enskilda Bank extended its loans to Tetra Pak to the utmost limit.

structure of the Bank has changed; but what is now Skandinaviska Enskilda Banken is still Tetra Pak's major partner where Swedish banking business is concerned.

When, 40 years later, another kind of merger was proposed, it was greeted by keen Wallenberg interest, however. The biggest business acquisition that Sweden had so far seen took place in the summer of 1991 when Tetra Pak bought the venerable company called Alfa-Laval, one of the most cherished members of the Wallenberg group. The preliminaries of this vast deal were negotiated with the utmost discretion, and it literally caught the market napping. On 28 January 1991, on the midday news programme of Swedish Broadcasting, it was announced that Tetra Pak had offered to acquire all shares in Alfa-Laval. The news burst like a bomb, and one of the switchboard operators at Alfa-Laval dashed upstairs and into the central management offices, exclaiming breathlessly, *"We've got to telephone the newsroom instantly and tell them to correct this misinformation! For surely it's Alfa-Laval that's going to buy Tetra Pak, isn't it?"*

Still, there it was – it was Tetra Pak that had decided to make a bid for Alfa-Laval. The hard times were long past. *Per aspera ad astra*; but at this point the cold star of want had moved away, and kinder stellar rays were shining on what was now a "house of plenty". The deal came to form the climax of a fortunate period in the history of the company, and a new day dawned with this acquisition which signified the achieving of a goal. Per aspera ad Alfa!

Both Alfa Laval and Tetra Pak contributed to the new, joint symbol of the Tetra Laval Group. The previous logotypes of the two companies provided a starting-point.

Both Alfa Laval
and Tetra Pak con-
tributed to the new,
joint symbol of the
Tetra Laval Group.
The previous logo-
types of the two
companies provided
a starting-point.

Stony Places

"Some fell upon stony places". Both the quotation and its meaning are familiar; not all seeds ripen to make a handsome crop. Of course, Tetra Pak has bumped into hard rock from time to time in the course of the years. Many projects, many new departures, never came to fruition.

This chapter deals with dashed hopes.

Tetra Pak has usually been successful in achieving its aims, partly by virtue of sheer persistence. Still, it would have been a strange state of affairs indeed if *all* ideas and aspirations had been crowned with success, and there have been failures: a fair number of notions and projects, some of them far advanced, had to be dropped in the end.

One factor should be observed in this context, though: it has always been a fundamental company policy to run competing development projects alongside one another up to a certain point, in full awareness of the fact that only one variant would ultimately be considered for mass production. This approach has constituted a safeguarding measure as well as a way of gaining time: in the early stages of a project, it has rarely been possible to foresee which option would turn out to be best in the long run. If one process failed, another solution would already be well under way. At times, the psychological consequences of this policy would be embarrassing; thus, for instance, a highly motivated development group would find it hard to come to terms with being told, without much ado, that their project had been removed from the list of priorities and would not be pursued further. Fortunately, though, new problems would be waiting around the corner; the company never suffered from a dearth of ideas or from the danger that inventive capacity would run dry.

"Buy Tetra Pak, and you'll always have milk on the table!" The joke had a basis in fact. There have been a large number of aids to handling, opening, and pouring, but Tetra Pak has not had a hand in them. However, the company now offers easily opened and resealable packages.

Having said this, it is only proper to include some of those development processes and products which seemed convincing at the outset and were taken way past the experimental stage, sometimes even brought out into the market at considerable expense – but which ultimately had to be withdrawn and discontinued. By far the biggest enterprise in this category was *Rigello*, the package for carbonated drinks. But a few examples from the area in which Tetra Pak ambitions originated should be mentioned first.

An essential developmental issue, constantly on the agenda, is that of *opening gadgets*, especially for the Tetra Brik package. Innumerable solutions have been proposed throughout the years, most of them falling short of the requirements of harsh reality. In the very last few years, however, novelties have emerged able to satisfy the most demanding clientèle. Another perpetual problem has been the *capacity* of filling machinery. One far-reaching attempt to create a faster Tetra Brik machine was the HCB project (short for High Capacity Brik), which ran for several years in the mid-1970s. It was supposed to be the answer to those fast-operating machines which competitors were in a position to offer.

No answer ever appeared, though; the very complexity of the machine model became its downfall, ambitions were simply too exalted, and HCB never made it into the marketplace.

An entirely new approach was contributed by those unique projects that originated not in fibre materials, but in *plastic throughout*. Some important background facts must be mentioned first: All previous developments at Tetra Pak had proceeded from paper materials, coated with a thin plastic film. Even as long ago as the early 1960s, however, competing systems made entirely of plastic materials had emerged – bag-like packages, for instance, and moulded plastic bottles. These phenomena gave Tetra Pak staff much to think about. Maybe cellulose and fibre were not the sole, and best, base material for all purposes? There was reason to expect further development in the field of plastics; the trends were there and plain for all to see. And what would the relationship between the prices of plastic and paper materials look like in the years ahead? The feeling of being – to a great extent – at the mercy of the paper-and-pulp industry, without any alternative options, was not an altogether comfortable one.

A promising new material had started to appear in the late 1960s: expanded polystyrene (XPS), nowadays – a little carelessly – labelled "foam plastic". It was used for other products in the U.S.A.; but the idea was that it should also be be adaptable to packages of fluids. A couple of research groups, headed by engineers Olle Stark and Herwig Pupp, fell to work, and the early 1970s witnessed the birth of two new packaging systems, the *Tetra Cup* and the *Tetra King*. Both utilised this new plastic material instead of paper. As XPS was such a comparatively new phenomenon, the material itself had to undergo further development before being fit for the purpose. A unique, complex machine was put together for manufacturing the material, using plastic granules as a point of departure. With a slight exaggeration, the machinery could be compared to a young paper mill. No previous accumulated experience was available; this was to a large extent pioneering work.

The *Tetra Cup* was – as its name suggests – a kind of mug intended for yoghurt, ice-cream, beverages, and so on. A big, fast machine was built on the basis of extensive market research. The package had a number of virtues – it possessed thermoinsulating capacities, and it was easy to open as well as to stack. But in spite of extensive efforts the Tetra Cup was a short-lived object, and only a few prototypes of the machine were ever constructed. The *via dolorosa* of this project was bordered with com-

The XPS material, "foam plastic", was regarded as a useful complement to fibre-based packages.

The Tetra Cup was made of this material.

135

plicated technology, unfavourable financial prospects, and problems over patent rights.

By contrast, the *Tetra King* proved more viable. This package, with its characteristic horse-shoe shape, was also made of XPS. Apart from purely technical advantages, it was to provide a consumer-friendly compromise, something of a cross between a cup, a bottle, and a carton. The system was first demonstrated in the spring of 1976, and a fairly small number of machines were deployed in the next few years. There was a spirit of cautious optimism about; test sales began in Sweden, Denmark, France, and Germany, and many people were hoping for a decisive breakthrough for this new and different package. A practical opening device was a definite advantage, and the shape was an attractive one; but the package did not live up to expectations. Despite constant improvements, one of the basic difficulties remained: the material was brittle and fragile. Therefore, continued efforts were mainly devoted to portion packages, and with some measure of success. The system remained alive for many years among a few occasional customers – in Norway and Taiwan, for instance. But it never attained sufficient volumes and hence failed to generate acceptable manufacturing costs. In the end, hopes for the Tetra King – which was to have been the icing on the cake – were dashed. The Tetra King was obliged to abdicate, and the project was scrapped, but not until the early 1990s.

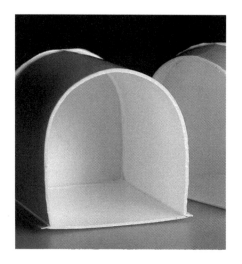

The horseshoe is said to be a lucky symbol. Despite its characteristic shape, however, the Tetra King package never caught on.

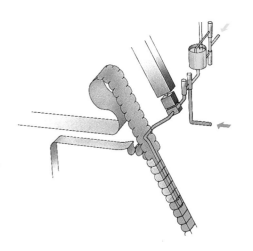

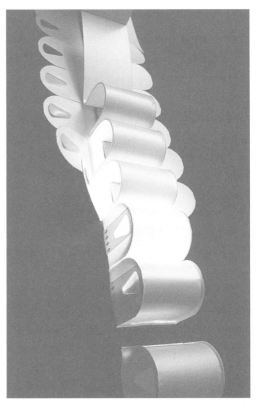

The Tetra King package was also manufactured in a continuous process. The machine utilised the opportunities in the form of thermo-shaping which the material provided, and thanks to a new sealing system it operated quickly. The packages were easy to handle and attractive to look at. Great effort was invested in sales; but the system did not live up to expectations.

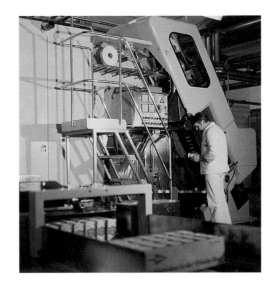

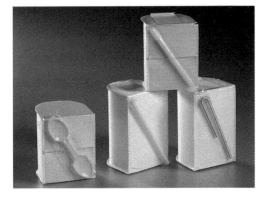

The Tetra King was certainly a demanding and long-standing commitment; but among the projects that came to naught, it was dwarfed by *Rigello*. In neither case would it be correct to speak of "failure" or "erroneous investment" in the ordinary sense of such expressions; complicated circumstances, some of them entirely uncontrollable, finally sealed their fate. The story of Rigello is, in brief outline, as follows.

In the mid-1960s, Tetra Pak was establishing a respectable position for itself in the field of dairy produce, fruit juices, and so on. Another alluring market which could not be conquered by existing or planned systems was the large market for carbonated beverages – beer and soft drinks. The Rausing family were interested in these products from an early stage, and in collaboration with a small group of engineers, they had given serious thought to a beer package way back in 1963. The very first proposal consisted of a simple plastic cylinder sealed with metal clamps at both ends. But how was the package to be opened and put on a table? After some further thought, a principal solution evolved which came to form the mainstay of subsequent developments. It amounted to casting a two-component bottle in a mould, then welding the components together, and finally inserting the cylindrical part into a paper casing. The outcome would be a thin-walled bottle made of cheap materials. Pressure from the carbon dioxide would be absorbed by the surrounding paper cylinder, which would also serve as a label and provide a certain, and desirable, protection against light. It was an elegant conception, and it had great potential.

The plastic material used for the bottle – the only conceivable one at the time – was polyvinyl chloride, PVC. Others had tried to manufacture bottles from the same material, but they were thick-walled and expensive. At first, there were no objections against PVC at all; the debate on it started several years later. A group, headed by Rolf Ignell, M.Eng., was set up and given the job of systematising work on this new, exciting project. In the late autumn of 1965, simple trial machines had proved able to manufacture bottles for storage tests. The results were reasonably encouraging, and construction work began on an experimental machine which was completed two years later. In the meantime, another machine had been built for the manufacture of PVC foil, the basic material for the production of the new bottle.

The Rausing family were keen to avoid "mixing milk with beer" as far as possible, feeling that it was important for the new development to possess independent status. A particular organisation was established

RIGELLO

At first, there were no clouds on the Rigello horizon.

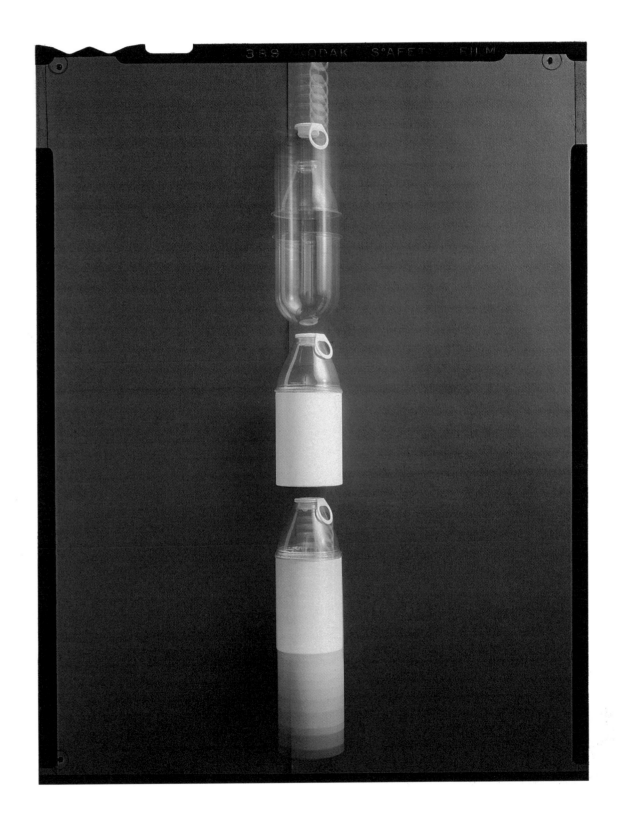

Like a three-stage rocket, the Rigello was intended to conquer the world market of beer and other carbonated beverages.

The bottle had an attractive shape which facilitated rational distribution.

In Sweden, alcoholic beverages are the subject of much political discussion. Here, the then Chancellor of the Exchequer, Mr Gunnar Sträng, is being persuaded that the new package for beer possesses all sorts of virtues.

In the field of soft drinks, too, the Rigello bottle was felt to have bright prospects.

with a view to making sure that Tetra Pak interests were not dissipated. Otherwise, a number of hard-bitten company salesmen would have been only too pleased at a chance to rush out into the attractive market for beer. But this was exactly what the rapid creation of a parallel organisation was intended to prevent – just as the family had been anxious to keep Åkerlund & Rausing and Tetra Pak separate in the early 1950s.

A special company was formed in July 1966. The product and company name was Rigello, R standing for Rausing and IG for Ignell. Hans Rausing was appointed Managing Director of this company; Erik Sandberg, Sales Manager at Tetra Pak, moved over to Rigello as Marketing Director, and Rolf Ignell himself was in charge of technology. Around Christmas 1967, the management of Pripps, the biggest brewery group in Sweden, had an opportunity to inspect the novelty, whose development had thitherto been conducted under the strictest secrecy. Six months later, in May 1968, about a hundred journalists attended a magnificent press conference which would resound all over the world. The biggest American brewery journal published an enthusiastic statement: *"After this, beer packaging will never be the same again."* The autumn months were spent making sundry alterations to the design and building new manufacturing machines. In the spring of 1969, test sales of the Rigello bottle began. The next few years were spent refining it; among other things, new bottle sizes were developed. Cautious market introductions started, the bottle was generally well received, sales figures rose, and everyone was relatively satisfied. In March 1971, the Pripps management went so far as to announce that *"We expect Rigello, following its introduction all over the country, to achieve a higher market share than any other individual form of packaging for beer."* However, there were two latent question-marks: the PVC material, and the durability of beer in Rigello bottles.

Soon enough, a number of clouds were seen to crowd into the field of vision at Rigello. A stubborn and protracted environmental debate started around PVC. When burnt, PVC could, under certain conditions, give off hydrochloric acid, and the media began to talk about "the acid beer". Canned beer continued to gain ground, light aluminium cans replacing the old sheet-metal variety. The market insisted on a wider range of package sizes. Another serious obstacle was created by new regulations within the framework of Swedish alcohol policies. All this was bad enough, but the question of the material was the greatest problem. True, things did look up when a new American plastic called Barex became

The three Rausings hoped that the Rigello project would be a genuine revolution.

Rolf Ignell, M. Eng., was Chief Designer of Rigello and prime mover of the project.

available. The relevant technology was improved, and the Rigello bottle was able to provide more durable beer. Even so, it still did not keep for as long as beer in cans. The calculated costs of the venture, pleasant to contemplate in the early days, had to be adjusted. European licence manufacturing of Barex, which had been going on for a couple of years, was discontinued. Despite powerful marketing efforts, the desired sales volumes failed to materialise. As time went by, the project suffered so badly as a result of mounting debts and unfavourable connotations that the Group Management reluctantly had to close it down. That decision was made in November 1982, and activities were wound up during the spring months of the following year. Reflecting on the sad fate of Rigello, more than one person will privately have been struck by the connection between the Swedish word for "bottle", *flaska*, and the corresponding borrowing from the Italian, a word used in an entirely different sense – *fiasco*.

Thus vanished a promising product which might have formed the basis for expansion on a scale comparable to that of Tetra Pak; as it was, the funeral baked meats had to be washed down with beverages served from other receptacles. Unforeseeable factors had come together, making the project infeasible. To recapitulate in a few words, one could justly claim that the whole thing was something of a premature delivery: if the Rigello bottle had been launched some six to eight years later, when technological and market conditions had changed, its chances of survival would have been much greater and the project could have been a success.

Today, only rough estimates can be made of the costs and losses incurred by Rigello over the years – and all such figures would be dismaying. Characteristically, the Rausing family did not refer to the matter again by so much as a word, and they never lamented the fate of the Rigello bottle. On the contrary, new ideas and technological solutions for carbonated-drinks packaging have always been welcomed. Who knows, it may one day be possible to invoke another Italian expression and exclaim *"Ecco fatto – Now it's been done!"*

Fair Winds

**The proverb – of English origin – which tells us that it is no use crying over spilt milk is uniquely apposite in relation to Tetra Pak, possessing both literal and metaphorical significance.
The determination not to mourn over past misfortunes, but to look ahead in a spirit of optimism, has always been something of a company hallmark.**

At last, the Tetra Pak ship began to sail with the wind astern; but she did not run free in earnest until the 1970s.

Many sections in this publication tell of problems with which the company had to grapple on its path towards success. At first, the difficulties were legion, and it would not do to pass them over; they are an integral part of the history of Tetra Pak. Apart from technological troubles, the main problem for years consisted in the necessity of heavy investment – in development work, marketing, and plants. Although the company returned a profit at a fairly early date, all funds were instantly devoured by its powerful expansion; the need for capital greatly exceeded the available assets. The lean years formed the substance of a previous chapter. In the last 25 years, however, the group has been able to show an unbroken period of growth, unparalleled in this line of business. It is time to devote some attention to these happier times.

The last profound crisis in the company history was over once the aseptic Tetra Brik system had become operable. Machines of this type began to be delivered in 1969, but it took time for their teething troubles to be overcome – board-meeting minutes regularly report on technical disruptions. As so often before, the organisation fought its way through

As time went by,
the original product –
milk – has gradually
been complemented
by other drinks, such
as fruit juices, table
wine, and mineral
water.

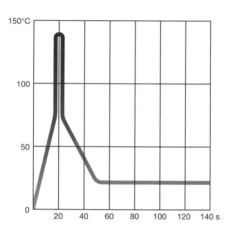

Ever since
the early 1970s,
the aseptic
Tetra Brik package
has been the com-
pany's best-selling
item. Swift heating
and chilling –
performed in a
matter of seconds –
ensure that the
UHT products
retain their high
quality for a long
time without
requiring refriger-
ation.

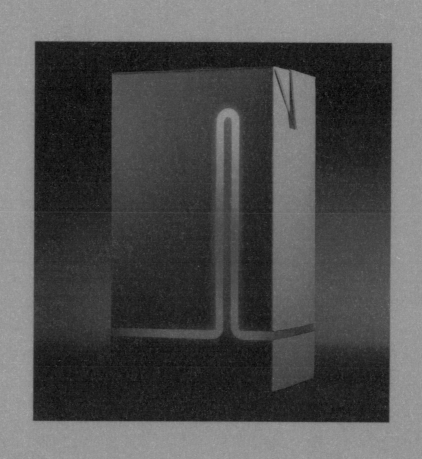

these tempestuous times with grim determination. The management, the marketing department, and all the technological subdivisions formed a united front. Heroic efforts were made everywhere, not least among the local Tetra Pak companies – after all, their staff were the people who actually patrolled the front line. By and by, operating conditions became acceptable, and an increasing number of machines were deployed. The machinery stocks, a drain on the company finances, decreased, and the system began to yield revenues. *Tetra Brik Aseptic* became the company flagship and has remained so ever since. The advantages that it brought to producers, distributors, and consumers – and to the community at large – cannot be overstressed. Distances in time and space have been made to disappear: milk, juice, and other liquid foods have become products that know no boundaries; they are accessible to everyone, not least to thirsty people in the Third World who require plenty of protein.

There is no Nobel Prize for foodstuffs technology, of course, but the Tetra Brik and the aseptic processing method have come as close to such a distinction as any product could: The American Institute of Food Technologists – numbering some 23,000 scientists and industrial leaders – has established that *"aseptic processing and packaging constitutes the most significant innovation in food technology in the last 50 years"*.

The second half of the 1960s saw a further system join the sales programme, the gable-top package called *Tetra Rex*. The background of this difficult but important decision can be outlined in a few words: it was triggered by competition from the Norwegian-American Pure Pak. The first confrontations between Pure Pak and Tetra Pak took place in the Scandinavian market, at a time when Tetra Pak was vulnerable. The tetrahedron was the sole saleable option, as the Tetra Brik was not yet established. Besides, there were no plans for a package larger than one litre. One of Pure Pak's strategies in Europe amounted to launching a two-litre carton, especially in high-consumption countries such as Sweden and the rest of Scandinavia. True, milk prices and packaging-materials costs were still subjected to tight control; but despite being more expensive, the American package had some points in its favour, and the dairy industry was interested. One argument among others was that the large two-litre package would save costs.

The situation was growing desperate. After rapid consultations, it was decided that Hans Rausing should go to America at once in order to look at the possibilities of collaborating with a modest-sized company which manufactured so-called gable-top machines, in direct competition with

Even in tough climatic conditions, milk and other drinks containing plenty of proteins can be distributed safely – to school dining halls, for instance.

For many years, Gösta Sevrell managed Tetra Pak's comprehensive patent activities. Many a ticklish issue landed on his desk.

A licence connection with interested parties in the United States was the first step towards the integration, in the mid-1960s, of the Tetra Rex package in the company's sales programme.

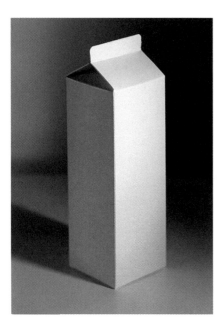

Pure Pak. A licence agreement was signed, and a few machines were imported. By way of this new alternative, named the Tetra Rex, Tetra Pak began to build up a market presence in the gable-top segment as well. However, the American machines did not come up to expectations where technology was concerned. After a couple of years, Tetra Pak decided to take matters into its own hands, terminate the licence relationship, and build its own machines. What began as a defensive measure gradually developed into a strong modern product line which soon proved able to conquer markets on its own merits.

There is no denying that it took a lot of nerve for Tetra Pak to challenge its main competitor by starting to sell a product which was almost undistinguishable from that of Pure Pak. Although the patent issues had been carefully studied and not found to constitute an obstacle, strongly emotional resistance from the competitor was to be expected; but that was not all: there would be unhappiness among customers, too, as well as among Tetra Pak's own staff. The latter factor turned out to be a major difficulty in this context. Now, in internal competition with their own company's Tetra Brik, technologists and marketing staff were asked to deal with a new package, an adopted child brought in from outside. It took several years for the psychological barriers to be conquered. In the light of history, though, this hard decision has proved justified – today, the Tetra Rex is a valuable component in the company product range.

One risk to which Tetra Pak was indirectly exposing itself by acting in this manner was that the company's own systems – the Tetra Brik especially – might be copied and pirated. No patent is sufficiently fortified to guarantee total protection in the end. Attempts at manufacturing copies have in fact been made, but so far without much success. In this context, the technological complexity which has imposed such hardships on Tetra Pak over the years has actually turned out to be an asset. What proved hard enough for the company's own technological experts to achieve has been even harder for others. Technological advantages and superior know-how have formed a strong safety net. For this reason, intensive efforts are being invested in further development, even of machines which might well seem perfect as they are.

In the early 1970s, the company possessed a solid systems programme: the tetrahedron and the Tetra Brik, both for pasteurised and aseptic products; and the Tetra Rex, a somewhat more costly option which still had certain advantages. In addition, Tetra Pak had some new and potentially interesting developments up its sleeve. Even if they did not all come

During the period
from 1970 to 1985,
no less than seven-
teen new plants were
built for the manu-
facture of packaging
materials.

BERLIN, GERMANY 1981

NAIROBI, KENYA 1983

XHAM, GREAT BRITAIN 1979

O, FINLAND 1983

ROMONT, SWITZERLAND 1975

IELD, AUSTRALIA 1974

MONTE MOR, BRAZIL 1978

NA, ITALY 1973

DENTON, U.S.A. 1984

LISBON, PORTUGAL 1980

SEISHIN, JAPAN 1981

JURONG, SINGAPORE 1981

GOTEMBA, JAPAN 1971

AURORA, CANADA 1985

MOERDIJK, THE NETHERLANDS 1975

ARGANDA DEL REY, SPAIN 1970

DIJON, FRANCE 1971

149

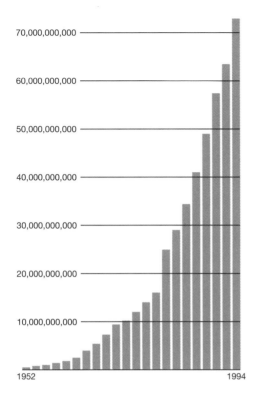

70,000,000,000

60,000,000,000

50,000,000,000

40,000,000,000

30,000,000,000

20,000,000,000

10,000,000,000

1952   1994

The diagram show-
ing the number of
packages produced
was always a crucial
indicator of how
things were going
at Tetra Pak. Here
is an illustration of
volume growth from
1952 to 1994.

Ever thoughtful
and far-sighted,
Lennart Ohlsson
laid the founda-
tion of the group's
control system
for financial
operations.

off, further expansion was a certainty. A wider range of machinery entailed steady growth and an increasing consumption of packaging materials. True, the relevant curve had already been rising for a number of years; but this was the time of the great volume increases, and capacity had to be extended without delay. The company was better equipped financially than it had been before; more than anything else, the years from 1970 to 1985 became the golden years of company-owned materials manufacturing. Occupying crucial terrain was, of course, a major ambition; it was essential to create the basis and volume which would be needed in harder times ahead. This expansion policy is still in evidence at Tetra Pak; everybody has long been aware that the future will be different from today. Competition is constantly increasing in the large and interesting drinks market, and it is vital to be in the lead.

This simple line of reasoning has resulted in a pattern of wide geographical distribution; new markets are constantly being added to a list of countries which was long already. Still, it is surprising to find what a vital role "old Europe" has continued to play in the performance statistics of the company. The relative share of the European market, above or around 50 per cent, has remained constant for decades. Where would the company have been today without such nations as France, Italy, and Germany, reliable and well established from an early point in time? Markets like these, characterised by powerful growth, formed the solid basis of Tetra Pak expansion. Together with other factors, they created the economic platform for the increasing requirements of the group.

Technological and market gains made it mandatory to devote plenty of energy to another field of activity: economic and financial resources. In earlier times, the person in charge of the company's financial affairs had not held an enviable position; the heroic exploits of people like Boris Carlsson and Ingvar Wenehed have already been mentioned. A new era began when, at long last, earnings covered expenses – not only the ones related to current operations, but also the large amounts that went into investment. Lennart Ohlsson was the man entrusted with the responsibility for designing a modern, efficient economic and financial company strategy. After a couple of years as an "apprentice" in Lund, he was appointed Controller in 1964 and put in charge of the financial department.

As the Rausing family drew up long-term plans for the company, one fundamental notion would always be part of their deliberations: the

creation of an independent financial centre outside Sweden, for the purpose of co-ordinating certain functions in the group of companies whose strength was continuously increasing. This ambition was realised when a modest-sized office was opened in Lausanne, Switzerland, in 1971. Its initial function was to handle purchases of raw materials for the plants owned by the group. Soon, however, it became necessary to add economically qualified reinforcements to the small office staff, and Lennart Ohlsson was chosen for the job. Having moved to Lausanne in 1973, he began to build up a financial structure and organisation which has afforded Tetra Pak a great deal of scope as regards cash-flow, funding, patent issues, and insurance activities. Outwardly sober and unremarkable, the new office quickly became a crucial factor in intra-group planning and policy-making.

After a couple of years on rented premises, the Lausanne staff was able to move into their new office in the autumn of 1983. An extension, opened in 1993, has since doubled its space.

Consequently, the next step in the organisational expansion seemed logical enough: that of choosing Lausanne as the domicile of the Tetra Pak international head office. Lennart Ohlsson and his staff had been asked to make all the necessary arrangements, including the construction of a suitably located office building. After years on the drawing-board, the move away from Sweden finally took place in the autumn of 1981. For an expansive decade, Lausanne was the seat of the group management. The office was extended in 1992–93; today it houses the European head office of Tetra Pak, as well as vital functions in what is now the Tetra Laval Group.

Many are those anxious company managers who have turned to "Uncle Lennart" for help in difficult moments. Understanding and assistance would always be forthcoming – and usually money as well. Always held in great esteem by members of the Rausing family, Lennart Ohlsson received a tangible acknowledgement of their appreciation on his retirement in 1991. He was elected Honorary Chairman of the company which was then called Tetra Laval Holdings & Finance SA.

These achievements with regard to financial planning have been essential to Tetra Pak's ability to bide its time in a large number of markets which only matured very slowly. The U.S.A., South America, the former Soviet Union, and Eastern Europe, India, and China are some examples. The element of long-term commitment which forms part of the general Tetra Pak philosophy has often been commented on, and it is pertinent in this context, too. The company would take an interest in certain markets long before they caught the public eye, small sales offices would struggle against the wind for years – and then one day circumstances would change and better conditions prevail. When the eyes of the world were turned towards one country or another, Tetra Pak was there already, all vital contacts in place. Nor have customers forgotten that the company was on the spot even when prospects looked less bright. Patience, the art of "waiting and letting time pass", has usually been rewarded. Naturally, such a policy calls for a liberal supply of funds and an express willingness to make sacrifices on the part of the owners. It is also necessary for a strong faith in the future to pervade the entire organisation.

Usually, bold speculations geared towards an uncertain future could not be realised straight away; that, after all, is in the nature of things. At times, technical and market gains have taken a long time to materialise. Hence, it is easy to perceive the connection between the pioneering spirit of the early years and results achieved at a later stage. In most cases, the seeds of the market conquests of the 1980s and 1990s were sown long before. One of the most recent developments, the *Tetra Top*, may serve as an example.

The idea for this new combination package was born in the late 1970s. A proposal was put forward for equipping a paper package with a suitable plastic lid, thereby providing a truly serviceable opening and resealing device. Development groups in Germany and Sweden were involved in the project, but work on it took time. In 1986, prototype machines came into the market in Belgium and Spain; but not until the 1990s was the new system widely established. Thanks to this geographical expansion, it is one of the most recent promising additions to the company sales programme. With the intense research and development work now in progress, the Tetra Top will soon be accompanied by new, exciting systems and packaging solutions; an intriguing store of product and brand names is waiting for them! The decision, made in 1992, to deploy resources and move certain lines of development from Sweden to other countries (for instance Italy and the United States) has had a healthy, invigorating effect.

The company management has long been preoccupied with the continual adaptation of its industrial operations to ever-increasing environmental demands. In the last 15 years, as technological progress has made new solutions possible, manufacturing methods for the Tetra Pak material have undergone radical improvement. The carton used today is high-quality kraft paper, its main ingredient being unbleached pulp which contains no chlorine. In case anyone might have thought that wood from rainforests was being used, it is best to add that such a raw material would be entirely unsuitable for this purpose. The second main component is polythene, a material identical with that which is being used by the foodstuffs industry all over the world. Plastic coating takes place under strict supervision, ensuring that all current demands on the working environment, and on the product itself, are duly met. The same applies to the printing of the décor. Here, the company has come to rely more and more on water-borne paints, thereby steering clear of the use – and emission – of undesirable chemical solvents. Efficient ventilation and air purification are self-evident measures, in the interests of factory employees as well as of the people who live close to plants.

In research and development, as well as in the manufacturing process, it is essential to keep up a commitment to stringent and justified

The Tetra Top, a paper package with a spray-moulded plastic top, was introduced in 1986, elegantly solving the problem of opening and resealing.

environmental demands. Despite the superiority of paper-based packages, receptacles made of plastic throughout have become increasingly fashionable, both for beverages and for other foodstuffs. The discovery of new, considerable oil deposits and the development of acceptable recovery processes have persuaded present-day politicians and societies to look more favourably on plastic products than they used to. As one of the latest instances of developments that are in tune with the environment, the *Tetra Box* might be mentioned – a new package suitable for certain product segments in the area of non-liquid foods. This development is also a handsome example of the stimulation engendered by the merger with Alfa-Laval in the early 1990s.

The Tetra Box is a box- or trough-like plastic package intended for such products as margarine and ice-cream. One of its advantages in relation to existing variants is found in the composition of materials. Instead of PVC or other raw materials which impose strains on the environment, the Tetra Box is made of a simple homogeneous material largely derived from a natural mineral in abundant supply, namely chalk. Its virtues are numerous: the package is easy to manufacture, hygienic, practical in use, protective of its contents, and economically advantageous. Once empty, it can be re-used, and it goes into the dishwasher, the microwave, and the freezer. Finally, it only gives off carbon dioxide and water at the waste-disposal stage, and its high pH content helps to neutralise acid components in other refuse.

Thanks to this system, and several others that are being developed, the basis of operations in the Tetra Laval industrial groups is constantly being enlarged. With its combined expertise solidly behind it, the Group confidently faces that leap into another century which will also take it into the next millennium.

The Tetra Box is made of a new, environmentally-friendly material. These packages are chiefly intended for non-liquid foods.

Over the years,
the Tetra Pak
product range has
become more and
more comprehensive.
By way of a com-
plement to the
fibre-based systems,
Tetra Pak is now
also able to supply
packages made
of plastic materials
only.

The Springboard

Despite today's striving towards a global society, national currents are noticeable in many places – a development with both favourable and unfavourable aspects. Flags are hoisted and patriotic songs heard, and not only in the ice-hockey or football stadium. Tetra Pak certainly has reasons to rejoice in its Swedish origins, but those reasons have nothing to do with chauvinism. The country offered the company the best possible basis for expansion in the world market.

Sweden supplied the point of take-off, forming the springboard of Tetra Pak.

Tetra Pak is, of course, only one among many companies which have proved themselves as administrators of the Swedish business heritage – we need only think of AGA, Alfa-Laval, ASEA, Atlas Copco, Electrolux, Ericsson, SAAB, Sandvik, SKF, Volvo, and STORA, as well as of all the other firms that make up the Swedish paper-and-pulp industry. Many more might be mentioned; and all have contributed to turning the poverty-ridden agricultural society of old – in evidence as recently as the late 19th century – into the modern industrial nation that is Sweden today. This amounts to saying that most of these industrial companies can look back on a long evolution process, often beginning before 1900. During the post-war period, the country only produced two large business companies that grew from nothing and won a truly extensive international range – IKEA and Tetra Pak. Some of the circumstances which made Sweden fertile soil for Tetra Pak should be indicated at this point.

Without its secure anchorage in Swedish industrial traditions, the company would not have developed as swiftly and efficiently as it did. Tetra Pak was fortunate in being able to draw on Sweden's main natural resources – iron ore, steel for the filling machines, and paper for the packaging material, the latter supplied by the Swedish forests. Both iron

The secrets of the earth's surface are easily revealed by modern satellite photography. The picture illustrates the forested regions of Europe, explaining why Sweden and Finland are known as "the woodshed of Europe".

and paper are raw materials which Swedes have used for centuries. Availability breeds the desire to process and stimulates the necessary know-how, one skill leading on to the next. It is fascinating to contemplate the long chain of evolution in the iron industry – from bog ore to modern mining, from the simple weapons and tools of past ages to a present-day Tetra Pak machine. The evolution from the former to the latter was not an uncomplicated one; but fine craftsmanship gave rise to the engineering skills and well-developed manufacturing industry which made the high-technological products of today possible.

Swedish forestry supplied a corresponding basis of solid knowledge. Timber, wooden materials, pulp, and kraft paper – all are Swedish trump cards in the world market. The forests in the North European climate zone yields exactly that long-fibre pulp which the Tetra Pak carton needs. Thanks to suitable raw materials and skills provided by Swedish mills – Uddeholm, Billerud, Korsnäs, ASSI/Frövifors, and several others – it was possible to meet the relevant quality requirements. The demands made on a carton holding liquid are extremely high, but the Swedish paper industry has always supplied the best conditions imaginable for satisfying them. In fact, certain preliminary work had been done in advance: the first bleached kraft paper in the world was probably produced in Sweden – for Åkerlund & Rausing. This way, Tetra Pak developments received welcome assistance in the domestic market, particularly during the initial, crucial stage. During a subsequent phase, when the company was looking for suppliers abroad, it turned out – not surprisingly – that it was considerably harder for non-Scandinavian mills to manufacture an acceptable carton. Modern technology has ensured that it is no longer necessary to rely on Scandinavian raw paper only; but its significant contribution to the general development must not be forgotten.

The Swedish wood-pulp industry has also blazed a trail with regard to environmental issues. The manufacturing process has its unfavourable aspects, and paper mills all over the world have been held up as environmental "villains" due to the emission and discharge of pollutants. This picture was true enough; but it is fast becoming a legend. Now, the bleaching process utilises no chlorine, waste water is purified, and efficient re-planting schemes guarantee that forests are well sustained. As always, there is more to be done; but the major producers, Swedish mills in the lead, have taken vigorous steps to abolish the problems of earlier times. Anyone who is interested in these matters will easily find documentation to this effect.

Special mention must be made of two other sectors which influenced the growth of the company: the Swedish dairy trade and Swedish retailing. The parent company Åkerlund & Rausing had already acquired extensive insider know-how and useful individual contacts in both areas. As a result, the new Tetra Pak project had free access to these lines of business.

First, a few words concerning the handling of milk. It is a curious fact that a small number of small nations have acquired the status of international models and reference markets for developments in the dairy business – Denmark, Finland, the Netherlands, and Sweden might be mentioned as examples. It is less strange, though, to find three Scandinavian countries on this list: after all, production and consumption of milk are high up north. Domestic industry has been pressed into pushing ahead with modern technology. Both what was then Alfa-Laval and Tetra Pak found that Sweden offered an especially favourable climate for expansion and development; in Sweden, model units for consumer milk – and other processing branches relying on milk – were set up at an early point in time.

A large and vital foodstuff calls for rational handling in the retail trade, too. In respect of the restructuring of milk distribution, Sweden was a pioneer. As this development has been outlined elsewhere, it is enough to say that the advanced systematic solutions that emerged in the course of a few decades – the Tetra Brik forming the corner-stone – were soon imitated elsewhere. "The Swedish model" rapidly became an accepted designation as a point of reference in the context of market and distribution economics.

Ideal conditions thus enabled Sweden to provide all the components that were needed to help the Tetra Pak concept gain ground quickly. For a long time, this market became an example for the rest of the world to follow. It is important to remember that none of this could have been accomplished without the co-operativeness and forbearance of all the people and businesses involved: producers, retailing organisations, and consumers as well as public authorities and institutions. Certainly, criticism has sometimes been harsh, and many a gale has arisen; but in the end these disturbances amounted to little more than *"storms in a milk glass"*. Within its line of business, Tetra Pak has become a symbol for Swedish entrepreneurship. Today, its products are disseminated all over the world. Each market is governed by its own special characteristics, and all have come up with individual solutions to their problems. Even so, the

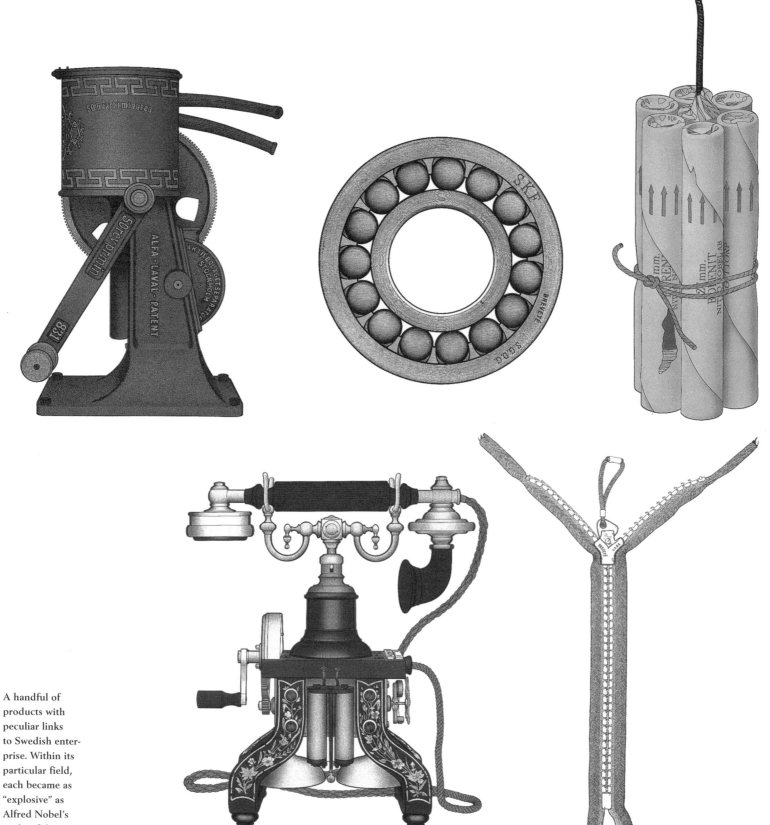

A handful of products with peculiar links to Swedish enterprise. Within its particular field, each became as "explosive" as Alfred Nobel's sticks of dynamite.

ANDERS ÖSTERLIN

basic inspiration, the very source of it all, is there in the background: the Swedish example.

The idea of opening the entire fan of experiences from international operations wide, describing the various and often truly exotic conditions under which they evolved, was a tempting one; but unfortunately it cannot be done. The ensuing chapters with their examples from international markets have, perforce, had to be restricted to mere glimpses from a small number of countries; and space only permitted the presentation of a few of all the key figures at Tetra Pak. Sales staff, engineers, service technicians and fitters, factory workers, administrative employees, assistants, secretaries – people whose intense and whole-hearted efforts brought about a long line of breakthroughs out there in the field – they have all contributed to the writing of decisive chapters in the many-faceted history of Tetra Pak. While the persons named in this publication have played significant roles, all those who cannot be quoted here are equally important; and the best proof of this is the highly successful presence of the company in no less than 125 countries (1995).

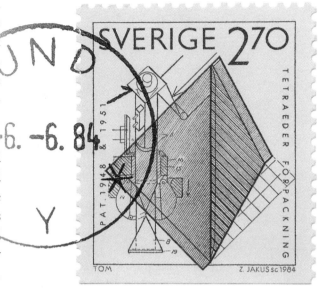

A series of stamps illustrating important Swedish industrial products was issued in 1984. The tetrahedron package was one of the six inventions to which the Swedish Post Office wished to pay tribute in this way.

The Larousse encyclopaedia aligns the characteristic milk package with these triangular French "rock" sweets.

The Larousse
encyclopaedia
aligns the cha-
racteristic milk
package with
these triangular
French "rock"
sweets.

French Connections

Everyone who ever had anything to do with the French language knows the Larousse encyclopaedia. The browser may amuse himself by looking up the word "berlingot", to be told that it is
– a well-known type of sweet, manufactured in the shape of a tetrahedron;
– the popular designation for a carton package, especially intended for milk. Nobody purchases advertising space in an encyclopaedia. If you wish to be mentioned in the Larousse, you want to be a household word among the French.

Like the sweet, the milk package can fairly claim such a position.

The Tetra Pak campaigns in the battle-fields of France form a thrilling story. In France, as in many other countries, a powerfully organised glass industry was the chief competitor during the early years. The path to victory and ultimate conquest of the market – and consequently to a mention in the Larousse – comprises all the classic features: revolt against the Establishment; persecution; the struggle for survival; cautious progress; and – at last – the rout of the adversary, in this case the glass bottle. Here, as so often in the tale of Tetra Pak's toddler years, one individual made the difference between market failure and success. His name was Pierre Schmit.

If there is any one product besides champagne, wine, and *foie gras* which has made France famous in the world of gastronomy, it is cheese – Brie, Camembert, Roquefort. France is also, of course, the home of café au lait, the well-known morning drink. In fact, France is one of the biggest milk producers in Europe. Normandy and Brittany are the most important "milk pockets". Even so, the French are not a nation of milk consumers in any generally accepted sense. Consumer milk used to lead

1. berlingot n. m. (ital. *berlingozzo*, sorte de gâteau). Bonbòn préparé avec du sucre caramélisé et aromatisé, dont la forme rappelle celle d'un tétraèdre régulier. ‖ *Fam.* Emballage en carton ou en matière plastique de forme généralement tétraédrique et de contenance normalisée, pour la vente de certains liquides, notamment du lait.

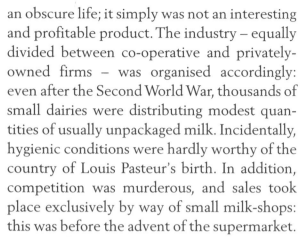

Pierre Schmit, "Monsieur Tetra Pak France", would speak with fervour in favour of his product, draining every last drop out of his arguments when talking with customers.

an obscure life; it simply was not an interesting and profitable product. The industry – equally divided between co-operative and privately-owned firms – was organised accordingly: even after the Second World War, thousands of small dairies were distributing modest quantities of usually unpackaged milk. Incidentally, hygienic conditions were hardly worthy of the country of Louis Pasteur's birth. In addition, competition was murderous, and sales took place exclusively by way of small milk-shops: this was before the advent of the supermarket.

In February 1950, a new Act stipulated that all milk sold in communities with more than 20,000 inhabitants had to be packaged. At this point in time, the glass bottle was the only existing receptacle, and the Act entailed a tremendous boom for the glassworks of France – especially the powerful St Gobain Group. Still, forward-looking men with plenty of fighting spirit sensed that there were different times ahead. One of them was a man named Pierre Schmit. Born in Paris in 1915, he became a B.Sc. (Econ.) in 1937. On the outbreak of war he was mobilised, fell into captivity in 1940, and did not come back to liberty until after the war. Following his return, he had to spend some time taking care of his health; but in the late 1940s he was fit for work again and joined a small packaging business in Grenoble. This was how, as early as 1949, he first came into contact with Åkerlund & Rausing. In the month of November that year, Schmit visited Lund. On that occasion Gad Rausing, dressed in a boiler-suit, showed him a super-secret novelty behind the closed doors of the Å&R special laboratory: the new milk carton.

Nothing was ready for production at that stage; but the demonstration had made an indelible impression, and Pierre Schmit went away "sucking the sweet". He kept in close touch with the Swedes over the next few years. When, halfway through 1952, the first tetrahedron machine could finally be demonstrated, Schmit tried to set up a contractual relationship with Tetra Pak. It failed – the company simply did not have enough cash. A "loose connection" was proposed instead: if Schmit managed to conduct any business, he would receive a certain remuneration after the event.

In the month of October that year, Pierre Schmit began to work on the market, without a contract. To begin with he arranged, at his own expense, a couple of information meetings in Paris, inviting interested representatives from industry and the public authorities. These conferences aroused a great deal of interest, but they roused a number of sleeping dogs, too. Suppliers of dishwashing machines, bottle-fillers, bottle-top sealing machines, distribution crates, and so on rushed in to protect their market. Besides, Tetra Pak still was not in a position to deliver; so far, everything was in the realm of fair words. There were many other impediments, too: an excessively revolutionary idea; the shape of the package; the rental agreement; the price level – but over and above everything else, a well-organised glass industry. The abovementioned St Gobain Group even went so far as to try to obtain the sales agency for Tetra Pak machines, in order to block developments. Another serious problem were the stringent restrictions on imports in force at that time, due to the economic difficulties of post-war France. The whole of 1953 went by without any results, and Pierre Schmit was beginning to abandon hope.

June 1954 saw a new Government take over, headed by Pierre Mendès-France. The new Prime Minister soon made himself known as something of an "ambassador of milk" – he wished to inculcate healthier drinking habits in France and was especially keen to persuade young people to drink milk in preference to wine. This situation was everything that Pierre Schmit could have wanted; but he realised that he was unlikely to get his message across if he were to proceed along the customary route, by way of ministries and bureaucratic administration. Instead, he decided to approach the Prime Minister in person, and one afternoon he plucked up his courage and called at Mendès-France's private residence. There he was received by Mrs Mendès-France, who listened attentively to the somewhat flustered door-to-door salesman. After a short while, she said: *"Please leave your documentation with me, for this is sure to interest my husband. In fact, I'll have a chance to talk with him tomorrow; we're taking the boat to America."*

Nothing venture, nothing have: in September 1954, the Tetra Pak machines were suddenly exempted from the prevailing restrictions on imports, and in October Pierre Schmit was able to record his first order, fourteen machines for half-litre packages. This made quite a stir in Lund, as it was the biggest order for machines ever to have been registered in one go. The customer was one of the major dairy groups in France at this

In the 1950s, Prime Minister Pierre Mendès-France made a name for himself as a veritable "milk imbiber".

LE "BERLINGOT"
TETRA PAK

En une SEULE OPÉRATION et de façon CONTINUE complètement automatique, cette machine :

- aseptise l'emballage,
- forme le récipient "autour" du liquide,
- le remplit sous vide,
- le ferme sous vide par scellage à chaud sous pression d'une tonne,
- le place dans le panier de transport.

pour les liquides

L'EMBALLAGE PERDU NON PREFABRIQUE

time, Les Fermiers Réunis, with plants in the Paris region as well as in the northern part of the country. The machines were intended for installation in several different dairies. The very first ended up in Rheims, the capital of champagne, which ensured that the venture got off to a sparkling start.

Once the tetrahedron packages – *les berlingots* – had gained a footing in the market, the champions of the glass bottle doubled their efforts to retain their positions. Nor were the dairies particularly enthusiastic about the novelty. The Act which had been passed a few years before had necessitated extensive investment in glass equipment, investment whose depreciation phase was still running. Retailers might have been expected to rave about the new package, but this was by no means the case. First, supermarkets and large sales premises had not arrived yet; second, the retailers – like the dairies and delivery men – earned money out of the deposit system that had been created for glass. And then, consumers

The big Paris dairies were among the first to introduce "le berlingot – the milk bonbon". Here are a couple of pictures from the early days in 1955.

Pierre Mendès-France and Ruben Rausing lunching together in Paris in 1954. Much water would flow under the bridges of Paris before Tetra Pak's break-through was a fact.

were less than jubilant; leaky packages were no help in persuading them to accept the tetrahedron, nor was its unusual shape.

Support from the powers that be was soon removed; the Mendès-France Cabinet fell from power as early as February 1955. Before that happened, though, Schmit had managed to establish a friendly personal relationship which enabled him to bring the Prime Minister and Ruben Rausing together over lunch in Paris. A few years later, and then in the capacity of an active general politician, Pierre Mendès-France paid a visit to Lund as the guest of the Rausing family. His interest in milky matters was still strong.

During the first few years, the Tetra Pak system played a fairly modest role in the French market. The reason was that 95 per cent of French consumer milk was sold by the litre; the half litre was hence a marginal product. The real struggle only began when the first one-litre machines went into operation in France, in the autumn of 1958. As before, the Fermiers Réunis Group was one of the major purchasers, and several installations were set in motion in the Paris region, to feed the multitudes of the metropolis. The first machines performed abysmally – why should France be an exception? The following episode throws stark light on these distressing times.

After long delays, the first one-litre machines were finally installed in one of the Parisian dairies, but production was uneven. Not many days had passed before the Lund employee responsible for contacts with France was ordered to come to Paris immediately, in order to take part in a meeting with the anything-but-happy customer. An appointment was made, but at the last moment Pierre Schmit was prevented from coming, and the Swedish visitor had to set off for the lion's den on his own.

Politely received, he was ushered into the presence of the senior Manager, Monsieur Godard. The latter turned out to be a distinguished-looking gentleman of about 60, with gold-rimmed spectacles and searching, but not unkind, eyes behind them. After a long silence, the following questions and answers ensued:

– *How do you do. May I ask how long you have been working for Tetra Pak?*
– *For about eighteen months, sir.*
– *Might this be your first employment after your studies?*
– *Yes, that's right, sir.*
– *Just what I thought … I had intended to inform Tetra Pak that we cannot possibly keep their machines here and that we intend to return them, as they do not work properly. We will also be claiming compensation. But I can hardly hold you accountable, young man. That discussion is one I wish to conduct with someone at a higher level. Still, do allow me, for the sake of your own future, to give you a piece of advice which I think you would be wise to adhere to – resign from Tetra Pak forthwith; that company will not survive! Goodbye.*

The visitor was seen out, as courteously as he had been admitted a short while before. He privately reflected that Pierre Schmit was sure to have known what he was doing in dispatching such an inexperienced messenger, thereby gaining a few precious days of grace in which technicians would have time to remedy the faults. But the well-meant exhortation had precisely the opposite effect – why, here was a situation where you had to stand and fight! The outcome was that both the machines and the employee stayed on – the former in the dairy, the latter in the company.

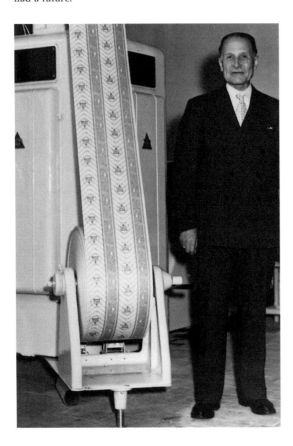

Monsieur Godard, manager of the biggest dairy group in Paris, was not convinced that Tetra Pak had a future.

Although foreign trade and imports were granted some relief, serious obstacles to a more liberal importation of goods remained. Tetra Pak paper was a particularly sensitive product, and demands for local manufacturing were soon heard. Volumes were far too small for any company-owned manufacturing to be feasible. It was hence necessary to look at the possibility of licence production, and as early as 1955 an agreement was made with the Polypapier works. Polypapier was willing to invest in the machines required for plastic-coating, printing, waxing, and cutting the material, which was derived from imported Swedish raw paper. All the necessary machinery, except the plastic-coating machine, was purchased from Lund; this formed part of the deal.

Polypapier had been started by Georges Illès, who originally came from Hungary. He turned out to be a staunch and faithful partner with whom it was a pleasure to collaborate. This did not prevent price negotiations – conducted once or twice a year – from turning into close fights over a penny or two. Hans Rausing would always take part in this combat, armed with his classic, hand-driven Facit calculator – it would be impossible to count the number of revs that it performed during the Polypapier negotiations. After long hours of discussion – sometimes in Lund, sometimes in Paris –, the parties would finally come to an agreement and be able to seal the outcome over a good dinner.

At first quantities were so small that there could not possibly be any money in it for Polypapier, but Illès was willing to invest in the future. Once business was picking up speed, during the first half of the 1960s, a serious competitor turned up in the form of plastic bags; they were soon followed by plastic bottles. With her potent petroleum industry, France became the mother country of these developments which would in due course enter markets worldwide. It was vital to prevent them from gaining too secure a foothold in the domestic market, and this aim could only be accomplished if Tetra Pak packages were cheap. Illès moaned during negotiations, eagerly supported by his own colleagues, but to little avail – the licensee was expected to shoulder his part of the responsibility. The calculator turned round and round, Polypapier groaned – and in the end a reasonable compromise was attained.

Volumes increased slowly in the early days, but after some time expansion proceeded apace. This was truly a victory won on points, and it had called for all the energy that Pierre Schmit and the French organisation were able to muster. Glass, plastic bags, and polythene bottles weakened the resolve of French dairies somewhat, but Tetra Pak

made extra efforts to convince them. The company also managed to win important allies by way of the retail trade, largely thanks to Schmit's brilliant tactics: he built up a very active sales support division which helped retailers and distribution networks – free of cost – to devise campaigns, to praise the virtues of their product, and to set up demonstrations in their shops, thereby persuading housewives to buy milk in cartons. *"Don't resort to the bottle – buy Tetra Pak!"* was a promotional slogan which caught on. For many years, the French company would run a large department devoted to this essential function. Other Tetra Pak organisations adhered to the pattern set by the French; but no sales-promoting operations anywhere else were ever as hard-hitting and successful as those in France.

This pioneering effort, especially necessary in the early 1960s, continued for a long time, even after the Tetra Brik and asepsis had emerged in

In France, sales support evolved into something of an art form as time went by, "imitated by many, surpassed by none".

Tetra Pak's "street salesmen" trying to convince sceptical house-wives of the advantages of the package: hermetically sealed, easy to carry, crushproof in their bags.

The Swedish-inspired GREDFIL was one of many special products.

While the Tetra Brik is by no means a "shady" phenomenon, it does protect the sensitive milk from light. In marketing, this point was made by means of attaching a pair of sun-glasses to the package.

In the mid-1960s, Nestlé launched flavoured condensed milk in a convenient mini-sized package. The product became a favourite "weekend sweet" among the children of Paris.

171

the market. France was always a country characterised by stiff competition. Pierre Schmit had every reason to exclaim, *"We won, despite the dairies, despite the retail trade, and despite the consumers!"* He might have added *"and despite the political, economic, and industrial establishment"*: the first 15 years had been tough ones. Today, for instance, it seems difficult to imagine that on three different occasions during this early stage, Pierre Schmit was subjected to anonymous telephone calls containing explicit threats and exhortations to take up a different line of work without delay ...

It was always fundamental Tetra Pak policy to manufacture materials under the company's own steam as soon as this was economically defensible. In spite of the many difficulties, the French market developed favourably, and a decision was made to build a plant just outside Dijon, the capital of French mustard. The factory was ready to open in 1971, and that was the beginning of the end of relations with Polypapier. It should be pointed out, however, that the winding-up took place over a period of several years; this gradual phasing-out was designed to give the loyal

Pierre Schmit greeting his guests at the opening of the Dijon factory.

The materials-processing plant is situated in Longvic, just outside Dijon.

172

Ruben Rausing
shaking hands
with Robert
Poujade, France's
first "Minister for
the Environment".

Monsieur Poujade,
likewise Mayor
of Dijon, was guest
of honour at the
factory opening.
Here he is flanked
by Ruben Rausing
and Pierre Schmit.

licensee the breathing-space he needed to find customers who could replace his Tetra Pak business.

Like any other company, Tetra Pak needed a firm of accountants to rely on in matters of taxation and for certain other expert evaluations. In the late 1950s, the company established contacts with Cabinet Sabatier, a firm which specialised in supplying guidance for entrepreneurs creating Franco-Swedish businesses. This relationship did not stop at conventional auditing: as time went by, it developed into a scheme of far-reaching collaboration. One of the firm's owners, Louis Faure, soon became Pierre Schmit's confidant and assisted Schmit on innumerable occasions in the course of the years. Annual accounts, commercial contracts, customs and tax matters, administrative procedures, licence agreements, international transactions, company structures – everything was discussed between them. Louis Faure's talents and expertise were invaluable: the knottier the problem, the greater the challenge to his powers. In recent years, he

For many years,
the company
profited from
the initiative and
resourcefulness
of its adviser
Louis Faure.

has also frequently been consulted over major international issues affecting the Group.

As the Larousse encyclopaedia implied, Tetra Pak was soon part of everyday life in France, even at the early stage when pasteurised milk was sold in the tetrahedron package. When aseptic, long-life milk came into being, the novelty was greeted with keen interest, as sterile products traditionally accounted for a large share of the French market. The Tetra Brik introduction in the mid-1960s consolidated positions further. In the meantime, the retail trade had undergone a restructuring process, too. Self-service shops and shopping centres emerged: Prisunic, Carrefour, Euromarché, and Radar are only a few examples of powerful chains of distribution which – thanks to Schmit's contacts – became valuable allies. Naturally, the construction of the Dijon plant helped in stabilising conditions.

When Pierre Schmit retired in 1985, he was in a position to look back proudly on a long line of years during which Tetra Pak France, his life's work, had grown from nothing into one of the most important and profitable companies in the Tetra Pak Group. Over the past decade, the market has continued to develop satisfactorily under new management. If we use turnover size as a basis for comparison, we find that France is now (1995) among the top five on the list. However, there were times in earlier years when Pierre Schmit and his colleagues had reason to ponder the motto in the city arms of Paris, which feature a ship in troubled waters. Beneath the picture is the Latin device *"Fluctuat nec mergitur"* – she tosses, but she does not sink.

The young people of today want to be able to greet tomorrow with a smile, too. Supermarkets are obliged to make substantial efforts to satisfy the demands of a public keenly aware of the importance of environmental issues. To an ever-increasing extent, rational packages requiring a minimum of materials consumption are coming to determine the purchasing habits of consumers.

The New Roman Empire

Italy, heiress of the superpower of classical antiquity. Rome, the Eternal City, the hub of a world empire for more than a thousand years. "La bella Italia" of today, a popular country among foreign visitors, sunny and smiling. When you sip a chilled Chianti wine in the pleasant shades of monuments and ruins, you do not associate this nation with milk and dairies.

And yet this was the country in which Tetra Pak built a new Roman Empire, raising monuments of its own.

Maybe there is a connection between the old and the new; perhaps Italy does have traditions with regard to milk? After all, it was milk from the illustrious she-wolf that ensured the survival of Romulus and Remus – legendary sons of Mars, the god of war, and a vestal virgin – after their adventures on the Tiber. Duly fortified by this nourishment, they embarked on their labours, and according to legend Romulus founded the Eternal City in 753 B.C. The she-wolf and the suckling brothers remain the symbol of present-day Rome, a latter-day gesture of gratitude.

Looking upwards on a starry night, we perceive the Milky Way, the Via Lactea of the Romans, extending across the night sky like a band of light. There is no doubt that the idea of milk as a product had a place of its own in the mythology as well as the everyday life of classical times. Even so, that heritage did not make any significant contributions to the creation of the Tetra Pak market in Italy. The company had to write its own, modern history there; and the author's name is Danilo Severi.

Towards the end
of the 1950s,
the new dairy
at Modena became
Tetra Pak's cradle
in Italy.

In the early 1950s, during the post-war boom, Danilo Severi (born in 1913) was working as a well-established agro-industrialist in the prosperous province of Emilia – in Modena, to be precise, some 90 English miles from Milan in a south-easterly direction. His business activities included the buying, storage, and re-sale of fruit, Parmesan cheese, and – brandy. As a counterweight to the latter product, however, he took an interest in milk and was one of the owners of the privately-owned dairy consortium in his city.

Among many other responsibilities, Severi had undertaken to examine the plans for a new Modena dairy project in the capacity of sole investigator. Keen to keep in touch with technological advances, he visited a number of fairs and exhibitions in 1953, such as the then well-known MACHEVO fair in Utrecht in the Netherlands. That was where he first caught sight of a Tetra Pak machine and quickly realised the potential of the system. In this context, one may well speak of what the Italians call *innamoramento* – but Tetra Pak let this love-at-first-sight languish unrequited for quite a while. In the following year, 1954, Severi went to Lund and was in due course received by the management of the day. His was a dual purpose: he wanted to order a couple of machines for the new Modena dairy; but he was also eager to obtain the Tetra Pak agency for Italy. However, the unresponsive Swedes were unenthusiastic about the Italian milk market and its possibilities. Severi did not give up – perseverance does it – and the minutes of a board meeting in February 1956 contain the following entry: *"It is agreed that Dottor Danilo Severi may be employed, on trial, as an agent for Italy during a period of twelve months."* Severi himself had anticipated developments and been able to place a couple of machines in northern Italy the year before, without possessing any formal contract with Tetra Pak.

During the world congress in Rome in 1956, Pope Pius XII received the participants and delivered a message emphasising the vital importance of milk.

In 1956, though, Tetra Pak had reason to take a special interest in Italy. That year, the world congress of the International Dairy Federation (IDF) – a congress arranged every third year – was to take place in Rome in the month of September. In connection with this congress, there was to be an exhibition of modern dairy-technological equipment. It was absolutely essential for Tetra Pak to display a machine there. After all, important scientists, technologists, and customers from all the corners of the earth were expected to visit the Italian capital; it was literally a case of all roads leading to Rome. It might be mentioned, by way of curiosity, that Pope Pius XII held an audience before the 3,000 congress participants, emphasising that it was vital for the distribution of such a fundamental foodstuff as milk to be both efficient and hygienic. His Holiness laid stress on the joint responsibilities of producers and distributors in the name of humanity. The delegates were also able to inspect the Tetra Pak machine which had been temporarily installed in the large but old-fashioned Roman dairy. In fact, the Pope's blessings were sorely needed: the machine was still suffering from teething troubles, and it was taken down after the congress. The Roman market was not yet ripe, and it would take years for this bastion to fall into the hands of Tetra Pak.

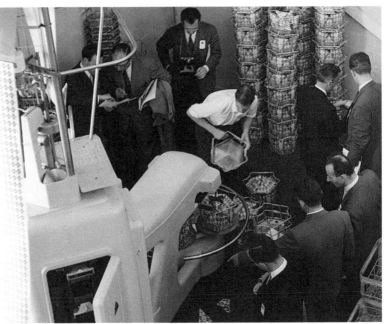

Alongside his usual operations, Severi continued – now in the capacity of agent – to exercise his persuasive talents on suitable clients, initially with modest success. The large, municipally-owned dairies were not

A demonstration machine was temporarily installed in the venerable Roman dairy.

likely to take an interest; the glass bottle was of course an excellent means of keeping competition away and preserving a local monopoly. Besides, "milk in paper" was a costly novelty. Consequently, the only dairies to take the bait were a small number of minor, privately-owned ones.

In the Italian dairy industry, Danilo Severi was already a well-respected name. That respect came in very useful indeed during attempts to persuade customers who took some convincing. When deals were struck, he often furnished a kind of personal guarantee which operated on the ethical rather than on the financial plane. Thus, for instance, the complicated rental agreement with all its clauses was not the sort of thing to present to a no-nonsense dairy manager without much formal schooling. Danilo repeatedly found himself in a position where he would exclaim, *"Never mind the small print in this contract, just sign, will you – and trust me!"* Another example of personal authority is found in his way of working on the market. He was unimpressed by sales methods which involved visiting, and canvassing, prospective clients: *"If people want to discuss Tetra Pak, and I'm sure they do, they'll know that I'm right here in my Modena office!"* This is the reasoning of a true feudalist; but these days such an attitude would be less appropriate. When customers came to Modena, they were courteously received and well fed, and they were given opportunities to discuss their problems in detail. A solution was always found. Not many returned home from such a visit without having signed some sort of Tetra Pak contract.

Relations with the Swedish head office were not altogether comfortable. The feeling in Lund was that Italy was no doubt a good producer of spaghetti, ice cream, and Gorgonzola cheese, but that the Italians did not take much interest in other types of dairy produce. In addition, they spoke *"a language difficult for Northerners to understand"*. Severi did not do much to rid the Swedes of their preconceived notions. His visits to the Lund office were few and far between; he did not like travelling, especially by air; and he spoke no English. Matters went as far as the dispatching of

Danilo Severi proudly indicating where Tetra Pak has gained ground in Italy. Temperamental "pointers" were occasionally flourished during internal discussions, too.

an emissary from the Swedish sales management, a representative charged with the task of investigating the state of affairs *in situ* and establishing whether there was really any point in continuing to waste time and resources in a market which had for years been promising more than it could perform. Fortunately, the management paid attention to the favourable report submitted by the emissary and resolved to evince a little patience. It was a very lucky decision, as Italy came to constitute one of the leading Tetra Pak markets for a number of years.

At this point, in the early 1960s, that development had only just started. A number of small private dairies made inroads into the distribution areas of the big urban dairies, generating unrest and irritation. The prime example was the little dairy just outside Rome called Fattoria Latte Sano. With the aid of a single Tetra Pak machine, this firm caused the largest municipally-owned fresh-milk dairy to take a sudden interest in the new carton system. The initial contracts were signed in the spring

Deliveries from the small, privately-owned Fattoria Latte Sano brought the new package to the attention of the central dairy in Rome. Dottor Fausto Bonetti, who managed the Roman dairy for years, was among Tetra Pak's chief supporters.

of 1962, six years after the world congress referred to above. A small number of machines were installed in the old, worn-down dairy in the middle of the city; the building was located right at the foot of an ancient aqueduct pillar and was, of course, listed. Now the ice was broken, and most of the big municipal dairies followed the Roman example: Milan, Florence, Bologna, Naples, Genoa, and others. In Venice, milk distribution would usually take place by gondola!

As we have seen, the decisive breakthrough did not come until ten years after the first tentative contacts between Severi and Tetra Pak. At that stage, the only saleable product was the tetrahedron package for pasteurised milk. To everybody's surprise, however, Italy turned out to be

Sweden's "export ambassador" *par excellence*, HRH Prince Bertil, left, cheerfully chatting to Danilo Severi during a trade fair in Milan.

In Venice there is every reason to talk about channels, or rather canals, of distribution. Shops would often have their milk delivered by gondola.

Reality past and
present. A succession
of pictures from
Naples, Milan, Parma,
and Florence.

"Autostrada" is,
of course, an Italian
loan-word. The
picture of "the milk
autostrada" shows
production on the
premises of one of
Tetra Pak's major
customers, Parmalat.

the most expansive market in the early 1960s. Consequently, this country was a natural option when Tetra Pak was considering the possibility of capacity extension outside Sweden. As volumes grew, it became increasingly difficult to convince Italian customers that their packaging materials had to come all the way from Sweden. Demands for local manufacturing – on the grounds of security as well as for economic reasons – began to be heard. At Tetra Pak, this became a major issue, as there were not as yet any company-owned factories outside Sweden. Hence the Board, headed by Ruben Rausing, travelled to Italy in the spring of 1963 in order to look into the matter on the spot. Several industrial sites were inspected in the northern part of the country. The final assessment only comprised two or three proposals. All preliminary investigations were already completed – in respect of land and soil conditions, power, labour supply, trade unions, transport optimising in relation to customers, and so on. One Wednesday morning, the decisive board meeting was to be held in the sales office at Modena. Everyone was counting on its being over before lunch, leaving participants free to return by an afternoon flight from Milan. The meeting began, and after some general discussion Ruben Rausing presented the following summary:

"Fundamental conditions pertaining to the matter in hand seem to favour our choosing the Rubiera site. But we have left an important topic out of account. In view of the fact that this factory will be an object of demonstration and a place of pilgrimage for our clients, internationally as well as locally, it is essential that there should be a first-class restaurant close by where we can entertain our guests. I propose that we make a study visit and have lunch in such a restaurant – assuming there is one, of course. Otherwise we must consider a different option."

Danilo Severi arranged a lunch reservation with all due dispatch, and his secretary was soon busy changing bookings for the board members so that they could catch later flights. At one p.m. precisely, the party sat down to lunch in a small village inn at Rubiera, called "da Arnaldo". A superb repast was consumed, and towards the end of the meal the formal decision was made to build the first foreign Tetra Pak plant at Rubiera. It was in fact Arnaldo's exquisite restaurant, even then aptly pet-named "Clinica Gastronomica", that tipped the balance. It turned out to be a wise and forward-looking decision – over the years, countless customers have been referred to this clinic for treatment!

In the mid-1960s, the system for pasteurised products was supplemented by a new development – the aseptic "triangle", designed for long-life milk free from bacteria. Here, too, Italy came to play the part of a pioneer. Even at an early stage, Severi had emphasised the importance of providing milk that would keep for a long time: milk which did not have to rely on the costly refrigeration chain as it was distributed over long distances, for example from the Po valley – where milk was in plentiful supply – down to southern Italy and Sicily, where production was slight. Besides, domestic refrigerators were still a luxury. As asepsis approached the marketing phase, Severi was hence in the forefront among those who were keen to install such machinery; and soon long-life milk spread like wildfire all over Italy. The system still had some way to go technologically speaking, but sales had begun and helped generate sufficient volumes for the new Rubiera factory which was ready to start operations in the spring of 1965.

Arnaldo's restaurant in Rubiera, now famous all over the world, is rightly described as a "gastronomic clinic". Many guests have received competent care within its walls.

As production started, it became necessary to establish prices pertaining to the locally-manufactured Tetra Pak paper. Everybody in Italy, but nobody in Lund, was of the opinion that prices must come down. Many tough and protracted discussions were devoted to this important topic. As so often before and later, Severi was assisted by his excellent adviser Luciano Tagliazucchi, a consultant on issues of a financial and/or legal nature and on matters of taxation. Tagliazucchi was also diligently employed as interpreter. On one such occasion, Severi delivered a long and eloquent discourse, whereupon Tagliazucchi rose to his feet and uttered the laconic recapitulation, *"Dottor Severi says no!"*

After a succession of Swedes had travelled to Italy and made repeated and abortive attempts to persuade Danilo Severi, he was finally

It had better be the right button – Danilo Severi starting the printing press when the Rubiera plant opened in 1965.

Italy is the home
of casuistry.
Sound legal advice
was hence essential,
and Dottor Luciano
Tagliazucchi invari-
ably supplied it.

summoned to Lund where the Board hoped to make him see reason. Long discussions and some private consultations were followed by a message from the Board to the effect that Dr Severi's arguments had at least partly succeeded in convincing the members, who were prepared to accept a trial year in the course of which the deployment of new filling machines would supply proof that the proposed cut-price policy was viable. Danilo Severi's reply was not long in coming: *"I cannot pursue collaborative efforts unless they are based on one-hundred-per-cent confidence. If no such confidence prevails, I'd rather drop the entire project. Incidentally, I'm not dependent on Tetra Pak for my subsistence."* An unmistakeable ultimatum, in other words, and it had the intended effect. Severi was given a free hand and proceeded to capture market shares with a price policy which was to prove very successful, but which would also come in for constant criticism and gradually cause considerable problems in the context of pan-European pricing. This was not the only occasion on which a firm and convinced Danilo Severi defended his notions against a unanimous board – and against the Rausings, too. It should be added, however, that among all the foreign Tetra Pak managers he was the one who came to be closest to the family, especially to Ruben Rausing. Contacts between them were particularly lively from 1969 to 1977, when Ruben Rausing lived in Rome.

But the two gentlemen liked and trusted each other well before that time. When, in the mid-1960s, the Rausing family faced the problem of possibly having to sell the well-established Åkerlund & Rausing in order to secure capital necessary for the expansion of Tetra Pak, they were confronting a very delicate and difficult issue. After all, the new company had hardly made any big waves yet. On one occasion, Ruben Rausing consulted Danilo Severi with a view to finding out what sort of market guarantees Italy would be able to provide. Severi was not a man for forecasts; indeed, he was even reluctant to make promises regarding the immediate future. In reply to a direct question, he made his one known exception from this principle and promised to *"place one hundred machines this year and the next"*. At that point in time, this was a mind-boggling number, and it came with the implicit promise of a marked increase in the sale of packaging materials, so vital to the company. Rightly or wrongly, this guarantee has been said to have contributed to the Rausings' decision to sell Åkerlund & Rausing to the future Swedish Match in the autumn of 1965, placing all their eggs in one basket – Tetra Pak.

Ruben Rausing was happy to receive visitors at Simontorp, his home outside Lund which was always dear to him. A particularly welcome guest was Danilo Severi. The discussions of the two men were conducted in a spirit of intimacy and confidence.

187

As we saw, the same year witnessed the starting-up of the first company-owned non-Swedish materials factory under the management of Ragnar Mandersson, M.Eng. Naturally enough, there were production problems at the outset; but the market was in a co-operative mood. At last, customers were able to rely on a supplier in their own country and had no need to worry about long-haul transport, delayed deliveries, or threats of strikes abroad. Payment routines were simplified and payments could be made in the domestic currency, which was no small relief. Skilfully led and managed by Mandersson, the Rubiera factory soon developed into a model plant. Part of the credit for this belongs to the workers of northern Italy, whose ability and diligence have long been generally recognised. The factory came to serve as a model for those plants that were planned and constructed all over the world as the years went by. In a few years the productive capacity of the Rubiera plant hit the ceiling, even after extensions, and it became necessary to plan for a second factory. This time the desire to optimise transports, and to cater to the needs of the growing number of clients in other parts of Italy, made it natural to look further south for a suitable location. Another important reason was the fact that the Italian state paid generous subsidies to companies investing in southern Italy, and Tetra Pak was keen to make use of them. An appropriate site was purchased in Latina, some 30 English miles south of Rome, and in 1973 the manufacturing company "Cartotecnica Pontina" was able to start operating. This second plant brought a necessary capacity expansion, but that was not all: it also helped to spread risks in view of contingencies such as labour-market conflicts, fire, and so on. For several years Italy was the only country outside Sweden to have two plants owned by Tetra Pak.

At the same time, in 1973, another and more monumental industrial achievement was beginning to take shape – the new super-dairy outside Rome. Alfa-Laval Italy was the sole contractor for this vast project, which entailed responsibility for planning and building the premises as well as for providing all the equipment, packaging machines included. This commitment caused Alfa-Laval virtually insurmountable problems: in Italy, milk is not always white; there are times when it comes tinged by special political and financial circumstances. At its initial stage the project comprised some 40 filling machines, and an entirely unrealistic schedule had been set for it. Gradually, it assumed more realistic proportions. When, after considerable delay, the dairy was opened in 1976, it contained 18 Tetra Pak machines.

Opposite page: A real treasure – Severi's pocket-sized "order-book" for the years 1960 to 1985. The original was presented to Hans Rausing on his 60th birthday in March 1986.

Are we right on schedule? Rubiera's manager Ragnar Mandersson is keen to demonstrate his model plant to Hans Rausing and Danilo Severi. France's Pierre Schmit in the background.

The fast growth of the market soon called for an expansion of manufacturing capacity, and the Latina factory, with the Apennines in the background, was completed in 1973. For many years, Sweden and Italy would remain the only countries with two plants.

When it was time to appoint a financial manager for the new Tetra Pak plant at Latina, Danilo Severi proposed that the post be given to his son Alfredo. Alfredo, in his mid-thirties at the time, had taken a degree in economics and then spent several years performing senior apprenticeship functions within the company. As a general assistant to his father and to Ragnar Mandersson at Rubiera, he had become thoroughly familiar with the business. Now Severi felt it was time he had a responsible post. The Rausings were not entirely convinced, however. Certainly, *"the lad might be promising"*, but surely he ought to have some international schooling first – preferably in the form of a year of two studying in the United States. Once again, Severi demonstrated his pertinacity and forcefulness. His final statement, somewhat condensed, ran as follows: *"No Harvard in the world measures up to our dinner conversations at home. That's where he learns something – I'm Alfredo's university!"* The matter does not seem to have been discussed further. Alfredo Severi went to Latina for a couple of years but then returned to Modena. When his father Danilo vacated

The new dairy outside Rome became a monument worthy of the city's traditions. Opened in 1976, it remains one of the major Tetra Pak customers for pasteurised products.

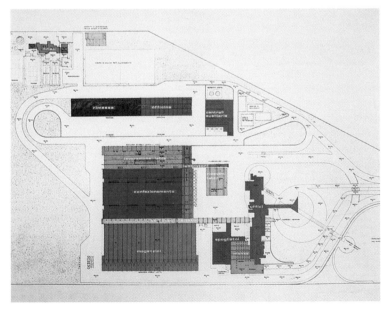

Thoroughly trained, in the spirit of patriarchy, Alfredo Severi was well placed to take over the post of Managing Director of the Italian group in 1982. The market has continued to expand under his management.

the M.D.'s chair in 1982, Alfredo took over responsibility for Tetra Pak Italy – still without an American degree. It should be added that he handled his duties impeccably; the market as well as the company has continued to develop satisfactorily year by year. In the spring of 1995 Italy passed a unique milestone: total production, from the beginning of operations in the country, exceeded a hundred billion packages.

Italy always, and deliberately, kept a low profile in the group. There was never much in the way of international exposure, and participation in exhibitions, fairs, and conferences has been reluctant and involved the smallest possible number of people. This was particularly the case under the reign of Danilo Severi – at that time Italy was sufficient unto herself. Nor did Severi's non-existent English assist the flow of communication. Put simply, he did not feel any need of those points of reference that an international market could provide; thus, for instance, his trips abroad with customers were few in number. Many other attitudes and values were peculiar to him – in his own day they were applicable, but they would not be very successful today.

Danilo Severi held a special position in the organisation of Tetra Pak. By dint of sheer intelligence and resourcefulness, he brought about a revolution in the Italian milk-and-juice market. He was never a man given to extravagant gestures. At his disposal he had – in addition to his son – a small number of co-workers who were unswervingly loyal to him. Of course, his intimate knowledge of the business and skill in handling political matters contributed to his success; but his biggest asset was his powerful personality. We have all been told that *Rome was not built in a day*. Even so, it is no great exaggeration to claim that the Roman Empire of Tetra Pak was built in the course of a single, if life-long, working day, and that it was the achievement of one man – Danilo Severi.

The master's touch shows in the ability to transcend narrow limits. With modest means and a small staff at his disposal, Danilo Severi accomplished the Italian miracle. For more than two decades, Italy was Tetra Pak's leading market from the point of view of volume.

German Business, Big Business

"Picasso-Euter", the Picasso udder, was the graphic pet name acquired by the tetrahedron package on its introduction in what was then West Germany. A peculiarly apt and telling description, as it happened: what followed turned out to be a colourful and artistic display of effective marketing.

The country soon became a stable point of reference and the company an impressive breeder of profits.

After the first, tentative launching in Sweden in 1952–53, what could have been more natural than letting one's eyes wander to the large market just south of the Baltic: to Germany, then undergoing a swift modernisation process? The industrial revolution in post-war Germany, "das Wirtschaftswunder", would amaze the world. The dairy industry had initiated a restructuring process where disposable packages might fit in nicely. In fact, Germany was at this time the only market in Europe to have tested an alternative to the glass bottle on a notable scale – a waxed carton called Perga, manufactured by the German company Jagenberg. As the years went by, subsequent products developed by the same company, the Blocpak and the Combibloc, became serious competitors.

Still, the idea of a throwaway package was after all a fairly new concept at that point in time, the mid-50s; and it was essential for Tetra Pak to secure a footing without delay. The first export deal was struck with the Alster Milchwerk in Hamburg, where a machine for half-litre packages was installed in the summer of 1954. The Managing Director of this dairy, Emil Dous, became a prominent figure among German customers. He was a truculent man of few words, with a sullen cast of mind and a more than slightly choleric temper; but as a client he was a rock whose loyalty was beyond question. That was exactly the kind of

The manager of the Hamburg dairy, Emil Dous, became Tetra Pak's very first customer outside Sweden.

customer Tetra Pak needed – a number of things went wrong during the phase of introduction. For instance, the printed décor on the rolls of paper stained the plastic inside of the material, and every now and then the milk would acquire a slightly greenish tinge as a result. Consumers failed to appreciate this special product, unmoved by the fact that green is the symbolic hue of Nature herself.

Further prospecting went ahead with efficiency and dispatch, Dr Carl-Axel Althin being the man in charge. His background was somewhat unusual for a businessman – an archaeologist, he belonged to the realm of the Humanities – but he was a particularly talented salesman, imaginative, persuasive, and eloquent. Domiciled in Lund, he spent a great deal of time travelling around Germany, setting up temporary offices in several of the great hotels of Hamburg, Düsseldorf, Frankfurt, and Munich. His hotel bills were sometimes hefty, but the outcome amply justified them. With the aid of a small local organisation and a couple of agents working on commission, Althin quickly managed to establish a respectable list of customers. A German company had been founded in the early 1950s, right at the beginning of operations in the country, its legal basis resting with a firm of lawyers in Hamburg which bore the awe-inspiring name of Martin Luther und Partner – yes, very possibly a direct descendant of the great 16th-century reformer! This company did not conduct any transactions during its first few years, though. Marketing work was done by way of Lund, and travelling fitters and engineers took care of technical maintenance. Soon, however, a local service office was opened in Frankfurt. Its first permanent Services Manager was Bertil Runow; but initially he worked under the formal authority of the Hamburg lawyers. The following exchange with one of them occurred during an early discussion on matters of organisation: *"Never forget, Herr Runow, that the company's seat is in Hamburg. – Yes, Herr Doktor, but its head is in Frankfurt!"*

Increasing volumes led to growing demands for the local manufacture of paper. The most expedient solution to the problem was to start co-operating with a well-established firm in that line of business; in Germany as elsewhere, quantities were still far too small for the building of an "own" factory to be defensible. Nor was there any money for such an investment. Hence, the Zellstoff-Fabrik Waldhof in Mannheim became the first Tetra Pak licensee in 1956, a step which heralded decades of collaboration – with modest success at first. Despite certain problems with quality, the "Milch-Tüte" ("milk cornet"), as it was also called, continued to gain ground, and a small, resourceful organisation evolved, still based in Frankfurt.

It soon became impractical to run this growing market from a distance – that is, from the sales department in Lund. Staff taken on along the way required permanent leadership on the spot. When Carl-Axel Althin left Tetra Pak in 1960, the time had come to appoint a Managing Director for the German company. The offer went to Bertil Turesson, a young, promising sales manager at Åkerlund & Rausing. Turesson left for Frankfurt in September that year, moving into office premises at 16 Schöne Aussicht, right in the heart of the city. He was not given much

From the first years in Germany, Martin Luther lent invaluable assistance on all legal issues. Tetra Pak's collaboration with his firm has continued into the next generation.

Bertil Turesson, the company's first manager permanently stationed in Germany from 1960 to 1966.

On hot summer days, machines at the Firma Rickertsen in Hamburg would run hot as well. Demand for Sunkist juice products was high all over Germany.

Since the mid-1960s, the German head office has been situated in Hochheim, near Frankfurt.

Munich became a pioneering customer for Tetra Brik Aseptic. "Long life" created new opportunities where transportation was concerned and made UHT milk a product that knows no boundaries.

opportunity to admire the beautiful view from his office windows, though; the move was followed by a couple of years of tireless field-work, with trips and visits to customers from morning till night, day after day. During this period, the market reputation of Tetra Pak was consolidated. Any disruptions were promptly dealt with by skilful technicians, and volumes kept increasing.

New opportunities opened up when asepsis was ready for introduction. In Germany, a so-called Marktordnung prevailed; it was, in practice, a local monopoly ensuring that dairies were protected from the competition of neighbours. This, however, only applied to pasteurised milk. Now that the new, long-life milk had arrived, many people saw a chance of extending their distribution and sales. A gradual loosening of the established zone monopolies began in the spring of 1964 as the first aseptic tetrahedron machine went into operation in Munich, an example soon followed by other dairies. One factor which contributed to its success was that still drinks and fruit juices began to be sold in the handy portion packages of Tetra Pak. The German pioneer in this respect was Firma Rickertsen in Hamburg, licensee of the American brand-name Sunkist.

Åkerlund & Rausing had not been slow to grasp the potential of the German market either. An Å&R plant in Germany was planned in the late 1950s; the question of where to put it was answered when Ruben Rausing declared, *"it will be located very close to the Frankfurt airport"*. Hochheim-am-Main was the ultimate choice, and a state-of-the-art factory went into business there in 1960. In addition to products belonging to the Å&R range, it was soon manufacturing paper for Tetra Pak purposes. After some time, the Hochheim plant led to Tetra Pak's moving its premises from the city centre of Frankfurt. An initial component in what was to become the German heart of the company was built in 1964–65, at which point the Tetra Pak office and service workshop were transferred to Hochheim.

In the autumn of 1965, Åkerlund & Rausing was sold to (the future) Swedish Match. The sale entailed a shift in the need for leadership and management in Lund. Bertil Turesson would be summoned back to Sweden, and the search for a new M.D. for Germany was on at once. Many Tetra Pak people were involved in this recruitment process, and finally they believed they had found the right man. The only member of the top management in Lund who had not seen the person in question was Erik Torudd, who was then sales manager in charge of non-European

German operations were closely monitored by Ruben Rausing, even in his old age. Here he is engaged in conversation with Gunther Luedecke. Both gentlemen appear to take an optimistic view of the future.

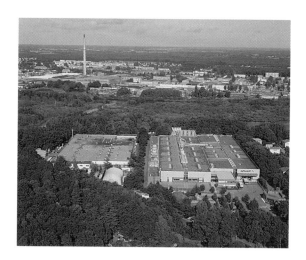

markets. The matter was becoming urgent – it was already summer – and the only chance of a brief interview came in connection with a big dairy congress in Munich, during a few unusually hot days in July. The meeting took place during a brief lunch break, beside the pool on the roof of the Hotel Bayerischer Hof. And that was how Gunther Alexander Luedecke (born in 1925), recruited from Remington of America, came to undergo the final stage in the protracted round of interviews under fairly extraordinary circumstances – wearing swimming-trunks, a white towelling bathrobe, and slippers! Even so, he sailed through both mental and physical "striptease" sessions and sat down in the German Managing Director's chair in October 1966.

This date marks a milestone in the history of the company. Energetic and dedicated, Luedecke continued the work of his predecessors, achieving great things during his 25 years as Manager of Tetra Pak in Germany. Asepsis went ahead, the Tetra Brik was launched, and soon the first factory for the processing of materials was on the drawing-board. Asked by Luedecke how large the factory site should be, Ruben Rausing allegedly replied, with a humorous twinkle, *"Buy all the land up to the horizon, that'll leave us room to expand and nobody will get in our way."* In 1969, the plant was completed in Limburg, near Frankfurt. When Tetra Brik Aseptic began to be marketed around 1970, the milk and juice markets were revolutionised, and volume growth continued with increasing speed. Despite having acquired a large site in Limburg and extended the plant there, the company soon found that it needed a second factory. It turned out that the City of Berlin offered interesting

The manufacturing plants for materials in Limburg (above left) and Berlin, completed in 1981, are two of the German company's centres. Their massive strength is partly due to their modern and highly effective manufacturing equipment.

The machinery of Firma Stute is a truly "succulent" spectacle; here, juices are being filled day and night during the peak season.

terms for industrial investment, which facilitated the decision as regards location. The Berlin manufacturing unit was opened in the autumn of 1981, and it did not take long for the newcomer's capacity to be fully utilised as well.

Of course, the preceding résumé does not do the German organisation justice. It might appear as if it had all been a bed of roses; reality was very different. A demanding clientèle has kept the organisation on its toes. A particularly German feature was the emergence of plants built on a truly massive scale. Several examples might be mentioned in the juice sector: while Rickertsen in Hamburg was the pioneer, Firma Stute, domiciled in Paderborn, occupies a special place. You would have to travel far and wide before seeing anything like it. At present (1995), Stute is Tetra Pak's biggest customer in the country.

In the past, however, thoughts of Germany would usually be associated with the large "H-milk dairies" – "H" standing for "haltbar", "long-lasting". Milchversorgung Bochum, Hansamolkerei of Hamburg, Südmilch in Stuttgart: many more could be listed. While long-life milk gained ground, it became increasingly difficult to maintain the zone-based monopoly which was mentioned above. As everybody was keen to cut slices from the same cake, and there was a hefty milk surplus in the background, dairies would occasionally make exaggerated investments; murderous competition would ensue. Nor were the big chain-stores – Aldi, EDEKA, and others too – slow to use long-life milk as a cut-price item or "loss leader". As a result, long-life milk has long been sold at lower prices than the pasteurised variety. Naturally, the fundamental reason was found in the flexible distribution opportunities created by the aseptic system. As a result, Tetra Pak frequently had to play the part of scapegoat in this context – the graphic German word *Prügelknabe*, "whipping-boy", is highly applicable here. At the same time, nobody could deny that the long-life products had their advantages. People soon came to appreciate the convenience of being able to buy and store their milk outside the refrigeration chain.

It would have been strange if such an important market as Germany had not been subjected to fierce competition. Domestic items competed against imported ones. The paper package Zupack came and went. Other cartons and plastic packages, from such producers as the powerful Bosch Hesser Group and the German plastics industry, put up a tough fight. Vigorous German companies have stood up to their foreign competitors. This is especially true of Firma Jagenberg, which has gradually developed new systems whose market adaptation has been increasingly successful. In the 1960s, their original, waxed Perga carton was successively replaced by Blocpak and, during the next phase, by the Combibloc system. The latter now also exists in an aseptic variant. The fact that the Combibloc is, as a finished product, virtually undistinguishable from the Tetra Brik – the same bottom size, the same measurements, the same appearance – has not made life any easier. It is not continuously manufactured from a roll of paper, though, as is the case with Tetra Pak, but from flat packaging materials, and the process does not permit filling without air. As we all know, pioneers are bound to have successors.

While competition has certainly hardened in a general sense, the collapse of the Berlin Wall in 1989 opened up greater potential. True, Tetra Pak had long maintained a certain, fairly modest, presence in the former GDR; a licence agreement was signed as early as 1968. Following

To Aldi and other large chain-stores, UHT milk has become an item with "magnetic" properties which is exposed to tough price competition among distributors.

The collapse
of the Berlin Wall
created new
potential for an
expansive market,
not least for daily
foods such as milk
products and juices.

political liberalisation, though, investments have shot up, especially in such a vital and literally down-to-earth sector as the dairy industry. Today, reunified Germany is the Group's most important market in western Europe.

With their stringent demands in most areas – technology, performance, hygiene, environment, cost effectiveness –, German customers always constituted a driving force impelling general development at Tetra Pak. The expressive term *Funktionstüchtigkeit* is an illuminating one. It has really been a matter of being *tüchtig*, "able" – no one English word fully corresponds to *Funktionstüchtigkeit*, and there is an element of passivity in the phrases "in good working order" and "capable of functioning" which is absent from the German concept. Meeting the frequently tough demands of the clientèle, and quickly too, became second nature. On the other hand, company staff knew that once a product had passed through the eye of the German needle, it had to be good enough for other markets – with the possible exception of Japan, which has been even more demanding in certain areas. Due to the great expectations which it has been required to meet, the German company's organisation has occasionally been felt to be oversized and too expensive compared to general Tetra Pak standards. Still, the fact remains – the company was always, and continues to be, one of the corner-stones in the Group. Every market has its own peculiar conditions which contribute to creating its particular profile. In the case of Germany, these circumstances have left traces in many different areas; only a few of them can be summarised here.

Germany became Tetra Pak's first export market, with the catalytic effect that this entailed in terms of work on several other countries in Europe. Besides, special ownership conditions were conducive to rapid development. The company was not a regular subsidiary in the Swedish group. Consequently, it enjoyed considerable freedom of action whose benefits were felt by the entire Tetra Pak Group, not least during the creation of legal and financial structures in the 1960s and 1970s.

In the field of technology, Germany became an important partner. The Bundesforschungsanstalt in Kiel – an institution with special competence in advanced agricultural research – was often consulted on matters of dairy hygiene, especially while asepsis was being developed. In this particular field, certain schemes of co-operation with other German firms were set up as well. Tetra Pak created its own "school of technology" and a machine-manufacturing department, both in Hochheim. Under

The German company frequently employed the designer Wilhelm Reil, far right.

the management of Wilhelm Reil, an engineering specialist, teams working on development and production were established in Darmstadt and Pfungstadt. In addition, Dr Erwin Wartenberg was asked to head a centre of materials research in Stuttgart. The Limburg and Berlin factories have already been mentioned.

Commercial operations in Germany were always characterised by a certain grandeur – but then this was a large, demanding, and expansive market from the start. Sales have usually been supported by vigorous media campaigns with a "modernist" tinge. *"Das Ding, Kamingespräche, Stunde der Wahrheit"* – these slogans, and others too, have passed into Tetra Pak history, bearing the stamp of Gunther Luedecke. During the big international Frankfurt exhibitions, there was never any doubt as to who was *best in show*. The German organisation worked miracles, and the Tetra Pak exhibition area soon became a major attraction drawing customers from all over the world.

Erwin Wartenberg founded, developed, and extended a laboratory for research on materials. Other companies in the European group have relied on it as well.

Concern for the environment arose at an earlier point in Germany than anywhere else. That concern was reflected in the attempt to re-launch milk in returnable bottles, a project undertaken in the early 1980s with a view to reducing the size of the "refuse mountain". As a shape and a phenomenon, the bottle has such a solid position in society and among consumers that nobody seriously questions its existence. For many people, the bottle has an aura of "the natural alternative"; it is recycled – not forever, it is true, but a certain number of times. Having served its primary purpose, it ends up in a glass container whereupon it is melted down and then resurrected as a new bottle; what could be better? After an initial period during which the green light of early environmental awareness – and a pricing policy which the dairy and retailing trades found interesting – prevailed, the facts of "glass milk" began to emerge. Even with modern manufacturing methods, making glass costs a great deal of energy; the melting of sand, soda, and lime into glass-in-the-mass still requires temperatures of 1,100 degrees centigrade at least. A return bottle must be washed before it can be re-used. With its residues of content and detergent, the hot washing-up water cannot be discharged into the sewage system without prior purification. The collection of returned glass receptacles is a laborious and energy-consuming business; so is the handling and distribution of filled bottles. The bottle entails additional inconvenience for the consumer, who has to carry it home and then rinse it, sort it, and carry it back. With today's life-styles this becomes a problem, especially in respect of milk which is consumed in such large quantities. The German experience showed that the large-scale implementation of a returnable-bottles scheme was not a feasible option: costs are simply too high; neither the retailing trade nor the consumer will, in the end, be prepared to foot the bill. "Glass milk" has become something of a luxury for the few. In this regard, consumer milk differs from the rest of the drinks market.

The Hochheim office was the first to employ experts and develop strategies to deal with these issues. In many ways the German company became a pioneer, working under constant pressure from the authorities as well as from society at large. At first this work was undertaken in a defensive spirit. As in so many other places, environmental discussions would be characterised by lack of objectivity, emotional arguments, personal likes and dislikes, and political bias. Gradually, however, this debate has become more disciplined and matter-of-fact, although it must be granted that it is hard to reconcile environmental *and* economic

Hard-hitting
advertising
campaigns often
lent support
to marketing
efforts; here are
some examples.

The advantages of cartons for beverages are appreciated by people with ministerial responsibility for environmental matters, too – on condition that the demand for energy recovery, or some other recycling option, has been met.

Opposite page: A couple of years ago, there was an international competition for young designers. They were asked to come up with attractive décor specimens for a series of milk glasses manufactured by a German glassworks.

interests in a fair and balanced legal framework. Discussions have brought increased awareness to all strata of society. At the same time, many political decisions in this problematic area – and not only in Germany – have proved too hasty and are now in need of revision. These days, the former German Secretary of State for the Environment, Mr Klaus Töpfer – at one time a committed environmental politician with a special interest in the packaging industry –, can be seen drinking milk from a Tetra Brik package. It has to be a good omen.

True, the foundations of Tetra Pak's German "empire" were laid at an early stage; but the man who administered and extended the market for more than 25 years, along the lines drawn up above, was Gunther Luedecke. A tribute to his way of discharging his duties is in order at this point. Born and bred in Berlin, young Gunther had plans to become an actor before the world of business claimed him. Those early ambitions were not entirely thwarted, though: there was plenty of scope for his histrionic talents within the Tetra Pak framework. He was frequently the only begetter of various well-directed events in connection with exhibitions, conferences, jubilees, or other celebratory arrangements in the Group. When he retired in 1992, his ability to bring light relief into the arduous business of every day by means of little humorous pranks was part of the legacy he bequeathed to his organisation. Business should, at its best, contain a generous streak of show business; and Gunther Luedecke is a fine example of how people in business may succeed in fusing, and balancing, seriousness and a sense of fun. *The show must go on:* Germany, the biggest company in the Group in respect of turnover (1995), continues to think, act, and produce big – while pleasing everyone by yielding a handsome surplus.

At the Heart of Europe

Switzerland, that industrious nation in the middle of Europe, is "a land of milk and honey" – well, milk, at least. Verdant alpine pastures, jingling cowbells, hard-working farmers, Swiss cheese, and milk chocolate: such images tend to spring to mind when we think of Switzerland. In a country with few other natural assets, agriculture – comprising milk and dairy products – is a cherished base industry.

Consequently, Switzerland has long been at the heart of Tetra Pak's development in Europe.

When Tetra Pak was presented in the mid-1950s, "milk in paper" did not generate much interest in a country where the home distribution of unpasteurised loose milk was still the rule. Even today, visitors to fairly modern Swiss blocks of flats can see a space in the vestibule, behind the letter-boxes, intended for the bucket or jug which "the milkman" would top up during his daily round in the neighbourhood. The people who sold milk had a strong organisation behind them, and there could be no talk of selling it in ordinary groceries or in those self-service shops which were coming into existence. When the first Tetra Pak machine was set up in Lausanne in the autumn of 1957, this was a venture preceded by much discussion. The dairy had taken the precaution of signing a guarantee agreement with the neighbouring cities of Berne and Geneva, thereby giving the project a solid foundation and spreading the risks associated with it. It would take another year or so before the market picked up in earnest.

The catalyst in that process was the powerful Migros organisation, which accounts for approx. 35 per cent of food distribution in Switzerland today (1995). Migros had been planning to apply for permission to sell milk in its supermarkets for a long time. But "loose" or glass-bottled milk was out of the question; both systems would have been too awkward to handle. When the weapon of disposability became available,

The Lausanne dairy was the first in the country that ventured to present an alternative to the glass bottle.

For a long time, Migros has been a leading force in Swiss foodstuffs industry and retailing. Pierre Arnold, its manager for many years, was instrumental in persuading Swiss customers to accept the new package when Tetra Pak was widely introduced in the late 1950s.

Opposite page: Pictures from the 1960s. In its heyday, the tetrahedron attained dizzying heights.

it was hence natural for Migros to seize it and, brandishing it, to declare war on the establishment: the dairy and milk-trader organisations. On the quiet, a small, modern dairy was installed in Zurich, and a veritable milk war erupted in the autumn of 1958. Migros had promised the authorities to raise the consumption of milk in the city by two per cent in the course of one year. Such arguments would fall on willing ears, as the country was burdened by its surplus production. A vigorous advertising campaign was set in motion to support the project, which had been named Grossversuch Zürich. The person in charge at the very top was the dynamic Pierre Arnold, Managing Director of the Migros Group and a strong supporter of Tetra Pak's ideas. Those days on the barricades engendered a long-lasting and close relationship between customer and supplier, benefiting and giving pleasure to both. In order to deal with the competition, all major dairies soon equipped themselves with Tetra Pak machines, as soon as the delivery programme allowed it. In a matter of months, "paper milk" had been introduced in Basle, Berne, Geneva, Lucerne, Winterthur, Zurich, and several smaller cities and towns. The machine system had not yet been perfected, though, and as a result of the rapid rate of installation the small service staff suffered severe trials. It would not be correct to say that everything went according to plan: an episode illustrating the early tribulations may be mentioned.

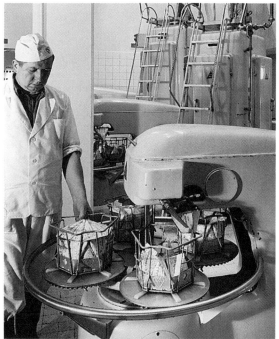

At last, and after much hesitation, the large dairy of Geneva had decided to order a machine for half-litre tetrahedrons. It was installed in November 1958 and expected to operate in plenty of time before the Christmas rush. The machine was duly started a few days into December. Expectations were high, and a big introductory campaign had been prepared. During trial runs, the machine – like so many others at that time – proved a trifle whimsical, and the results were not entirely convincing. The Technical Manager at the dairy, Arthur Grandjean, was palpably nervous. Even so, he was persuaded that the machine could go into operation, and the new packages were to be introduced on 13 December, a Saturday. At the same time – on St Lucy's Day – the Sales Manager, Lars Leander, was married in Lund. The next morning, the newlyweds were due to set off for a couple of days' honeymoon in Copenhagen, not being able to afford more time-consuming or expensive celebrations. On the Sunday morning, at 6.20 a.m., the telephone rings:

– *Allô Monsieur?! This is Directeur Grandjean of Geneva. I just wanted to tell you that we've got a disaster on our hands here – your wretched machine doesn't work. You have to take steps at once, and send someone with the required technical competence, the technician we've got can't cope. In addition, I want you yourself here first thing tomorrow morning!*

The monologue continues for several minutes. When, at long last, the irate client falls silent, the poor bridegroom gets a word in edgeways. He blurts out the truth:

– *I'm terribly sorry to hear this – of course, I'll do all I can to set matters straight. It's just that I got married yesterday, and we were just about to go away for a few days.*

– *What's that you're saying? For Heaven's sake, man, couldn't you have said that before? I apologise, forget what I said, we'll sort it out ourselves, things aren't too bad after all. You might get in touch when you have a moment. Besides, why not come to Geneva on your honeymoon – you'd be most welcome!*

Copenhagen remained the destination after all; but the episode heralded a lasting friendship with the management of the dairy, which became a good and faithful customer. Being married to one's company and its customers is a phrase often heard among businesspeople; this is a tangible illustration of what the expression may mean in practice.

Back to realities, as they were then: the monopoly was broken; home deliveries and loose-milk sales were declining rapidly: *"The milkman*

The procession up to the rich alpine pastures, confirming the arrival of summer, was always a special occasion for Swiss farmers. The event is often depicted in folk art.

Home delivery of loose milk was a form of distribution which was still around throughout the 1960s, even in cities.

doesn't come any more" was a frequent headline in advertisements. Packaged milk could be sold freely; and this was the beginning of a market development which has no known parallel in Tetra Pak history and was to lead to world records in terms of market shares for a number of consecutive years.

At that time, the Swiss milk industry was well organised, and the national federation of Swiss dairies in Berne was a power to be reckoned with. True, the transition to cartons was under way, by dint of gentle violence; but not all parties were convinced that it was a blessing. Above all, customers did not approve of being dependent on imports for such a vital daily food as milk: what would happen if there was a long delay in the delivery of paper, or a strike, or even a state of emergency – mobilisation, for instance – somewhere in Europe? As volumes grew, demand for domestic materials production increased. Even if the actual raw paper could not, for quality reasons, be manufactured locally, much

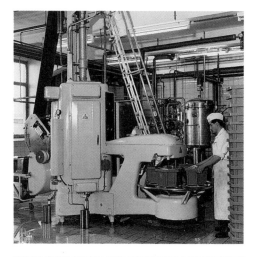

The first tetrahedron machine for commercial production was installed in Berne.

The Tetra Brik introduction, several years later, was a nation-wide scheme. The dairies chose a uniform décor, which is why the text is in the three main languages of Switzerland.

would be gained if the plastic coating, printing, cutting, and some storage could be located in Switzerland. Negotiations concerning licence manufacturing were conducted, and as an alternative Tetra Pak considered – as early as the autumn of 1959 – building its own factory. A site was purchased outside Zurich, and plans were set in motion. Fortunately, though, something happened that changed the situation, saving both Tetra Pak and the market from a premature and less than profitable investment: the European Free Trade Association (EFTA) was created, and both Sweden and Switzerland joined. As import duties fell and far-reaching promises were made to the effect that prices would remain stable, customers were content for the time being, and the factory project could be postponed.

Relations between clients and their Swedish supplier developed favourably. In many respects, the two countries are similar in potential and outlook; mutual understanding and respect blossomed in consequence. Other and more tangible bonds created special goodwill for Tetra Pak, too. As early as the mid-1950s, Lund had started a scheme of technological collaboration with a Swiss industrial group, Ursina outside Berne, for the development of bacteria-free, long-lasting milk products. When this new type of milk was presented in the early 1960s – *"the most important thing since Pasteur"* – the news was received with great interest, but also, in some quarters, with suspicion. Now it was essential to create a reference market and to do it fast, and here Swiss dairies were eager to help. Test sales started in Berne, where UHT milk was sneaked on to the market alongside the ordinary, pasteurised variety. The idea was to have the taste evaluated; after all, there was a certain difference in comparison with the pasteurised type, which was also referred to as "fresh milk". There were no unfavourable responses, and distribution was soon extended.

The Swiss market continued to expand. While a technical organisation for service and maintenance was now in place, sales activities were still run from Sweden – an arrangement the inconveniences of which were beginning to be felt. The market demanded a permanent commercial presence, especially in respect to the monitoring of orders and general customer contacts, as well as help with campaigns and sales promotion measures. In other words, the search was on for a marketing assistant, and advertisements had appeared, but without success. In the late spring of 1961, however, the following incident took place – a true story straight from life:

After a long and weary day, the Marketing Director, who had travelled down to Switzerland from Sweden, was sitting in the vestibule of the Hotel St Gotthard in Zurich. In the hotel foyer, the television set was on – this was before there were TV sets in rooms. The Swede watched the news in a desultory fashion, but all of a sudden he sat up. The newsreader was saying that attempts had been made in the Berne region to deploy milk vending machines in petrol stations, and a few pictures from the field were flashed across the screen. They showed a young man who argued in favour of the machine vending of milk products in filling stations, volubly, with fiery enthusiasm and eloquent gestures. The presentation was so vivid that the spectator was captivated. He instantly resolved to find out who this person was and how he might be approached. Inquiries yielded the information that the TV star was a consultant with the Swiss Milk Propaganda in Berne. The young man was contacted, interviewed, hired – and became one of Tetra Pak's most successful managers, Marcel Zbinden. He is the sole executive to have been discovered in this somewhat unorthodox manner. He is probably also the only M.D. in the group who has a very special occupational link with the dairy industry: as a very young man, Zbinden acquired the diploma of a cheese master; but he subsequently went on to study economics and commercial subjects.

The hiring of Marcel Zbinden towards the end of 1961 gave sales a further boost. Zbinden's initial duties lay in the field of sales promotion and support. During his first few years on the job, he visited virtually every retailer who sold milk in Switzerland – at that time, the estimated number of shops selling milk was 3,000. At the same time he continued to maintain and extend his contacts with dairies, leaving no stone unturned. The goodwill capital amassed during these years would prove invaluable when new systems were introduced and when increased competition brought on harder times.

The whiff of a colder climate was sensed when, around 1965, the largest dairy association in Switzerland, Milchverband Winterthur, suddenly decided to start using the German Zupack system in its Zurich dairy. The Zupack was a glorified paper bag, thin-walled, wobbly, and not very practical. Still, it had the advantage of being rectangular, and it was definitely easier to handle than the rather inconvenient one-litre triangle. Zbinden lost no time in launching countermeasures which succeeded in limiting the damage. In consequence of this incident, the introduction of the Tetra Brik was accelerated. Otherwise, the Tetra Pak strategy – with

It was with the aid of television that Tetra Pak managed to discover, track down, and employ Marcel Zbinden – a somewhat unusual mode of recruitment.

217

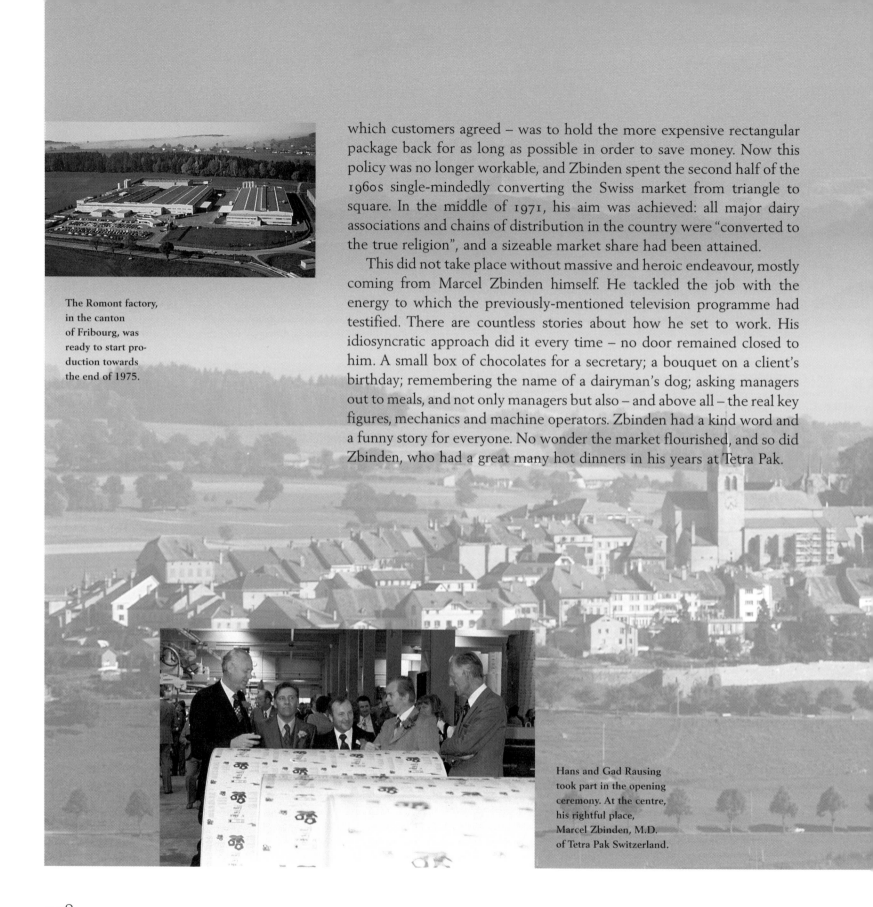

The Romont factory, in the canton of Fribourg, was ready to start production towards the end of 1975.

which customers agreed – was to hold the more expensive rectangular package back for as long as possible in order to save money. Now this policy was no longer workable, and Zbinden spent the second half of the 1960s single-mindedly converting the Swiss market from triangle to square. In the middle of 1971, his aim was achieved: all major dairy associations and chains of distribution in the country were "converted to the true religion", and a sizeable market share had been attained.

This did not take place without massive and heroic endeavour, mostly coming from Marcel Zbinden himself. He tackled the job with the energy to which the previously-mentioned television programme had testified. There are countless stories about how he set to work. His idiosyncratic approach did it every time – no door remained closed to him. A small box of chocolates for a secretary; a bouquet on a client's birthday; remembering the name of a dairyman's dog; asking managers out to meals, and not only managers but also – and above all – the real key figures, mechanics and machine operators. Zbinden had a kind word and a funny story for everyone. No wonder the market flourished, and so did Zbinden, who had a great many hot dinners in his years at Tetra Pak.

Hans and Gad Rausing took part in the opening ceremony. At the centre, his rightful place, Marcel Zbinden, M.D. of Tetra Pak Switzerland.

218

By this time package volumes had increased to the point where it made sense to go ahead with the planning of the factory which had been talked about before but which was – luckily, as it turned out – postponed. Now, however, an increasingly vociferous market insisted on having paper manufactured in the country. A couple of site options were evaluated. In May 1974, the decision was made to build a modern plant in Romont, in the canton of Fribourg, and in December of the following year manufacturing was ready to start. When Tetra Pak Switzerland celebrated its 25th anniversary in 1982, the festivities took place at Romont. In his welcoming address, Zbinden pronounced a special word of thanks: *"Today, we are passing a milestone in the history of our company. Here and now, I would like to pay special tribute to some of those who made it all possible, first of all Dr Ruben Rausing and his sons Hans and Gad. But I've got someone else in mind, too – without her, nothing very much would have happened."* The room was all agog, and curiosity was intense. And then, a splendid Swiss milch cow was led on to the rostrum, adorned with flowers and with an enormous bell around her neck, accompanied by an alpenhorn player!

The Romont factory became an attractive showplace for demonstrations to customers, non-Swiss ones as well as domestic clients. The market situation resulted in Marcel Zbinden's having to receive a very large number of foreign visitors. On these occasions, he would happily show off his culinary accomplishments. Wearing a chef's cap, he composed delicious menus, often served in the small special dining-room which he had caused to be built on the factory premises. Warmth, geniality, and considerateness were always characteristic of him. Another example of his way of looking after customer contacts might be mentioned: a small group of dairy managers and others, long retired, would be invited to an annual excursion featuring much friendly talk and a good lunch. Although these gentlemen were no longer on active service, they were not forgotten, and this special attentiveness was soon talked about throughout the industry.

And the outcome, the reward? First creating and then maintaining – for nearly 20 years, and under constantly increasing pressure from competitors – a virtually unbeatable market share. In 1991, Marcel Zbinden retired from his post as Managing Director of the Swiss company; but he has remained a welcome guest among customers and colleagues alike. *"As a man sows, so shall he reap."*

The poster below stresses the stimulating properties of milk. Marcel Zbinden must have consumed large quantities of it over the years. Always a bundle of energy and a much-appreciated supplier of good cheer in the Tetra Pak Group, he can look back on his 30 years in the company with satisfaction.

MILCH. MUNTERMACHER DER NATUR.

Sunrise over Japan

Nippon, land of the rising sun, with bearers of an ancient culture: pagodas, samurai swords, kabuki drama, sumo wrestlers, the geishas of tea ceremonies. But an ultra-modern industrial society, too: Canon, Mitsubishi, Sony, Toyota. The old and the new, inscrutably interlaced.

Maybe they were brought together in a dream of "the best of all possible worlds"?

At a cursory glance, it might look like two contrasting, indeed irreconcilable, worlds. And yet the two could be, and have been, combined. In less than a generation, a miracle happened: Japan, one of the defeated nations at the end of the Second World War, economically and otherwise encumbered with the burdens of war, grew into one of the major industrial nations in the modern world, a country of seemingly inexhaustible financial strength. Japan's success has been phenomenal; but it required a great deal of stamina.

For Tetra Pak, it took years of waiting before hopeful expectations could be realised. Some years after the end of the war, when trade between Japan and the rest of the world had been established, a Danish trading company – Wohlhardt Bros. – was appointed to represent Tetra Pak in Japan. The business was headed by the brothers Kaj and Hugo Wohlhardt, whose activities in Japan rested on a firm footing and were to some extent orientated towards the dairy industry. A Tetra Pak machine was exhibited at the international trading fair in Osaka in 1956, where-

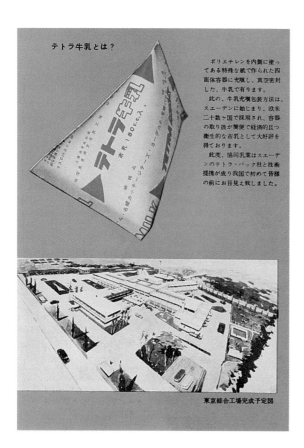

テトラ牛乳とは？

ポリエチレンを内側に塗って
ある特殊な紙で作られた四
面体容器に充填し、真空密封
した、牛乳で有ります。

此の、牛乳充填包装方法は、
スエーデンに始まり、欧米
二十数ケ国で採用され、容器
の取り扱が簡便で経済的且つ
衛生的な市乳として大好評を
得ております。

此度、協同乳業はスエーデ
ンのテトラ・パック社と技術
提携が成り我国で初めて皆様
の前にお目見え致しました。

東京綜合工場完成予定図

As the first Japanese
customer in 1956,
Kyodo Nyugyo
invested praiseworthy
efforts in the
marketing of the
new package; but
it would take years
before sales shot up.

Technical problems
were of a tangible
nature, and they
were numerous.
Hence, the former
fighter pilot Tetsuo
Yaegashi could
hardly speak of
having had a flying
start with Tetra Pak.

upon it went off to one of the big Japanese dairy businesses, Kyodo Nyugyo. Some further installations followed in the next few years, but developments were sluggish. There were a number of technical problems. A clever Japanese technician was employed in order to overcome them: Tetsuo Yaegashi, a former fighter pilot in the Japanese Air Force. If the Japanese surrender – on 2 September 1945 – had occurred only a day or two later, the Wohlhardts would have had to look round for another service engineer: in the last days of the war, Yaegashi was a kamikaze pilot and had been ready to depart on a suicide mission when the end came. Now Providence enabled him to move on to other, more peaceful, targets. For many years he was responsible for Tetra Pak's technical services in Japan.

As in so many other countries, it turned out that employing sales agents was not the ideal method for a foreign company bent on swift market conquests. It has to be said, though, that Japan was, and has remained, a particularly difficult market. Be that as it may, Lund decision-makers were resolved to effect a change and take matters into their own hands. At the beginning of 1961, the fairly recently employed sales manager Bertil Paulson was instructed to visit Japan and conduct a thorough investigation of conditions there. On coming back to Lund, he presented a report which strengthened the management's determination to set up its own office in Japan. Paulson moved to Tokyo in the spring of 1962. Drawing on his previous Asian experiences, he lost no time in establishing an initial, modest basis for what was, about a decade later, to become the biggest Tetra Pak investment outside Europe. Small office premises were rented, legal advisers were consulted, the agency agreement was terminated, the technician Yaegashi was taken over and given regular employment, and routines for calling on customers were laid down. Reinforcements were needed, however, especially someone who would be able to serve as a sales assistant and an interpreter. Now, how was a suitable person to be found? Once again, Providence intervened.

One day Bertil Paulson was sitting in his car on his way to a meeting with a client. Traffic was heavy; in Tokyo, the number of inhabitants had just passed the ten-million mark; he was a little late already; and he was not entirely sure of where he was going – the address, written in characters incomprehensible to him, had been jotted down on a piece of paper. Waiting at a red light, he wound down the car window to make contact with the driver of the car beside him. In excellent English, the young man asked if he could be of any assistance. Instead of uttering a string of directions, he offered to take the lead and show Paulson the way. When the cars finally arrived a good half hour later, Bertil Paulson asked his guide to contact him whenever convenient. He had a feeling that this was a person one should take a closer look at, and not simply because he had been so helpful – there was something special about this man. Some time later, Yasunori Katsuyama came up to see Paulson, who had not had time to consider the matter further. After talking for a while, the two gentlemen had come to an understanding, and Katsuyama's employment began – initially, for a trial period, as a driver and messenger. He turned out to be a prime asset and was quickly promoted to salesman. It did not take many years for him to become Marketing Director and later Deputy Managing Director of the company. Today (1995), he manages another company in the Group, Tetra Laval Food Japan.

Ever since the war ended, the Japanese government had been anxious to catch up with economic developments, to modernise industry, to open the country to foreign investment, and to join the IMF (the International Monetary Fund). For a time, protectionist policies were interrupted, and it became possible for non-Japanese enterprises to set up business in

It was Bertil Paulson who began to build up Tetra Pak's own organisation in Japan.

Human lives are often decisively influenced by coincidence. The recruitment of Yasunori Katsuyama is an example of this.

225

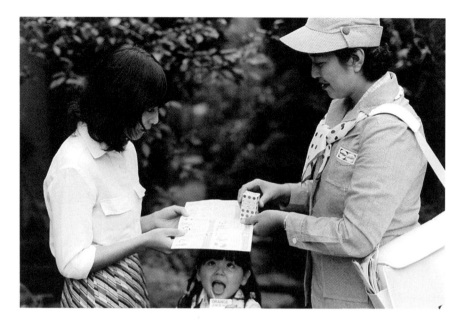

Yakult Honsha specialises in health drinks, sold in individual portions. Home delivery is not unusual. At first, these products were launched in the tetra-hedron package; but nowadays they come in small, attractive Tetra Brik packages.

Japan. Tetra Pak seized the opportunity. But procedures were complicated and expert assistance sorely needed. Throughout this process, Tetra Pak received valuable advice from Fumio Takashima, better known as the Chairman of the Japanese Olympic Committee. He may well have been the original source of that sportsmanlike fighting spirit which has since imbued the company. The decision to set up a business in Japan was by no means self-evident, and it came in for a good deal of criticism: *"How can you possibly be so careless as to start your own company in Japan, with a currency so feeble that it will never become convertible?"* But the necessary faith in the future was there, and the leap was taken: as the first Swedish-owned company in the country, Nihon Tetra Pak was registered in October 1962. Only a few weeks later, the national boundaries were once more closed to one-hundred-per-cent foreign ownership, and they remained shut for a considerable period of time.

At last, here was a platform which would support further efforts to work on the market. Another problem had been solved as well: that of domestic materials manufacturing. The ground having been recon-noitred, discussions led on to a licence agreement with the Fujimori Kogyo firm, supplier of Tetra Pak paper in Japan for many years. Now sales could be expected to shoot up – but it still did not happen. There were many obstacles to overcome. Japanese milk consumption was low, only just under two litres per person and year. There were not a great many refrigerators or cold-transport and storage facilities around. In 1962 not a single machine went out into the market, and the few which had existed previously were in such poor technical condition that they were returned to Sweden.

The 1960s became a decade of anticipation and preparation; but there were bright spots, too. During the Olympic Summer Games of 1964 Tetra Pak was often if not on, then at least very close to, the winners' stand. That was not primarily due to the company's dealings with Mr Takashima, however; there was another reason: the Yakult Honsha company, later a major client, had just received its first machine and decided to distribute a yoghurt-based health drink free of charge to participants and stewards. On television and in newspapers, smiling winners were seen refreshing themselves out of the new, triangular

Bertil Paulson thanking the Tetra Pak licensee, Mr Fujimori, for fruitful co-operation.

From a first modest appearance at the 1966 Tokyo Pack, the Tetra Pak exhibition area at this biennial fair has grown to imposing proportions, along with the market.

The Olympic Games of 1964 took place in Tokyo. Thirsty spectators and participants were able to refresh themselves with drinks in Tetra Pak packages.

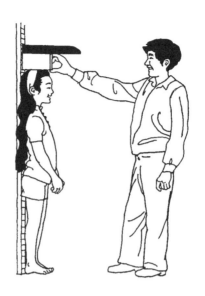

Health-care
authorities have
long realised the
importance of having
milk distributed
to schools and day
nurseries, thereby
ensuring that healthy
eating habits are
established from
the outset.

portion package from Yakult. A couple of years later, in the autumn of 1966, Tetra Pak took part in the Tokyo Pack biennial fair for the first time. Since then, the company has featured on the list of exhibitors every year for a quarter of a century.

In the meantime the distribution of school milk had begun, especially in cities. The milk came in portion-sized glass bottles – an awkward form of distribution, but the only possible option at the time. In consequence of improved eating habits – and greater consumption of milk –, the average height of teenagers increased by as much as four inches in the course of a single decade. No wonder the authorities suddenly became interested in supplying protein to the young. The new paper package began to "go to school" where it evinced a number of advantages in comparison with the glass bottle, and not just with regard to easy handling. Packages would often carry little messages for the children, who were given useful instructions both in words and pictures: *"Wash your hands before you eat. When you cross the street, use a zebra crossing. Don't throw litter around you."* Patterns of consumption were changing outside the school world as well, and milk, juices, and health beverages were becoming more popular. Physical distribution was modernised. One of the results of altered mealtime habits and increased consumption away from home was the abundant deployment of vending machines for milk and other drinks in all major cities. In this context, aseptic packaging was particularly appropriate. Importation was liberalised; the Ministry of Agriculture and other authorities were keen not to counteract the process of modernisation in the foodstuffs industry and in the distribution and retailing trades. The market was maturing.

In other words, conditions were favourable when the 1970s dawned. Japan was not the only non-European market that was looking up; so did several other Far East markets. This called for reinforcements in Tetra Pak's Asian organisation, and Bertil Paulson, who had so far been responsible for co-ordination in Japan, received an offer to head the company's organisational expansion in South-East Asia, using Hong Kong as his base. His one-time colleague and assistant from the Lund marketing division, Bertil Hagman, was put in charge of sales in Tokyo.

Up to that point, Bertil Hagman's career at Tetra Pak had been short and steep; it went on to become considerably longer and, if possible, steeper still. When first taken on in 1967, Hagman had just completed his law degree at Lund University. He had made good use of his student years, and not only in an academic sense: at an early stage in life he had

All the posts held by Bertil Hagman during his career in the Tetra Pak Group have involved great responsibilities. His Japanese period from 1971 to 1981, with six years as M.D., was his first great challenge.

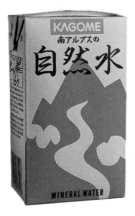

gained an international outlook, partly as a travel guide, partly as a U.N. soldier in the Gaza strip following his training as an officer in the reserve. During his years at university, Bertil Hagman held several commissions of trust; they provided him with other experiences which proved valuable throughout his years at Tetra Pak.

Hagman began in the overseas department in Lund, working as a contact and sales manager for a large number of countries, mostly in the Middle East and Asia. He spent much time travelling around, and it was not always easy to find time to deal with the piles of paperwork in the office at home. "The Hagman Hillocks" became a fixed concept in his department, and Hagman spent many a weary weekend perusing reports, answering letters, preparing tenders, and planning calls on customers. In 1971 Hagman was stationed in Tokyo, first as Marketing Director and then, from 1975, as the company M.D. In the autumn of 1981 he was summoned back to Europe to take up the post of Sales Director at the then head office in Lausanne, Switzerland, a position he left some time later on being appointed M.D. of the Tetra Pak company in Britain. In September 1985 he returned to Lausanne to succeed Hans Rausing as President of the entire Tetra Pak Group. He surrounded himself with a small, efficient management team, remaining President for six eventful and expansive years, up to September 1991.

Bertil Hagman's 24 years in the Group have been characterised by exceptional variety, and his career has been a truly remarkable one. In the free, sometimes fierce, interpersonal competition that prevails in a company such as Tetra Pak, a person who rises to the posts held by Hagman must possess extraordinary qualities. The keywords of his success were always old-fashioned respect and good manners, imagination and empathy, a sense of humour, tough demands both on himself and on those around him, considerateness extending to "the little things", attention to detail, and finally – a stupendous verbal talent, proving that the noble and ancient art of rhetoric is still alive. To sum up: leadership qualities, and an ability to dispense hospitality, which were just right for the global arena. Nor could Bertil Hagman have had a better second and helper than his wife Margareta, who stood by his side with unfailing enthusiasm and patience.

With such a background, it is hardly surprising that the Japan years were so successful. The first domestic materials factory was opened in 1971 in Gotemba, at the foot of the sacred Mount Fuji. Its snowy peak is usually wrapped in clouds, but they dispersed during the actual opening

Lausanne in
September 1985.
The handshake
that confirmed
the succession:
Bertil Hagman
takes over after
Hans Rausing as
President of the
Tetra Pak Group.

Mount Fuji's majestic silhouette rises behind Tetra Pak's Gotemba plant, opened in 1971. The inserted group photo was taken in connection with the "topping-out" ceremony the year before, when the roof was just in place.

ceremony – a good omen, according to the Shinto priests who attended the inauguration. Gotemba became a genuine pilot factory for the whole Tetra Pak Group, not least because of the far-reaching demands made by Japanese customers in respect of quality and hygiene. Increasing volumes tested the mettle of the factory staff: it was imperative to raise productivity. On one occasion, a Swedish visitor to the plant saw that all the workers were wearing an armband with characters on it. He was not a little surprised when told that the text said, *"Today we are working on strike."* That day, instead of sitting arms crossed calling for higher wages, the staff were making an extra effort, showing that they could do even better if paid a little more!

The market grew quickly, but not without complications. For instance, great efforts were made to introduce long-life milk products, but current regulations created impediments and matters made little progress. A report was sent home to Lund, explaining that a legal rule precluded the distribution of aseptic milk outside the refrigeration chain, and that this made sales work and argumentation pointless. The telex reply from Lund was not long in coming: *"Change the law! Yours, …"*

Towards the end of the decade Tetra Pak filling machines, about a hundred around 1970, had increased to five times that number. All the big dairies – Meiji, Morinaga, Snow Brand, and many others – were on the list of customers. So were plenty of other companies in various lines of business: juices, soya-bean products, coffee, tea, mineral water, even sake, the famous alcoholic beverage made from rice. In many cases, special developments were required in order to satisfy customer demands. The best example of this kind is probably the new machine model built, in record time, for the previously-mentioned client Yakult Honsha in the late 1970s. Yakult wanted a fast machine for a wholly new concept: easy-to-open one-decilitre portion packages of the Tetra Brik type for one of the company's new health drinks. A co-operation agreement was signed during a visit to Lund, and ten months later the first packages were produced. The project was a notable success.

Another example is the collaboration that was simultaneously set up with the large Meiji Group. Here, customer and supplier faced the task of solving the packaging problem posed by the distribution of milk and flavoured milk products via a comprehensive network of vending machines. The option that was chosen in the end was a two-decilitre Tetra Brik package which proved ideal for the purpose. In three years, Meiji installed over 50 packaging machines for the vending-machine market.

Nomu – Beverage

Japanese characters are beautiful examples of the fine traditional art of calligraphy.

233

The compact, brick-shaped portion package is eminently suitable for distribution by way of the countless vending machines in Tokyo.

The small, handy package has become a real best-seller in connection with a large number of products, many of them manufactured by other customers.

Despite the extension of the Gotemba plant, it soon became necessary to start making plans for a second manufacturing unit. The preparatory documentation was complete when Hagman requested an extra board meeting, so that the decision to build could be made. The reply was brief and came by telex from the Group President, Hans Rausing, in Lund: *"The responsibility is yours. If a factory is needed, it's got to be built. If so, there's no need for a board meeting. Incidentally, what's the thing going to cost?"* The M.D. faced up to his responsibility. The new plant in Seishin, close to the city of Kobe, was opened in May 1981, just a few months before Bertil Hagman left Japan.

In the meantime, the market has continued to expand. A wave of modernisation is still sweeping over Japan; life-styles are changing, purchasing power is growing, the flow of distribution is widening, and an increasingly fastidious public is calling for an ever-larger supply of goods. For Tetra Pak and its customers, developments have brought a veritable revolution – new packaging alternatives, a wider range of sizes, new products. In response to the frequent specific requirements articulated by Japanese clients, Tetra Pak has augmented its commitment to research and development. In February 1995, a new technological centre was opened at Haneda, Tokyo. The centre is firmly rooted in Tetra Pak traditions, priding itself on pioneering developments which may in due course benefit the entire Group.

The Group Executive Board was well represented when the company's technological centre in Haneda was opened in 1983. In February 1995, it moved to larger, newly-constructed premises.

Handy portion packages have led to a marked increase in the sales of a number of products. An emphasis on youth and fashion is noticeable in marketing.

Tetra Pak Japan celebrated its 25th anniversary in the autumn of 1987. At a splendid banquet, to which all customers had been invited, the first speaker on the list was Mr Takio Oda, Chairman of the Board for many years. On this occasion, Chairman Oda – a distinguished former diplomat who had been, among other things, Ambassor to Denmark, Indonesia, and the United States – emphasised that the company would go on making every conceivable effort to serve its clients and Japanese society at large. At the same time, it was established that *"Tetra Pak needs Japan; let us try to prove that Japan will need Tetra Pak in future, too, and need it more and more."* This aspiration has been achieved: the figures recorded since then are unambiguous. Today (1995), the company has the second biggest turnover among the Group's local marketing companies; and it is defending its position successfully despite harder times with fiercer competition, from domestic as well as foreign firms. It has performed the remarkable feat of adapting to Japanese conditions while safeguarding its original and peculiar character. Two flags fly side by side outside the various buildings owned by Nihon Tetra Pak: the Swedish one, blue with a yellow cross, and the red-and-white Japanese flag, bearing the symbol of the sun. *Ex oriente lux – light comes from the East!*

Japan, the country where past and present manage to coexist side by side as young people look ahead to the future.

237

The Super Market

Impressions and impulses – both as regards marketing and technology – had come from The Great Nation in the West in the early years. So what would be more natural than assuming that Tetra Pak developments would, in their turn, generate a great deal of interest in the United States of America? But this important market turned out to be a hard nut.

For decades, until well into the 1980s, the U.S.A. represented a semi-failure.

Ruben Rausing's stay in America in 1919–20 had engendered the initial ideas for the industrial activities that were later conducted under the roof of Åkerlund & Rausing. Besides, the American example provided inspiration for the idea of a Swedish milk package. Milk in cartons had begun to be sold in the United States as early as the 1930s. The trend had continued, and several systems were established after the Second World War – Canco, Sealking, Pure Pak, and a couple of others as well. In addition, the technologies applied in the plastic coating of Tetra Pak's packaging material were partly derived from America.

Simple logic would hence suggest that this market should have been particularly open to those technological gains and advances which the Swedish system entailed. To be sure, Tetra Pak staff were aware that American consumers were generally demanding, and that they were especially hard to please where the convenience and manageability of a package were concerned. All the cartons mentioned above were conventionally designed, rectangular or cylindrical, and passably easy to open. Nor was the U.S. quart, the package size which corresponded to the European litre and was the most popular one in America, part of the Tetra Pak range at the relevant time, around 1955. Even so, general interest in Tetra Pak had been roused; developments were becoming known, and some inquiries were coming in.

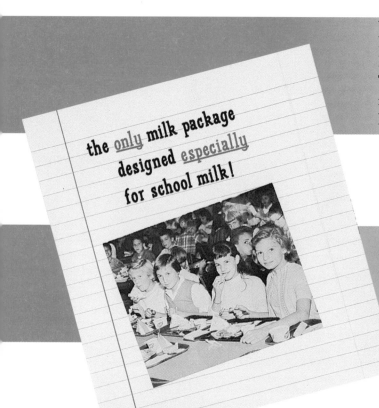

the <u>only</u> milk package designed <u>especially</u> for school milk!

"Tetra Pak goes to school" – the package soon became popular in school dining halls and canteen kitchens.

The shape of a better way to cream your coffee: Tetra Pak

Easy to use . . . cream to your taste

Hold at edge . . . pull tab   . . squeeze gently.

Another novelty that caught on was the small creamer, ideal for a cup of tea or coffee.

Above all, there was one "niche" which ought to respond to treatment, namely that of portion packages for the institutional market: schools, factory and office canteens, military dining halls, hospitals, and so on. Here, a cheaper alternative should stand a chance. Another serviceable weapon might be found in the so-called jigger, the mini package of milk or cream accompanying a cup of coffee or tea. *"The smallest package in the world for the world's biggest market"* – that notion ought to help in picking the lock of the promised land. Everybody was sure that market presence in the United States was the key to success in other parts of the world.

Sales efforts began around 1954–55, as soon as reasonably well-functioning machines were available. Åkerlund & Rausing, which had long been maintaining good relations with both people and firms in America, was helpful over contacts. It was hence natural for the initial market work to take place by way of key figures at Å&R, particularly its M.D., Holger Crafoord, the company lawyer Carl Borgström, the sub-managers Erik Torudd and Lars Hallberg, and several others, technicians included. On the other side of the Atlantic, a leading role was played by Charles Southwick. A few years before, he had been instrumental in finding suitable locations and methods for materials manufacturing. The able and well-informed editor of the prominent periodical *Modern Packaging* was frequently consulted by Tetra Pak. It was also partly thanks to Southwick's intermediary assistance that the first machines were contracted in the States.

Soon enough it became necessary to have "own" Tetra Pak technicians on the spot. Two engineers hence went off to America in August 1956, their mission being to install and supervise production in the first few machines. One of them was Stig Runnström, one of the few engineers in the company to undergo a "conversion" to sales work. Runnström was to remain in charge of market contacts for years, in Canada as well as in the United States. At this point, there were only a few reference plants in the U.S.A. The Cornell University installation was of particular significance; that was where the system was evaluated with reference to hygiene and performance generally.

One question very soon became an acute problem: how would materials be delivered to the machines? In the long run, it was obvious that paper could not keep coming from far-away Sweden; local sources were a must. In practice, the competing firms in the U.S. market had already established the pattern of sales in that country. Machines were

Charles Southwick advised Tetra Pak from an early stage and helped the company find its feet in the United States.

At first, technology was Stig Runnström's area of responsibility; but he was soon asked to assist in sales work as well.

241

In the early years, Crown Zellerbach was the licensee with the most lively interaction with Tetra Pak.

As far back as the Å&R days, Lars Hallberg was involved in Tetra Pak sales activities. In the late 1950s, he was appointed Manager of American operations.

provided by one supplier; cartons came from somewhere else. Actually, the sale of materials was an exclusive papermill affair, with several businesses competing among themselves. Consequently, it became impossible for Tetra Pak to introduce its systems policy – about to start operating in other countries – according to which machines, materials, and services were supplied by a single company. This was one of the main reasons for Tetra Pak's American failure in the early years. Divided responsibility for machines and paper led to complications which impeded swift and effective market developments, though circumstances were in fact quite favourable.

In order to make some sort of headway, Tetra Pak decided to make the best of a bad job and sign licence agreements with several paper groups. In rapid succession, negotiations were conducted with such companies as Dobeckmun, International Paper, Marathon, Olin Mathiesen, and Crown Zellerbach. The only agreement which led to concrete, ongoing collaboration was the one entered into with Crown Zellerbach; at one point, too, the latter company assisted in the placing of Tetra Pak machines by way of its sales organisation. This licence manufacturing called for many and detailed technical discussions; the Tetra Pak paper had to satisfy particular requirements with regard to stiffness, malleability, substance, thickness, and so on. On one occasion, the matter of thickness was being discussed and the point made that all paper had to be of equal thickness, whereupon one of the Crown Zellerbach managers, slightly hard of hearing, exclaimed: *"The sickness of the paper, what the hell is wrong with that paper?"*

Marketing efforts were intensified, and two local salesmen were employed – one stationed on the West Coast, in San Francisco; the other in New Jersey on the East Coast. A few additional machines were installed, but in order to get business moving faster a decision was made in the spring of 1959: the former Å&R salesman Lars Hallberg from Lund was to move to the States as General Manager of Tetra Pak Co. Inc. and set up an office in New Jersey.

All ways and means of influencing high-up decision-makers were tried. One example might be mentioned: At one point, members of the U.S. Dairy Federation's top management were in Sweden on a fact-finding trip. Their programme comprised a visit to Stockholm, where rooms had been booked at the Grand Hotel. The day before the group's arrival, a Tetra Pak employee in Lund was commanded to go up to Stockholm. Under an agreement with the hotel, he was to function as a

A co-operation agreement with the Milliken Group brought reinforcements in the U.S. market.

Kaj Wahlgren, a key person when the new Milliken materials plant was set in motion – as well as in connection with other factory installations all over the world.

room-service waiter on the floor where the Americans were staying, making sure that their breakfast trays featured milk, juice, and cream in Tetra packages! Tetra Pak did not trust the hotel staff to act with sufficient dedication in this respect.

Despite all the hard work, expectations were not realised: the market did grow, but only slowly. Office and staff cost a good deal of money, and the Lund management began to consider other solutions. The ideal one would consist in linking the sale of machines to a specially-equipped materials factory and then marketing the total concept, as was being done elsewhere. The volumes achieved so far did not warrant the construction of an "own" plant; besides, there were no funds for such an investment. That was how the co-operation of Tetra Pak and the Deering Milliken Group – mostly active in the textile industry – came about. Agreements were signed authorising Milliken to market the Tetra Pak system in the United States and to manufacture the packaging material. A new company, Milliken Tetra Pak, was set up in 1961. With help from Sweden, its bold-hearted staff began working on the market and erecting a conversion plant for Tetra Pak paper in Spartanburg, South Carolina. It was completed in 1962, and the start-up of production was supervised by specialists from Lund.

A large-scale
investment in
a tiny thing.
The mini pack
was a popular
object for years.
("Half & half"
refers to the com-
position of milk
and cream in the
package.)

The card
of invitation
for the Chicago
Fair displays
a slightly
"seductive"
picture of the
new, aseptic
rectangular
package.

Sales were still rather moderate, in spite of the new partner's endeavours. In this context, an unusual routine on the part of the Milliken Group must be described. For many years, it had been the custom for senior executives responsible for budgets and expenditure to "show their colours" publicly on the days immediately after the balancing of the books for a particular period. This was done in the following way: managers whose figures showed a surplus were allowed to sport a handsome green tie; those who had only just managed to achieve their budgets would wear a yellow one; whereas those who had not succeeded in living up to expectations were obliged to put on glaringly red ones. It is not hard to guess which colour the executive in charge of Tetra Pak had to show, for several years running. Still, diligent market work did yield some results. Milliken established a presence in portion packages for a number of special products, the small "creamer" being a particular success. At times the Spartanburg factory was producing materials both for the U.S.A. and Canada, and when sales were at a peak total quantities for this tiny package passed the thousand-million mark. Milliken made vigorous contributions to technological development and even built its own, faster, machine for small packages.

Shapes and formats contained built-in restrictions and limitations, though: no firm which based its efforts on the tetrahedron could hope to conquer the really large market, that of consumer milk for households. At a pinch, a rectangular one-litre package might be considered; but tendencies favouring even bigger units – two and even four litres – were already distinguishable. Even so, Milliken were keen to get their hands on the one-litre Tetra Brik when it began to be sold in the mid-1960s. Complicated negotiations took place over this issue, as the parties did not agree on the rights contained in the original agreement, nor on the formulae that would apply to a supplementary Tetra Brik agreement. The package was first shown during a large exhibition in Chicago in the autumn of 1968, arousing a great deal of interest among people in the business. Milliken appetite was growing, but negotiations were slow to make headway, which was not really a disadvantage to Tetra Pak. In December 1968, the Board in Sweden decided to *"shelve the present negotiations with Milliken, U.S.A., as the Tetra Brik package is not yet technically fit for successful marketing in the United States."* In actual fact, people in Lund did not feel total confidence in Milliken's ability to move ahead with this business under its own steam, especially as aseptic Tetra Brik developments had now begun to take shape and the American

Chicago, a city of bustle and energy, was the place where Tetra Pak was first publicly presented in the United States, displayed in an impressive exhibition case. Twenty years later, the company head office would be located in that very city.

In the time of Hellmut Kirchdorfer, from 1977 to 1984, considerable advances were achieved, but the decisive market breakthrough was long in coming.

Bernhard von Bockelmann, scientific asepsis specialist, was Tetra Pak's main representative in discussions with the FDA.

The final FDA approval of the asepsis system was a vital step forward.

BRIK PAK IS IN BALANCE WITH F.D.A.

Brik Pak Inc. has been working with the U.S. Food and Drug Administration since 1978 to establish proper regulations for the introduction of aseptic packaging to the United States market. On January 9, 1981, the FDA issued the regulation. Brik Pak Inc. has furnished data to the FDA proving it complies fully with this regulation.

Brik Pak Inc. is the acknowledged innovator and leader in the field of aseptic packaging. Companies in 67 countries are currently realizing the benefits of BRIK PAK® packaging systems.

Now our 20 years of experience and expertise offer you the most technically advanced method of packaging liquid foods in the world.

The most modern, most efficient, and most profitable packaging is now in America.

Brik Pak® outweighs the competition.

Brik Pak Inc.
A TETRA PAK COMPANY

prospects of asepsis looked good. Tetra Pak should, it was felt, display more in the way of hands-on commitment. The decision was hence made to protract negotiations with the American partner further still, while impatience grew at Milliken. Things staggered along over the next few years, and in the spring of 1973 negotiations were broken off without having led to any results.

In consequence of that decision, Lund began – with no undue haste – to prepare for taking care of the vast, still dormant, American market without outside involvement. Once the decision to establish a Tetra Pak office had been made, Hellmut Kirchdorfer, who had been the successful M.D. of Tetra Pak in Austria for a couple of years, was asked to be the first manager in charge of the new company registered in 1977, Brik Pak Inc. At that time, the Tetra Pak trademark was still being blocked by Milliken; hence the somewhat unusual variant of the company name. Kirchdorfer attacked the job with gusto, rented an office in Dallas, built up his own organisation, and gradually created a market. In that market, juices and special products still predominated; consumer milk did not play a very large part in it.

One potential obstacle had to be taken into account: the possibility that the powerful F.D.A., the Food and Drug Administration, might oppose the aseptic Tetra Pak system. The company decided to go for the safe option and submit to any tests that might be called for. The health authorities wanted absolute guarantees to the effect that no harmful residues of hydrogen peroxide, nor of any other chemical, could remain in the milk after packaging. The matter was subjected to careful investigations which lasted for several years. Finally, in the beginning of 1981, the F.D.A. let it be known that the Administration was happy with results and able to set the seal of its approval on the system. Reactions were prompt. The American press carried numerous references to the breakthrough, and there were many eulogies on new, long-life milk: *"Up to 1981, the most highly developed nation in the world was still a developing country with regard to the market for aseptic packages."* In the following year, the highly respected commercial publication *Fortune* chose the Tetra Brik Aseptic – along with a very small selection of other industrial items – as *"Product of the Year"*. Thanks to such encouraging signs, Tetra Pak devoted more serious thought to the possibility of building its own materials factory, and a team was appointed to look into the matter.

During the next few years, many machines were sent out to customers. In the spring of 1984, there were reports on about a hundred

In Texas, everything has a way of being "the biggest in the world". Not unexpectedly, then, the Tetra Pak plant, completed in 1984, was of considerable proportions.

Even the construction sign was a sizeable object.

Future Home Of
BRIK PAK, INC.
Denton, Texas Plant
Supplier Of Packaging Machines And Material For Liquid Food

LOCKWOOD GREENE
Planners / Engineers / Architects / Managers
Dallas, Texas

SITE CONTRACTOR
CANTERBURY
EXCAVATING
CO.

Contractors :

A day of celebration. Both Gad Rausing and his wife Birgit, right, attended the magnificent opening ceremony.

operating installations. In addition, Lund had given a firm promise to tackle the development of a large package – about two litres – without delay. Sadly, the project foundered due to insurmountable technical problems. No half-gallon Tetra Brik package ever saw the light of day, and the American organisation was reduced to selling what was available. This was a severe blow affecting the company's plans for the future.

In spite of everything, Tetra Pak's own materials factory could be inaugurated in Denton, Texas, in June 1984. It was a splendid occasion, and a couple of months later – following an agreement with previous partners – the company could be registered under its own, still valid, name: Tetra Pak Inc. In the autumn of the same year, a technology centre, Las Colinas, was opened, also in Texas. The idea was that the sales office would move there as well. In the meantime, however, total investment had – despite the hundred machines – grown to alarming proportions. All expensive measures were halted for the time being. Costs had increased ahead of volumes, and U.S. activities were running at a loss which cried out for remedial action. In the next few years, the company continued to struggle against poor profitability.

Not until Uno Kjellberg was put in charge of the U.S. market, at the beginning of 1988, did American business take a turn for the better. Kjellberg knew precisely how he wanted to deal with the problems, and during the just over three years of his Managing Directorship radical changes were implemented. He put the company on a firm footing; activities were rendered more effective; a main office was planned in Chicago; the development and manufacture of filling machines started on previously-acquired premises in St Paul, Minnesota; and the list of customers grew. Besides, Kjellberg launched an interesting strategy of acquisitions geared to creating swiftly increasing volumes and market presence. That strategy was heralded by the purchase of Tetra Pak's first American materials-processing plant in the northwest, near Seattle, in the early months of 1989. It has been pursued in more recent years, and today (1995) Tetra Pak U.S.A. operates seven carefully deployed units for the manufacture of packaging materials, mainly for the so-called gable-top model. Finally, after over 30 laborious years, the company has acquired a secure foothold.

When Kjellberg came to the States, he already had a solid background at Tetra Pak. Hired in 1970, he was appointed Manager of the company's Belgian business after a few years in Lund. In due course he returned to a central post in the Lund marketing division, but in the spring of 1979

Even the most succulent hamburger requires a drink to wind safely through to the stomach. Beverages in disposable packages command a large market in connection with quick meals out on the town.

249

Compact drinks
in Tetra Briks suit
the youthful life-
style of the States.

Columbus, as we
recall, discovered
America in 1492.
500 years later,
during the
commemorative
celebrations,
Columbian eggs
had assumed a
different guise.
Fluid egg mixture
is a popular special
product.

he was offered the M.D.'s chair in Spain. After nine prosperous years in Madrid, he was put in charge of the American company. With such a record, it was natural for the next step to be the offer of the post as Managing Director (President) of the entire Tetra Pak Group when that position fell vacant in September 1991. Perspicacity, strategic comprehension of operations as a whole, unconventional thinking, and a will of iron characterised Kjellberg's activities throughout the three years of his Presidentship. With the same vigour and eagerness as before, and without a moment's indecision, he altered and trimmed Group routines in essential respects. For all these forward-looking labours the Group will have reason to be grateful in the harder times ahead.

Finally, here are some reflections from Uno Kjellberg around a specific question: Why did it take so long for Tetra Pak to "make it" in the United States; why do so many foreign companies fail in America?

"This certainly doesn't apply to Tetra Pak alone but to many other firms as well, Swedish and European ones alike. Manufacturing industries, especially the ones that started in a small country, like to apply a niche-orientated approach; with the aid of patents protection, they believe they will be able to keep prices high and margins wide. But American industry is always aiming to produce more cheaply; costs and prices form the protective mechanism involved. The fundamental difference is that Americans start out from the notion of 250 million consumers, accept the idea of competition, and do not count their profit margins in percentages but in dollars. If you want to stand any sort of chance, you have to learn profitability 'the American way' and break free from 'the curse of wide margins'. At Tetra Pak, these insights have partly led on to fresh strategies.

To those who come to the United States as outsiders, the American market is a difficult and demanding one – not only for reasons to do with costs and prices, but also because American industries regard their domestic market as the most important and are resolved to defend it by all and any means. This is where they wish to establish volume and create springboards to the rest of the world. At the same time, the personal angle does not play such an important part in sales activities here; their orientation is more factual – products should sell themselves, be so good that people will want to buy them. Consequently, market research is often an important link in the sales process. This, too, was something of a new experience for Tetra Pak, for whose staff close and personal relations with customers always used to be crucial." Dixit Uno Kjellberg.

The carton offers excellent opportunities to convey information about the product, thereby encouraging the creation of new beverages. This coffee-and-chocolate mixture is one of them.

Now, however, the years of apprenticeship are long gone, as the rate of growth in America shows at a glance. Step by step, Tetra Pak has moved closer to the heart of this giant market by adopting a number of measures. The national organisation has been extended on the local plane, the Chicago office serving as a point of departure. The Tetra Pak materials factory in Denton has been supplemented by the acquisitions referred to above; today, big companies dealing with the development and manufacture of machinery are located in the U.S.A. Finally, one of the Group's four regional offices has been placed in Atlanta, Georgia, and given co-ordinating responsibility for *the three Americas*: North, South, and Central. At last, those wistful dreams of the mid-1950s are coming true. On Tetra Pak's own map, as on so many others, the United States has now become "The Big Country in the West".

The market continues to develop in a favourable direction. Slowly but surely, Tetra Pak is building its very own American skyscraper.

253

The Russian Evolution

The Bolsheviks and the 1917 revolution, the fall of the Tsar régime, Lenin and Stalin, the emergence of Communism, and the ultimate disintegration of the Soviet Union – all these are well-known historical facts. The writing of another history has only just begun: that of laborious liberation, a process whose purposes are détente, openness, and developments in the direction of a modern market economy. 300 million people have caught a glimpse of a new and different future; but it remains a distant prospect. Throughout this difficult process, support from the surrounding world will be more necessary than ever before.

Some have to move ahead, forming a vanguard. Paving the way for others calls for generosity, courage – and patience.

When Hans Rausing first visited the Soviet Union, around 1955, he certainly needed both courage and patience – particularly the latter. His aim was to establish contacts in Moscow and to rouse the interest of central authorities in the new milk package. It took time for him to find his way around the administrative jungle; the matter would be referred to one office and then passed on to another while days slipped by. Despite the fact that discussions were conducted in the national language – Hans Rausing speaks impeccable Russian –, ministries were uninterested. The well-known word *njet* was frequently heard. Many trips were necessary in the next few years before the first business deal could be concluded, in the autumn of 1959. It comprised eight tetra-hedron machines. Leasing the machines, according to normal practice everywhere else, was not to be thought of. The Russians rejected every notion of such a deal –*"njet, njet!"* At this time, the Soviet Union still had not joined the so-called Paris convention, which regulates matters concerning patent rights. Consequently, worrying about the danger of

copying, the Tetra Pak management had been reluctant to sell the machines. Nevertheless, the Board's decision was a favourable one in the end: *"A shipment should be sent in view of the possibility that continuing business communications might be established."* However, what there was in the way of continuing business communications during the 1960s was decidedly modest. True, equipment for the manufacture of packaging materials was ordered as well; but there were no further orders for filling machines.

The next notable deal took place in 1968. Development work on the aseptic triangular package was finished, and the problems with distribution in the Soviet Union made it a very interesting object there. Some twenty machines were ordered, to be followed by equipment for no less than six new packaging factories intended for the manufacture of materials for the tetrahedron package. The entire deal earned Tetra Pak nearly SEK 45 million – a staggering amount in those days. In addition, the first payment came to the company like a gift from the gods: at that moment, it hardly had enough to keep body and soul together. Both Hans Rausing and the Sales Director Erik Sandberg, who had been slaving over tenders and endless negotiations, were treated like heroes, especially by staff in the financial division, who knew just how meagre the company's funds were. As so often, Tetra Pak was in a position to confirm that however

In 1967,
a big foodstuffs
fair was arranged
in Moscow.
Tetra Pak was
there – even on
the advertising
poster.

The Chairman
of the Supreme
Soviet, M. I.
Paletskis, dis-
cussing the
virtues of the
tetrahedron with
Ruben Rausing
during a visit
to Lund in 1967.

Hans Rausing
was the host of
the Russian de-
legation, whose
members subjected
the plant installa-
tions to attentive
scrutiny.

257

Right:
A low-capacity
Tetra Brik machine
was developed
at the special
request of
the Russians.

Top-level
politicians took
an interest
in Tetra Pak during
the Inprodmash
Fair in 1967.
Here the exhibi-
tion is being visited
by General
Secretary Leonid
Brezhnev and
Alexei Kosygin,
Chairman of the
Council of Minis-
ters (right).

A peaceful every-
day scene from
Red Square
in Moscow. The
gently curving
outlines of the
bulbous domes
and the Russian
housewife set
off the distinctive
tetrahedron shape.

tough the Russians could be during business talks, they were equally scrupulous about paying once contracts were signed.

Most of us were told as children that if we decided to join in a game, we could not complain if the going got rough; and it was soon obvious that the Russians wanted to be self-sufficient in respect of filling machines. As time went by, there were large quantities of them in Soviet Union dairies. Someone at Tetra Pak described the situation in a nutshell: *"We delivered 28 tetrahedron machines, 1,350 of which are now installed!"* Local manufacture was definitely not a success. These machines, intended for pasteurised products, had been built without the participation and guarantees of Tetra Pak, which did not receive much information on materials manufacture either. As a result, it was impossible to satisfy necessary quality criteria. The system functioned poorly and acquired a bad reputation. The Russians had underestimated the technological complexity involved.

Slowly but surely, however, conditions changed from the early 1970s onwards. By this time, the Soviet Union – now itself eager to sell its own patents in the world market – had become a member of the international patents union. Besides, the new Tetra Brik model was so complicated that it was not worth anybody's while to try to copy it. The first deliveries took place in 1973, and orders have been coming in ever since. A particularly important one was processed in 1976, as the new, big dairy in Moscow installed 20 Tetra Brik machines. Here, as in several other cases, the deal was carried out in close co-operation with Alfa-Laval, which had long been a well-established supplier to the Soviet foodstuffs industry. These business deals would usually concern complete, "turnkey" plants, Alfa-Laval being responsible for the project and Tetra Pak acting as a sub-contractor. Among other big deals, equipment for a large baby-food factory outside Moscow should be mentioned. A total of 23 machines were delivered to it, in 1982 and 1986.

For less demanding conditions, mainly in the countless small dairies, there was a need for a more slow-moving model which would be easier to run. At the request of the Russians, such a model was developed. It did not have to be operated by staff with advanced training; the sales brochure described it as

Milk products in cartons – both portion-sized and larger ones – soon became popular, especially in schools and nurseries.

259

President Mikhail Gorbachev, accompanied by Prime Minister Nikolai Ryzhkov (centre), visiting the Tetra Pak exhibition area at a 1987 fair in Moscow. The man speaking on behalf of Tetra Pak is Sune Wejstorp, at that point Deputy Managing Director of the local marketing company.

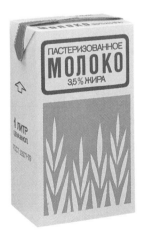

"the machine for unsophisticated markets". There has been a certain demand for it in other countries as well. Despite the Russian interest in this machine type, and in others, the number of installations at the end of the 1980s was nothing to write home about in view of the colossal potential of the Soviet Union. To be sure, the foodstuffs industry had been given priority, and Tetra Pak had long featured in the notorious Russian five-year plans which were intended to accelerate the country's industrial progress. Things had not, however, advanced far beyond praiseworthy aspirations which to a great extent remained unrealised. Insufficient technological expertise, a complicated, confusing, and awkward central administration, and lack of foreign currency were some of the worst obstacles.

Today, new developments are under way. The non-aggressive slogans which were heard during the second half of the 1980s, *glasnost* and *perestroika*, became the signals that started the "Russian evolution" – a slow and difficult process of liberation which is now beginning to bear fruit. One partial goal was achieved when the Soviet Union was finally dissolved in 1991. Since then, the world has been able to watch the former Soviet republics move towards a more liberal organisation in which Russia and Ukraine, with over 200 million inhabitants between them, are particularly prominent. For industry and commerce, it is hard to assess the consequences and the temporal aspects of this process. But Tetra Pak resolutely moved ahead of events to meet the future halfway – *"it's got to happen, and it's got to happen right now!"* In the last six to seven years, very significant investments have been made in several major projects. They are all, in their different ways, pioneering efforts, which makes it appropriate to supply brief sketches of them. The projects are based on the *"joint venture"* idea, a concept unknown in the old Soviet Union.

As soon as the new form of co-operation, which entails foreign part-ownership, became officially accepted, Tetra Pak took action in a number of ways. The company was keen to make the best of the new opportunities. The first of several projects was the joint creation of a syndicate together with interested parties from Russia and Brazil. The syndicate, optimistically named Progress, set out to teach the Russian people to drink juices – partly manufactured from their own apple harvests, partly based on orange concentrate from Brazil. Incidentally, the orange had up

Hans Rausing on the platform during the opening of the Progress plant at Lipetsk. The impressive new construction was completed in 1990.

The Podolsk
factory had housed
another business
before the
manufacture
of Tetra Pak equip-
ment started there.

The whole staff
posing proudly
in front of the
office block of
the new materials
factory in Kiev,
in connection with
the 1992 opening.

to that point been a virtually unknown fruit in Russia. The factory is situated in Lipetsk, 300 miles south of Moscow, and it started production in the autumn of 1990. The plant manufactures vegetable juices, too. For the younger generation, these products are becoming an alternative to such traditional national beverages as kvass and vodka.

At the same time, a further joint venture was launched, bearing yet another inspiring name – *Tetra Pak Lutch*, which means *ray of light*. The word itself was inherited: before the new company took over the plant, laser equipment for military purposes had been manufactured there. And indeed the factory, situated in Podolsk near Moscow, has managed to shed new light on the old problem of how to deal with packaging machines and spare parts made in Russia. It has undergone modernisation and is thoroughly adapted to current requirements. Several of Tetra Pak's machine models and related distribution equipment are now being assembled there. Parts of the Podolsk production are exported, and these days the plant is wholly-owned by Tetra Pak.

A couple of years later, in the autumn of 1992, a factory for the manufacture of materials was opened in Kiev, capital of Ukraine. It produces materials for Tetra Brik packages, both for pasteurised and aseptic products. The equipment supplied before, in the 1960s, had only been intended for the manufacture of tetrahedron packages. Now materials for other machine models all over the country can be ordered directly from Kiev; the customer need not pay in foreign currency, which is forever in short supply. At one stage, a complication arose due to the fact that Russia and Ukraine are now two separate nations; this led to difficulties over mutual import-and-export activities. However, the Kiev

At last!
Lars-Erik Janson,
standing behind
Hans Rausing,
was in charge
of the Tetra Pak
side during
negotiations
for the agreement
on the Kiev plant.
He had spent
a long time waiting
for the moment
when the
Ukrainian Deputy
Minister of
Agriculture,
A. N. Tkachenko,
would put his
name to the con-
tract.

In the Kiev factory,
materials are manu-
factured by modern
high-performance
machinery.

263

264

factory, majority-owned by Tetra Pak, is intended to serve both countries.

These days, the market is able to tap another source of supplies: the factory in Kuban, in southern Russia, where Tetra Pak came in as a partner in 1992. The plant – biggest of its kind in the country – was originally planned and constructed by others, but the Russian authorities asked for assistance over management and administration. Manufacture in Kuban comprises various kinds of packaging materials, cartons for milk and juice playing a prominent part. Vigorous efforts have been made in Kuban: there is a tangible commitment to quality improvements in production, connected with an interest in providing attractive packages for other kinds of goods besides milk products and juices. Today, this plant is also owned and run by Tetra Pak.

One large and painful problem always overshadowed operations in the then Soviet Union: the supply of raw paper for Tetra Pak purposes. There was never enough hard currency for the continuous importation of foreign paper. Attempts to manufacture a basic paper of good quality in the country had only been partly successful. As a result, production in dairies suffered; efficiency was low and product wastage inevitable. In its search for a remedy, Tetra Pak has now finally found a passable route. In the beginning of 1993, a co-operation agreement was signed with the

The company flag flying in front of the Tetra Pak plant in Kuban.

The factory building is at the centre of the picture. It houses the manufacture of carton materials for milk and juice. Other types of packaging are supplied as well.

Pleasures at work and leisure. The artefact on the opposite page comes from Krasnodar, on the River Kuban close to the Black Sea.

Karelia still offers examples of traditional architectural styles peculiar to the region.

The Svetogorsk papermill belongs to a more modern, industrial era.

Svetogorsk Papermill, situated in Karelia on the Fenno-Russian border. This mill was once built and run by the Finnish timber company Enso. In the early stages of World War II, the area fell into the hands of the Soviet Union, and the papermill was taken over by Russians. With Finnish assistance, it has gradually been extended and modernised over the past 20 years, and today it is one of the biggest wood-processing industries in Russia.

The first step in Tetra Pak-Svetogorsk collaboration was taken when Tetra Pak funded the reconstruction of a paper machine for the manufacture of suitable raw paper. This aim has been achieved; these days Tetra Brik machines in Russia are being supplied with domestic packaging material of good quality. When, in 1994, there were opportunities to acquire shares in the company in a stage-by-stage process, Tetra Pak did not hesitate to step in – first as a part-owner, later with a majority interest. Consequently, Tetra Pak is now carrying out its biggest undertaking so far (1995) in this part of the world. The strategy is clearly defined: creating a model plant; demonstrating modern methods of production and administrative management; obtaining a permanent source of supplies, of a high standard, for Russian paper requirements; and, finally, proving that locally manufactured paper may also be an attractive item in the world market. The Russian forests are waiting out there; anyone who ever flew across the country realises its as-yet-unexploited assets in that respect.

Concrete initiatives have been taken with regard to process equipment, too, in this case on the part of Alfa-Laval. The company recently acquired the majority in an existing plant which manufactures, among other things, heat-exchangers and cooling installations for the foodstuffs industry. New investments are currently being made in order to modernise the production process. As a result, it is now possible to provide good-quality process machines within the country, complementing the packaging systems. Alfa Laval Potok, as the company is called, is situated near Moscow.

A summary examination of Tetra Laval's capital commitments in the former Soviet Union and Eastern Europe speedily reveals that the Group has spent billions of Swedish crowns in this part of the world. Regardless of whether one calculates expenditure with reference to money, time, or personal efforts, the resulting figures are almost impossible to grasp. Of course, many people have helped in this tremendous endeavour; but the "chief ideologist" and tireless prime mover behind it all was always Hans

Alfa Laval Potok, situated in a Moscow suburb, is a big supplier of equipment to the Russian foodstuffs industry.

267

Rausing. During innumerable visits to these countries, he personally created the conditions that made the realised projects possible. In Russia particularly, his is a well-known and respected name, and in recent years he has been the recipient of many tokens of appreciation. In 1994, for instance, by direction of President Yeltsin, he was invested with a distinction rarely conferred on foreigners, the Order of the Friendship of the People. The spring of 1995 saw his election to the Russian Business Council, which numbers 25 members only.

Hans Rausing has frequently been asked at what point he believes that the rouble and other Eastern currencies will become convertible, so that profits can be transferred abroad. His answer was always the same, but it was never a routine reply. Expressing a firm personal conviction, it would run: *"I don't really find this question interesting. All profits are needed locally, for the continued expansion of foodstuffs industries in these countries. They are in desperate need of our help, and of our products. It is our duty to assist them."*

Hans Rausing has made full use of every opportunity to persuade the people he meets to take their responsibility – but also to perceive their opportunities – with regard to the markets in the East. Speaking in Stockholm a couple of years ago, addressing representatives of small and medium-sized Swedish industrial companies, he reminded his audience that Swedes were encouraged to go to America and seek their fortunes during the latter half of the nineteenth century. *"Young man, go West"* – that was the watchword in those days. Hans Rausing's own exhortation is headed in the opposite direction. As early as the 1950s – when he was himself a very young man – he personally showed the way. He was hence speaking from experience when concluding his address in the following manner: *"Young man, go East. With the addition of the old Eastern bloc, Russia, and Ukraine, Europe is more than twice the size it was. There, in the East, is where you're needed; that's where your particular competence is urgently wanted and your value fully recognised. Right now, you have a historic, fantastic opportunity; but the door won't remain open forever. Young man, go East!"*

During a solemn ceremony in Stockholm in February 1994, Hans Rausing received the Order of the Friendship of the People from His Excellency the Russian Ambassador, Mr Oleg Grinevsky. In awarding him the Order, the Russian Federation expressed its appreciation of the efforts which Hans Rausing had devoted to their country.

A Wall Fell Down in China

**China – also, and from ancient times, called The Middle Kingdom –
is the "Celestial Empire" which for nearly two thousand years
remained the centre of its own world, proud, sovereign, and sufficient
to itself, shut off from outside influence for long periods of time.
As The People's Republic, China is once again very much at the
centre of events, this time before the eyes of the whole world.
The Chinese Wall still stands, a historic marvel, while other walls
separating the country from the outside world are being torn down,
and at a tearing pace, too. In a few decades, China may have over-
taken the United States of America as an economic superpower.**

A market economy is taking shape.

The long, mythical epoch of the Imperial dynasties belongs to the past,
and so do the struggles, plots, and intense political turbulence of the last
hundred years. When Mao Tse Tung proclaimed the People's Republic of
China (the P.R.C.) in October 1949, using the slogan *"China has arisen"*,
he was signalling the beginning of a new era; but in what direction would
it be heading? Towards accessibility and international exchange? The
new régime had an inheritance to administer; it continued to conduct
isolationist policies and did not look for wide-ranging outside contacts. In
the early days, however, an agreement of co-operation with Moscow was
signed, and several far-reaching programmes of reform were implemented. The people's communes were set up, agriculture was collec-
tivised, an industrial programme was established – all with a view to
raising China from poverty as quickly as possible and creating a self-
sufficient, prosperous industrial nation. The Soviet experts were soon

Agriculture feeds and occupies most of the Chinese population. Cultivation on terraces helps preserve the precious arable soil. The soya bean, "the cow of China", is a vital source of protein.

272

superfluous. Having received initial help in getting their schemes off the ground, the Chinese leaders wanted to take the social policies, and the destiny, of their country into their own hands.

The great cultural revolution was set in motion during the second half of the 1960s, the outside world failing to grasp its full significance at the time. Not until several years after Mao's death in 1976 did the unhappy conditions in the country become apparent. Reform policies were partly re-directed, not always successfully. Internal power struggles paralysed economic developments, and criticism against the régime became stronger and more vocal. It culminated in the 1989 demonstrations for freedom and democracy in Peking and in the Tiananmen riots – the name of the square, meaning "the place of celestial peace", must be one of the most jarring misnomers in history. These events resounded all over the world and led to the imposition of international sanctions. The liberalisation programme which had started some time previously ground to a halt.

Not until the last few years, from the early 1990s onwards, has economic growth picked up speed again and international trade with it. Now, however, the process is accelerating at a tremendous rate, and the Chinese are determined to make up for decades of lagging behind. Industrial expansion, especially in the coastal regions, is forging ahead; the country has adopted helpful export policies; and GNP has gone up by 10 to 12 per cent a year during the last five-year period. Success has been hard-won, though. Unemployment and social unrest are worrying phenomena. Despite the industrial boom, China remains an agrarian nation; nearly 60 per cent of the working population are dependent on agriculture for their upkeep, and in this area poverty and squalor still exist.

Despite its enormous potential, with 1,200 million inhabitants (1994), the P.R.C. is a relative newcomer in Tetra Pak's sphere of influence. There are several reasons for this. While agriculture still dominates the country's economy, China is not, and has never been, a major milk producer. Besides, she could not afford the detour which animal proteins would entail; her protein needs are chiefly met by vegetable means. The soya bean particularly goes back to time immemorial. People will sometimes say jokingly that *the soya bean is China's cow."* Nor has interest in disposable packages been very great; the levels of income and purchasing power have not allowed for such extravagances. Like all other foreign companies, Tetra Pak was shut out for a long time and unable to establish

北　京
瑞　典　工　業　展　覽　會
SWEDISH INDUSTRIAL EXHIBITION, PEKING

In 1972, the General Association of Swedish Exporters arranged an industrial fair in Peking. The Tetra Pak exhibition drew many visitors. A wide audience, many of whom were obviously curious, wanted to acquaint themselves with the package.

273

During his visit to China in February 1972, President Nixon and Prime Minister Zhou En-Lai drank a toast to the common future of their two countries. It took decades, though, before the co-operative schemes envisaged at that time began to be realised in earnest.

Gad Rausing has been the host of countless groups of Chinese visitors. Here, an interested Beijing delegation is paying a visit to Lund.

the necessary contacts in an unwieldy, centrally-governed administration. True, company sales managers regularly attended the industrial fair in Canton; but things did not advance beyond the exchange of a plethora of cards and some polite conversation.

The first serious attempt to take soundings on the market was made in the spring of 1972, when Tetra Pak and other Swedish companies took part in an industrial fair in the capital Peking, nowadays – following a spelling reform – known as Beijing. The President of the United States, Richard Nixon, had just paid his historic visit to the P.R.C., and hopes for more relaxed commercial policies were burgeoning. The exhibition area, with three Tetra Pak machines one of which was shown in operation, was practically overrun by curious visitors. A few of these were genuinely interested specialists; but most were keen to get hold of a water-filled carton to bring home. Throughout the ten days of the fair, there was not a single package around to clear away when it was time to close the stand for the day.

But the machines needed someone to look after them once the exhibition was over. Nobody had expressed any serious interest in buying them, and all the equipment was shipped back to Sweden. Not until 1979 was the very first machine installed in Canton, for the production of juices. The same customer ordered a second machine in 1981, and a few other occasional installations were made in the next few years. Nevertheless, China was very far from being a booming market in any sense. As had been the case in so many other countries, Tetra Pak was caught up in a vicious circle: the market demanded paper manufacture in the country, before customers would be willing to invest in more machines; and at the same time the company needed larger volumes to justify any sort of domestic materials production. In the early 1980s, in order to break this deadlock and anticipate any initiative on the part of the Chinese, Tetra Pak decided to look into the possibilities of manufacturing packaging materials in China.

The P.R.C. has long been considered the greatest business opportunity for Western industry, its promise extending far into the twenty-first century. As Tetra Pak was facing the prospect of making big, strategically significant decisions regarding a market with such a potential, it seemed advisable to involve the topmost management in the process. Thus it came about that Gad Rausing assumed the responsibility for finding the proper channels in Chinese administration. He took to visiting China regularly and soon managed to establish necessary contacts. With his

Over the years, Gad Rausing has established good relations with top-level Chinese politicians. Gates have been opened, and not only to the Forbidden City.

Lars-Göran Andersson spent many hours, on many occasions, at the negotiating table, pursuing discussions about joint ventures and licence agreements in China.

impressive knowledge of archaeology and history, Gad Rausing became a welcome guest among political leaders at high levels. Doors were opened to him, and not only to the Forbidden City. The *"past and present"* theme turned out to be a highly practicable combination. His Chinese interlocutors would also pay close attention to what he was saying with reference to future industrial developments.

In the early months of 1984, discussions were going on with Beijing Pulp and Paper Mill concerning a licence agreement, the only possible form of collaboration at this point in time. The chief negotiator on behalf of Tetra Pak was Lars-Göran Andersson, M.D. of the organisation then in charge of the Eastern-bloc countries and China. Relying on his long experience of business deals with government-owned companies, he was firmly resolved to safeguard Tetra Pak's technology and demanded guarantees which the other side was reluctant to grant. The talks were protracted and difficult; they took a long time, and the negotiations were about to reach an impasse. At that precise moment, in June 1984, the Party Leader and Prime Minister Zhao Ziyang came to Sweden on a state visit. At the dinner hosted by the Swedish Foreign Secretary, it was natural for Gad Rausing to be among the guests. Earlier that day, he had handed over a personal letter, translated into Chinese, in which he described Tetra Pak's situation and plans for China. After dinner, the Prime Minister asked for a private conversation with Gad Rausing, and apparently the two gentlemen agreed on a joint line of action. When, a few weeks later, licence discussions were resumed in Beijing, the matter

During his visit to Stockholm in 1984, Prime Minister Zhao Ziyang was received by the King and Queen of Sweden. Here he is flanked by Queen Silvia and King Carl XVI Gustaf.

With the silhouette of Beijing's modern buildings in the background, the first factory for Tetra Pak paper is taking shape. Pictures from 1986.

In 1985 a Sino-Swedish initiative led to the construction, for educational purposes, of an experimental dairy with modern Swedish equipment.

Raw-material supplies were not a problem. With its 4,000 cows, a collective farm – now reorganised – in the vicinity was able to provide the dairy school with milk.

advanced with astonishing speed, and the deal was finalised in December 1984. Planning, construction, and installations took time, however, and the factory was not opened until the spring of 1987.

Now the ice was broken, and Tetra Pak China, established in 1985 and located in Hong Kong, has been able to continue working on the Chinese market with energy and determination. As part of these efforts, Tetra Pak was actively involved in the setting-up of the first experimental dairy in the country, the outcome of an agreement of co-operation between the Chinese and Swedish governments. The dairy was ready to start in the autumn of 1985, and it has since played an essential role as a centre of training and product development for this industry which is, after all, relatively new to China. In earlier times, the only people who had wanted consumer milk were Western expatriates living in cities on the coast. Not until recently has milk begun to attract general interest as a drink. In 1985, the total number of dairies was estimated at about 500, reasonably widely scattered over the country but with low capacity. But thanks to soya-milk products, coconut milk, juices, herbal teas, and several other beverages, Tetra Pak was able to develop, and in 1988 its volume was swiftly approaching a thousand million packages. It was high time to plan a second factory.

Discussions about a licence agreement began with the authorities of Foshan, a city situated in southern China, near Canton. This time around, negotiations were less complicated, and the deal was soon concluded; documents were signed in December 1988. However, Tetra Pak business was affected by the political troubles of 1989–90, and the factory project was delayed. At long last, the plant was able to start in the summer of 1991, and Gad Rausing invited the city elders to a traditional

An umbilical cord is cut – the first plant for the manu-facture of materials is opened in Beijing in 1987. Soon the market will begin to see paper carry-ing the inscription "Made in China".

The Swedish Prime Minister, Mr Ingvar Carlsson, receiving expert information from Gad Rausing during a tour of the new factory.

Swedish midsummer lunch with the classic ingredients: new potatoes, herring, and Swedish aquavit. The impressive-looking Chinese dragon dancers expressed their thanks by putting on a particularly fiery display.

Since then all figures have been heading in the desired direction, although a number of issues remain to be resolved. The biggest problem, of a practical nature, is how to organise effective distribution in this giant market where the bicycle remains the predominant means of transport. Things are not so difficult in the cities; it is the countryside, with poor roads and enormous distances, that suffers. In view of these conditions, aseptic, long-life products become vital. The infrastructure is rapidly being extended and improved: these days China has both motorways and express railways, but watercourses are still of great importance in the transportation of goods. Here, a construction which is in its own way as admirable as the famous Chinese Wall plays a key role, not as a barrier

Watercourses remain unsurpassed links. The Imperial Canal is a much-used route of transport.

On shore, the transportation of small quantities of goods still frequently relies on the bicycle – an adaptable and environmentally friendly vehicle. In the modern flow of goods, however, trucks and lorries are becoming increasingly common.

but as a link: the Imperial Canal, nearly 1,500 years old. Running from north to south, it connects the major rivers of China.

Since the start of the second manufacturing unit in 1991, expansion has increased even faster. Only a year later, the planning of a third factory was held to be necessary; a location close to Shanghai was proposed for it. This time, too, Gad Rausing came to have a hand in the process. The then Mayor of Shanghai, Mr Zhu Rongji, had been invited to Sweden on a semi-official visit. A short time before his trip to Sweden, he was appointed Deputy Prime Minister, and it was with this new title that he arrived in Gothenburg in November 1992. During an informal breakfast meeting at the distinguished guest's hotel, Gad Rausing presented a programme for the distribution of protein-packed drinks to China's approx. 170 million schoolchildren in the lower age groups, 7–14. The plans for a third Tetra Pak plant in the Shanghai district were also mentioned. The gentlemen got on well, and by way of sealing their personal friendship Gad Rausing handed over his own cuff-links to the Chinese visitor – a spur-of-the-moment gesture which was much appreciated. On a later occasion, the hospitality was returned on Chinese soil. At present, Zhu Rongji is one of the three or four most influential people in China. If his economic reform programme succeeds, the country is heading for a brighter future in the twenty-first century.

In the meantime, Tetra Pak is doing its bit to help. The two previous licence agreements have been re-negotiated and the plants are being run as *joint ventures*, with a Tetra Pak majority and full control of production. Sales and services offices have been opened in several places. The customer list is swelling, the number of machines is approaching 200, and the market is expected to consume two billion packages once the third factory – also majority-owned by Tetra Pak – has gone into production in mid-1996. Its location is ideal. There are nearly 75 million people living in the Shanghai area, and Shanghai itself is fast becoming a super-modern city of vast dimensions – the true Megalopolis of today's China. Alongside Hong Kong, which will be returned to China in 1997, Shanghai will become the most important node for commercial activities and streams of commodities in relation to the world outside the P.R.C.

And yet this is only a beginning. Although the Chinese government holds on to a monopoly of power which is based on strong one-party rule, it is determined to go ahead with the current reform plan under the designation "a Socialist market economy". If this difficult programme is to be implemented, however, powerful internal forces and continued

As newly-appointed Deputy Prime Minister, Zhu Rongji visited Sweden in the autumn of 1992. On that occasion, he had a meeting with Gad Rausing, and the two have remained in touch.

Shanghai, already the largest city in China, soon one of the biggest in the world. The population of the province is approaching 75 million.

Drinking-vessels, past and present. Noble, classic shapes are increasingly being made to yield to those demands for compact, convenient packages which are part and parcel of modern everyday life.

regeneration in the highest stratum of government will be required. Improving the living conditions of citizens and curing the social ills of China is a gigantic task. Both the people's communes and collective farming have now been abolished, but farmers remain the most vulnerable group in Chinese society. Better methods of production have caused mass unemployment in rural areas; as a result, country folk have flocked into the cities. Crime and continued social upheaval have followed in the wake of such developments. The authorities are hoping that these are merely transitional troubles and that rapid economic growth will provide the means to feed all mouths. That will not be possible without assistance from the outside, though, and the invitations extended to foreign investors deliver a clear message. Here all the experiences, products, and systems solutions of the Tetra Laval Group will be able to make a substantial contribution.

Large sections of the walls that used to shut China off from the rest of the world are now in ruins. The time has come to build something different – a new, modern, and stable society for the world's most populous nation, whose citizens make up nearly one fourth of the total population of the globe. In less than half a century China's population has doubled, and despite rigorous family planning it is currently (1995) increasing by one million people every month. The mind boggles at it. The national reform programme is ambitious and admirable, but global efforts of hitherto unknown proportions will be required as well. *"China has arisen"*, indeed; but the country needs help to move forward – and succeed.

The Soul Basis of This Company: A Portrait

"Body and Soul" – some may remember that insistently memorable tune, one hit among many in the realm of classic jazz music. It is not so hard to talk about the body and muscle of a company: figures, structures, products, markets.

The soul of a company is a different matter. How does one go about describing the spirit of the thing?

Every self-respecting company feels that it possesses a business culture of its very own, a special *esprit de corps* to be guarded with jealous care. Atmospheres and values make up the soul, the driving force, of a company. Still, it is not always easy to pinpoint the actual constituents of such a cultural treasure. It tends to resist slogans and rules. When people have come to the point where they are beginning to formalise the message of a company, putting it into print, mischief is already afoot.

The Latin word *cultura* implies sowing or planting, tending and watching, and finally harvesting. The culture of a company lives along similar lines. It does not sow itself; somebody has to initiate it. It is a product which grows as time passes, nothing you invent or command into existence. Nor are there any short cuts. We are talking about a process – a lasting, profound, and characteristically spontaneous one that will not submit to external control. In the happiest kind of situation, a company's business culture becomes an identity evolved from within: it is a natural pattern of behaviour that permeates the entire organisation.

The person who creates the culture of a business company may be its founder, or a small management group who supplied the initial enthusiasm and provided the original impetus. Some companies have been fortunate in having been run for years by such fiery spirits, benefiting from their example. This has, for instance, been the case with the two large industrial groups, Tetra Pak and IKEA, that were created in post-war Sweden. Ingvar Kamprad's overriding personal commitment to the development of his creation IKEA is well known – the commitment of the stubborn, economical native of the rural, wooded Swedish province of Småland. The entire IKEA business concept is based on this attitude: *"Our business language is English, but our culture speaks the Swedish of Småland"*.

Tetra Pak, the other group, was lucky in that it was able to develop its culture under the leadership of two generations of Rausings, assisted by a small set of colourful groundbreakers. More than anything else, the unconventional leadership of Hans and Gad gave Tetra Pak its particular profile. Their personalities have left an unmistakeable stamp on the organisation, engendering the special "Tetra spirit" – a concept that has become common currency in the company. The life of the company was always imbued by it, which means that it is not a matter for discussion in a separate chapter. That is why most sections in this volume contain examples of attitudes, values, and actions that bespeak a distinct company culture.

Thanks to dynamic approaches, optimism, and faith in the future, Tetra Pak has usually – despite many difficulties – succeeded in its various pursuits. Anyone who wants to find rather more concrete answers to the questions of how and why all this happened must try to capture something which is particularly hard to lay one's finger on: the very spirit, or soul, of a company. The pitfalls are obvious and best avoided by sticking to tangible practical examples which elucidate essential principles – things that were never strictly formulated, but passed into the realm of unwritten rules. The ensuing discussion focuses on a few key concepts and aims at conveying tones, moods, and ideas with a bearing on highly disparate matters. Decision-making, investment issues, the significance of intuition and humour, customer contacts, leadership styles, risk evaluation, and recruitment are some of the topics which are briefly illustrated by instances drawn from real life: instances that give rise to simple reflections around those golden rules that paved the way to success.

Decision-making

Everyday life in a business enterprise is full of situations which call for decisions to be made, by people from senior management downwards. The patterns applied at the top often create norms guiding decision-making activities in the organisation as a whole. Reality at Tetra Pak was always characterised by flexibility and swiftness in decisions, but also by careful contemplation whenever necessary.

"The best decisions are those that make themselves" – a favourite Rausing expression. It amounts to a contention that however urgent a matter is, it will not do to dispose of it in haste, forcing oneself to settle it one way or another. Far better to let the issue wait a bit, allow it to mature, turn it upside down and inside out, until one option has crystallised as the best or even the only sensible one. So many portentous decisions at Tetra Pak have been made in this way over the years – based, of course, on thorough analyses and investigations, but without being attended by coercion, formalistic awkwardness, or the solemn thud of the chairman's hammer.

Another characteristic feature was always found in Tetra Pak's dedication to training employees for their duties at an early stage, teaching them to rely on their own judgement, and giving them scope for decision-making and action as individuals. A brief episode from the late 1950s might serve as an example.

One staff member, recently employed in the European sales division, was intensely occupied with replying to incoming telexes, writing order confirmations, and calling Production for delivery dates – this was long before the age of the computer. Suddenly there was a knock on the door, brief but firm. In came Hans Rausing, not much more than thirty years old at the time. The following exchange ensued:

– *Hello, how are things, what's that you're doing?*

The salesman replied, in a somewhat circumstantial manner, what he was up to.

– *Fine, but do you never look out of the window?*

– *Not often, really – there's no time.*

– *Well, you should. If you don't take the time to take a look around you, to think about the problems and how best to solve them, then there's something wrong – and that's not the way to make good decisions!*

For many years Lidia Saarman, competent, efficient, and appreciated, played a demanding "double part" as secretary to Hans and Gad Rausing.

Discussions on the factory floor – a smooth, flexible way to cut corners in decision-making and steer clear of red tape.

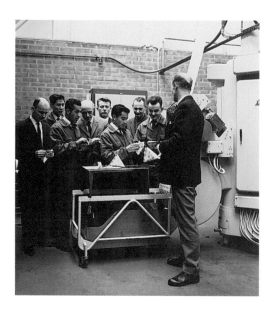

He was off a moment later, the door banging shut as he left – but a lesson was left behind: take the time to reflect ahead of events, rather than after the fact.

The road to independent decision-making as staked out at Tetra Pak cannot but lead to erroneous decisions from time to time. Whenever such a situation has occurred, the management has been understanding. After all, experience always has to be paid for one way or another. Employees and co-workers, senior as well as junior ones, have been entitled to make mistakes – within the bounds of reason.

Accessibility

When a business grows, so do distances between people working in it. What was possible in a small team is no longer feasible – we all know the telltale signs that insinuate themselves into the company's operations: committees, working groups, meetings, conferences, inquiries, and reports, and no end to them. The bureaucratic hydra is a particularly robust monster.

What can be done about it? Tetra Pak's formula was to take all possible steps to counteract dragged-out procedures, which inevitably decrease efficiency. The organisation must remain forceful and hard-hitting. It sounds simple, and every management aspires to it. Countless books have been written on the subject. But how has Tetra Pak applied theories in practice, how has the company managed to retain its youthful vigour even in the years of maturity? There are many partial answers to those questions; but one fundamental policy was always present: that of safeguarding flexibility and the existence of direct, uncomplicated channels of communication. A few examples will illustrate this point.

"Hello, Lidia, so where are the gentlemen today?" Lidia Saarman, Tetra Pak employee from 1950 to 1982, spent all those years acting as the superb secretary of Hans and Gad Rausing. Anyone at all familiar with the capabilities of these two men will be able to form an impression of what it meant to serve in that dual capacity. A frequent reply would be: *"They're out there in the factory and will be back in half an hour"*. It would mean that the Rausing brothers had, without any immediate reason, left their desks during a busy working day, taking time to go down into production to observe operations and listen to employees on the floor. They would never fail to pick up an issue worth discussing.

During one of these rounds of inspection, a shift foreman brought up an interesting proposal which might have a considerable impact on production. The snag was that a practical trial would require rather expensive experimental equipment. The annual budget for development work had already been presented, so surely the only solution would be to wait until the next budget was being prepared and try to find the necessary funding at that point? By no means. Instead, the answer was, *"Bring us an estimate of costs, and we'll arrange for an additional sum to be allocated."* After all, if everyone involved was reasonably certain that the proposal made sense, it was essential to proceed with it, and no complicated bureaucracy could be allowed to stand in the way. In addition, engineers, technicians, foremen, and workers knew that they were welcome up to the managers' floor, in overalls and clogs, to continue an ongoing discussion. Clear and swift replies could be had without unnecessary middleman involvement. And the red lamp outside the office door was never lit: nothing that shut management off from the vital nerve of reality could be tolerated.

For decades, Tetra Pak has regularly taken part in big international fairs and exhibitions attended by suppliers in the dairy and foodstuffs industries. Salon Laitier in Paris, the DLG Fair of Frankfurt, PAKEX in Birmingham, Tokyo Pack in Japan, the Dairy Show in America – every one of them was an excellent opportunity to display the latest technological novelties to a wide circle of customers. In due course, the Tetra Pak stands would become great attractions for other reasons as well: everything was done to take care of customers in a considerate and personal manner. This was a place where people could take off their coats and park their cases, sit down and take a breather, and have a good lunch in the specially installed restaurant which would frequently take up nearly half the space of the Tetra Pak exhibition area.

But the most important thing was that throughout the hectic days of exhibition, Hans and Gad Rausing would be present from early morning till late afternoon. Not only were they accessible in daytime; the Rausing brothers would always host the banquets and big dinners for customers which took place in the evenings. If there is any one quality which has been characteristic of Tetra Pak from the very beginning, it is accessibility, the realisation that managers must live in close contact with current events and not retire into their sanctum, cutting themselves off in the splendid isolation of the ivory tower.

DAIRY SHOW, CHICAGO 1979

Major exhibitions were always an essential way of communicating. For a few, intensely busy days, Tetra Pak receives customers from all over the globe in its exhibition area, showing them the latest technological novelties and exchanging fruitful ideas.

TOKYO PACK 1984

PAKEX, BIRMINGHAM 1986

THE DLG EXHIBITION, FRANKFURT 1992

Unpretentious habits

The constant lack of capital during Tetra Pak's early years ensured that its activities adhered to a plain, in some ways almost Spartan, style. The only exception was customer relations. Circumstances made economies mandatory, and the company climate did not encourage extravagance. The first office premises at Tetra Pak may be mentioned as a good example of this unpretentious life-style. Even at that time, one would have had to go far to find more modest offices.

The Publicity Manager in those days, Sixten Nilsson, who worked for Tetra Pak from 1956 to 1983, was a master of repartee. In his inimitable way, he would capture atmospheres and situations in brief, telling sentences accompanied by the humorous, sometimes ironical, touch of the born comedian. It was Sixten Nilsson who provided the following account:

"In the autumn of 1956, the new factory stood there, ready and waiting, in the middle of an enormous field of sugar-beet. This meant that the umbilical cord that tied us to the parent company, Åkerlund & Rausing, was cut; we were spared lots of well-meaning advice and became independent. The office was set up inside the factory.

We were all aware that Tetra Pak was unique in the world, but we couldn't help being surprised when we found that ours was the only known company that would experience snow showers indoors. In winter, great drifts of snow would occasionally slide from the roof windows, a procedure that engendered light, intermittent falls of snow below. To protect themselves against floor draughts, secretaries would sit with their feet in their waste-paper baskets, a somewhat peculiar sight to behold.

The office was divided into cubicles with partition walls 2.5 metres high. If these walls had been 1.9 metres high instead, a genuinely Kafkaesque atmosphere could have been created in which only Hans and Gad would have been able to step inside and look at the diligent office slaves, and nobody else would have been able to see a thing.

In those days, internal communication functioned perfectly: all conversations were overheard by everybody. To remedy this, someone had a jamming station installed in the form of a fan which put a damper on the entire hall. Internal memos could be circulated in the form of paper swallows which you'd just toss into the air; they'd be sure to land on somebody's desk.

At this time, Hans was busy working with coin-counting machines. We used to hear him pouring coins in his room, like Uncle Scrooge in Donald

Sixten Nilsson, a master of style, a humorist, and a "tetrapakist" as well. A genuine transmitter of cultural values during all his years as Publicity and Information Manager.

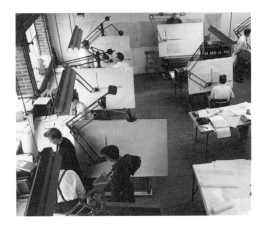

Duck. Of course we needed to improve our creditworthiness, suppliers would be queuing with their bills, and we were still dependent on our 'child benefit' payments from the Östanå papermill. They were amusing times, though, the days when Hans and Gad were able to pot at rabbits in the factory grounds."

Such were the premises where the office staff spent their working days for quite some time. In due course, new office space was created, initially by means of a plain construction which looked like a barracks. The mid-1960s saw the addition of the three-storey building which was the group head office for the next fifteen years. That house was hardly the lap of luxury either. There were no special rooms for meetings to be held in. Important ones would take place in the Rausings' own offices, which meant that groups had to be small and concentrated. Nor did conditions in general smack of ostentatiousness. There was, quite simply, no room for the usual status attributes, attended by prestige, hierarchy, and bureaucracy. Organisational barriers were unacceptable. *"It won't do for us to be swanning around acting the fine gentlemen"* sums up a typical Rausing attitude. Besides, the design of offices was not a vital matter – after all, people should not spend more time there than they had to. The management would maintain, with a touch of facetiousness, that one of the company principles was *"Management by absence – from office"*. The important thing was to be where one was needed: in production, in the field, with customers.

Throughout the pioneering years, office premises and drawing-boards were simple in the extreme.

293

One message which was never expressly formulated, but whose relevance was constantly felt, was that the good things of this life should be enjoyed in moderation. Employees had to be able to show restraint in respect of their everyday consumption of food and drink, particularly if they were frequent travellers or in charge of customers. An anecdote illustrating this policy may be added at this point.

In the new office building mentioned above, a small kitchen was fitted up on the second floor, and so was a modest-sized dining-room for clients and other prominent guests. Mrs Anna Larsson, a special-occasions cook famous all over Scania, was contracted to provide the meals. When the kitchen and dining-room were ready for use, Ruben Rausing invited the members of management to an inaugural lunch. Mrs Larsson had done her best, and an excellent meal was enjoyed by all. While coffee was being drunk, Mrs Larsson was summoned, and she entered expecting to be thanked for a superb lunch. So she was; but Ruben Rausing's address to her contained an additional exhortation:

"Dear Mrs Larsson, as you know I've devoted all my life to industrial activities. I've invested my efforts and my money in developing new products, building factories, and creating an able international organisation. But my most important asset is right here in this dining-room – it is made up of the people sitting round our lunch table at this very moment. Now you must promise not to ruin that capital for me. Therefore, I ask you not to put any butter on the table in future, and make sure that your sauces don't contain too much cream – but mind you, the food has got to be good!"

Nor was there any luxury around in 1965 when this head office was built.

Mrs Larsson bobbed and promised. From that day onward, there has never been any butter on the table, not even when important dairy customers were visiting. The matter of cream in sauces has not been quite so easy to control.

Humour

Jocularity and laughter are vital ingredients, both in the lives of individuals and in those of business companies. We must have some fun while we keep the treadmill moving – the harder we work, the more we need it. But humour is not to be had for the asking; it emanates from individuals, and it is to a large extent a matter of temperament. Besides, humour cannot flourish unless it is rooted in the right kind of soil.

Conditions at Tetra Pak have been favourable in this respect. A touch of roguishness, a readiness to perceive the comic aspects of a situation and not to regard every single matter as meriting the utmost seriousness, have been part of the company profile from the start. By happy coincidence, Tetra Pak was a nursling of the university city of Lund, a place of youthful high spirits and student playfulness; naturally enough, these surroundings have influenced the atmosphere in the company. Even so, the fundamental impetus was supplied by the sense of humour of the Rausings themselves – slightly sarcastic at times, though basically well-meaning and always stimulating. This humorous undertone has spread among close co-workers as a healthy impulse, encouraging the development of their own sense of fun; as a result, a spirit of jocularity has percolated throughout the entire company, all the way out into far-away local branches.

It is time to give the floor back to the Publicity Manager, subsequently Director of Information, Sixten Nilsson. This graphic description of Tetra Pak's European M.D.s as they were in the late 1960s is the outcome of Sixten's keen powers of observation and lively imagination:

"Watching the participants in the early sales conferences, you would have thought the aim of conquering the world a virtually unattainable one. We all scraped along somehow in various kinds of broken English, liberally mixed with savage native tongues. In some peculiar way, too, we had managed to hire a collection of caricatures of national characters. There was Danilo Severi with his Latin lover's moustache and eyes which would wander the

moment a girl walked by. And there was Pierre Schmit, a kind of Charles de Gaulle of the packaging industry, magnificent and self-possessed. Norman Dixon, with his cropped moustache and his carefully smoke-cured tweed suit, never further than an arm's length from a whisky glass. He would squash us all with a vocabulary not too far behind Shakespeare's. Luuk van der Meer, living proof of Darwin's thesis of the survival of the fittest – all those who grow up in the swamps of Holland and take a smaller shoe size than 12 are doomed to sink into the mire and disappear before attaining the age of reproduction. Marcel Zbinden, who proved beyond doubt that all mountain folk have powerful trunks and short legs. He was given to demonstrating the latter by standing on his head. Nils Lindholm, large, kind, and honest, and usually no more drunk than the general run of his Finnish customers. Danish Helge Lei, the ex-hippie, surrounded by an atmosphere which was a cross between the wafts of pot smoke in Christiania and the rarefied air of the Louisiana art gallery, but brilliantly knowledgeable about marketing and sales strategy. Gunther Luedecke, the product of the German post-war generation who, begging for chewing-gum, had grown up behind American barracks, a man with a partly unrequited passion for show business. But it all happened – we did conquer the world. Whether that was thanks to or despite our little idiosyncrasies is for others to say." – Thus spake Sixten Nilsson.

Many hilarious contributions have enriched the tradition of humour at Tetra Pak over the years. In the course of this book, the occasional anecdote has testified to the sense of fun which was always present in the organisation and which brightened many a dark moment. A single episode from the 1950s will provide a concluding, and very tangible, illustration of the notion of humour used as a weapon.

As so often, this Saturday morning was a hectic one in the Lund office. All the packaging materials for which there had been no time earlier in the week had to be loaded prior to being carried to their destinations during the weekend; all documents were to be made out; customers had to be informed of what was going on. To make matters worse, a production machine had broken down this particular morning and there was an acute danger that an important export order was not going to be dispatched – in which case the customer would find himself without paper in a matter of days.

The man in charge of the order had already been down to Production and explained that the shipment would have to leave around noon, the point when the goods were to be cleared and the waggons would begin

DANILO

PIERRE

NORMAN

GUNTHER

MARCEL

LUUK

HELGE

NILS

297

to roll towards the Continent. However, he had not been able to obtain a guarantee to the effect that the material would in fact be ready on time, and he saw no possibility other than going to the top in his search for help. After a cautious tap on Director Gad Rausing's door, he stepped inside and explained his business. Without a word Gad rose from his chair, walked a few steps, took down one of the rifles that adorned his office wall, and asked the employee to accompany him into the factory. Once there he went up to the foreman in charge, open rifle in hand, explaining, with a wide smile, that that little matter of the delivery deadline *"was a deadly serious thing, you know"*.

It is easy to imagine the headlines on the tabloid front pages if such a thing had happened today. At the time, though, the incident was taken in the proper spirit; everyone in the factory guffawed at this Lundensian sally – and in the end the order was delivered on time!

Intuition

What exactly is intuition? We all know more or less what it means – a sixth sense, a "gut feeling". It tells us that we are right about something in spite of having no evidence, no facts or figures, to back us up.

In the history of Tetra Pak, intuitive assessments were often favoured in practice. Facing difficult considerations and decisions, the management more than once relied on emotional arguments with very little basis in fact; indeed, those arguments would sometimes run counter to what one would have regarded as sensible. Working in such a manner requires keen responsiveness and a sense of harmony in the decision-making team, as well as constant practice in this arduous form of balancing – being irrational in the right way, and on the appropriate occasion. But what an asset it has been, what an inspiration to co-workers! Being allowed to trust your own best judgement breeds self-confidence and the best kind of responsibility. An example might be adduced:

When, in the mid-1960s, one of the company's young managers was sent off on a six-week course in modern marketing, he found a brief letter from Hans Rausing in his mail on the first day:

"Good luck with your further training – I'm sure you'll pick up all sorts of useful things in the next few weeks.

By the way, I saw an interesting article in an American business paper the other day; I think you might find it useful."

The envelope contained a newspaper article bearing the somewhat provocative heading:

Good managers play it by ear – they just muddle through ...

The article was a tribute to the free, unconventional style of leadership, unrestricted by dogma and textbook knowledge – a style which resists definition in terms and concepts. Certainly, the weeks spent on the course yielded many substantial insights, but so did the "course letter". This unorthodox way of tackling issues has often proved extremely effective. It is a matter of not feeling tied down by established truths; of being able to peer curiously around the corner, trying to foresee what is going to happen before it actually does; and of speculating, but taking care not to take extrapolation too far.

One dictum that has often been quoted in the organisation is: *"Long-term forecasts are extremely dangerous – after all, you tend to believe in them!"* The point of the statement is that written figures, prognoses, and diagrams are easily elevated into law, and people still have faith in them long after the point where radical changes took place in the basis for assessments and in external conditions. Sensitivity to altered circumstances – perhaps with an intuitive dimension – leads to better decision-making processes. Of course, it is mandatory to think ahead and to see visions; but such perspectives should be concretised with some caution and rooted in tangible realities: *"Long-term views – yes, but long-term forecasts – no!"*

Customers

Over the years, Tetra Pak's relations with customers have been a very special matter. *The customer is king* – it was hardly ever necessary to remind anyone of this truism. From the very first, it was self-evident that the customer's place was at the centre of operations. There are particular reasons for the company's lively and attentive way of keeping in touch with its market and clients. It is a commitment which has developed into an art form, and it may serve some purpose to review its background.

All the original customers were firms and associations belonging to the dairy industry, and they were used to doing things their way. These customers were frequently co-operatives with boards made up of independent, often wilful, farmers. This initial group of clients, with their feet solidly on the ground, forced Tetra Pak to adapt to local conditions. After all, the company was selling packages for daily, cheap milk, not for a luxury item. The need to decentralise, assimilate, and integrate became a necessity from an early stage. In modern usage, the word "multinational" has sometimes had a somewhat pejorative ring to it. A better expression, and one which truly reflects Tetra Pak's ambitions, is *multi-domestic* – being at home everywhere. From the very first, milk, farmer boards, and agricultural policies have imposed that demand on the organisation.

Another important component was the rental agreement and its psychological significance in customer relations. Back in the 1950s, it was not the easiest thing in the world to call on a dairy board with entrenched traditions and try to sell – or rather rent out – a new, highly technological packaging system. The board would have to be persuaded to accept a machine which did not become the property of the dairy, as well as an intricate contract which gave Tetra Pak comprehensive rights: the delivery of materials and spare parts, service inspections, and so forth. And then, to cap it all, the end product had that extremely odd tetrahedron shape! We must bear in mind, too, that the rental agreement was introduced long before leasing – of cars, computer equipment, and so on – had become a run-of-the-mill affair.

At the same time, these tough sales terms were a necessity. The degree of technological complexity was such that specialist competence was a must if service and maintenance were to be properly run. As the years went by, dairy staff would be trained to cope, so that responsibility could gradually be transferred to customers. But that was a slow, painful, and laborious process, and further delays arose when new machine models

The first Tetra Pak customers were often dairy associations run by strong-willed farmers. Good customer relations called for an ability to deal with people both on the local and the national level.

were introduced – not least in respect of the aseptic system. For years, customer relations would be under strain because machines did not perform as well as they should have done; milk flowed across the floors of cooling chambers and storage rooms.

What would have happened if customers had been free to purchase packaging material from anyone they liked? There is no doubt whatever: Tetra Pak would have gone to the wall. As the chapter on America above pointed out, the early launching effort in the United States foundered on this very issue. For years, Tetra Pak's own experts were finding it hard enough to produce an acceptable material for the sensitive filling machines. It was hardly realistic to imagine that anybody else would be

Today leasing is a widely accepted business policy. When Tetra Pak introduced its lease, or rental, agreement, such systems were few and far between. They entailed far-reaching obligations for the supplier, for example in terms of technical service and spare parts.

able to come up with a wholly satisfactory quality, let alone at a lower price. Nevertheless, this was not something one could expect a clientèle unfamiliar with the relevant conditions to realise. Some customers experienced a psychological resistance to becoming involved in an "improper" liaison, comprising ties and obligations far beyond the usual run of business deals.

These days technological necessity is no longer a main argument, and customers have a great deal of choice in their business relationships. Even so, the market has turned out to appreciate the advantages of concentrated responsibility for deliveries. Bold as the company's business concept was, time and circumstance caught up with it long ago. It is felt to be preferable to deal with a single supplier, with total responsibility, of the complex equipment which a state-of-the-art processing and packaging system entails. The improper liaison has developed into a successful marriage, albeit one which still demands a great deal from the supplier.

The conditions outlined above formed a challenge which called for hard work at all levels. Persistent difficulties refined the organisation. Harsh reality came to be the school in which Tetra Pak's customer contacts, to whose excellence many have testified, evolved. It was imperative to make an effort, to bend over backwards, otherwise neither employee nor company would survive. A dedication to sterling standards of service has been kept alive: every day and in every way, business contacts must be looked after; *every* customer is a VIP, not just a few. Personal considerateness, lively interest, the design of visitors' programmes and customer seminars – everything works in the same direction. At Tetra Pak, the concept of *software services* was applied long before it came into general currency.

Trials and hardships have created a special atmosphere in relations: customers frequently felt that they themselves had a stake in the company's sometimes uneven struggle against technological, financial, political, and other problems. As a result, a sense of solidarity has developed, and strong mutual confidence could be created.

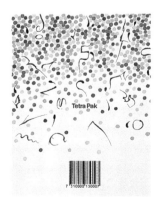

Tetra Pak's customer magazine, rich in traditions, has played a significant part in communication between the company and its market. Since the very beginning, the artist Carl-Otto Hultén has provided it with inspiring, varied, and original cover illustrations.

303

Einweihung der
Fabrik in Limburg

تاریخ

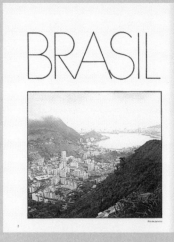

BRASIL

The Tetra Pak customer magazine has been issued since 1956. Printed in some ten languages, it has a circulation of approx. 30,000 copies. The contents, often organised around certain themes, are informative and tastefully presented. Conditions and environments in various parts of the world are lucidly described, and current problems are brought up for discussion.

PAPER

304

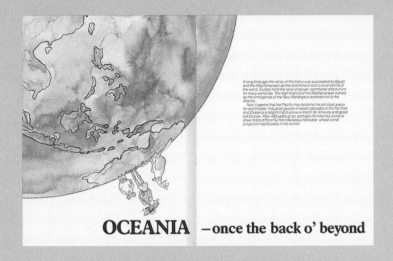

A long time ago the valley of the Indus was succeeded by Egypt and the Mediterranean as the commercial and cultural centre of the world. Europe held the reins of power, commerce and culture for many centuries. The significance of the Mediterranean waned as the emergence of the New World gave preconditions to the Atlantic.

Now it seems that the Pacific may become the principal arena for world trade. Industrial growth in recent decades in the Far East and Oceania is beginning to prove a match for America and good old Europe. After 400 years or so, perhaps the time has come to draw maps differently from Gerardus Mercator, whose world projection had Europe in the centre.

OCEANIA –once the back o' beyond

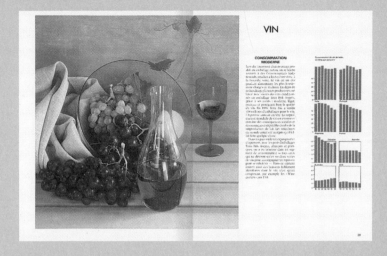

VIN

CONSOMMATION MODERNE

Förpackningens viktiga roll

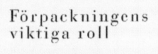

Det är en av de första kulturmänskliga fadäka i en förpackning. En tidiga människorna ...

Man kan säga att den första kulturmänniskan fadäka i en förpackning. De tidiga människorna försvarade upplevade en sten skap i inv-/skap i pruar specula av diasehudser, ofast gröbbon.

V älkanst resonerade – in fraga vasker per..., vanen av then usku är en förnecäts ersta... val, met i ken terrupher.

Lifestyle—a modern word, readily associated with youth and the hectic pace of the Western world.

救命的飲料

La forza dell'uomo, ma anche la sua debolezza, risiede nel nascere non ancora interamente plasmato. Il neonato viene dotato per la vita che gli offre l'ambiente, ma viene anche continuamente modificato dall'esistenza che conduce. La cura di un bambino comporta una grande responsabilità, ma rappresenta anche una sfida, la possibilità di creare, plasmare e strutturare qualcosa che continuerà oltre la propria vita, protettandosi nel futuro.

Nelle pagine che seguono abbiamo accentrato l'attenzione sul bambino, osservandolo da diversi punti di vista. Vogliamo sensibilizzare il lettore sulle condizioni di vita, diverse e spesso purtroppo difficili, dei bambini. Parliamo dei bambini della nuova era che apprendono le nozioni con i computer e i mass media. Passiamo quindi al mondo del commercio per presentare il potente gruppo di consumatori costituito proprio dai bambini. Concludiamo la rivista guardando al futuro secondo l'ottica dei bambini augurandoci che essi, indipendentemente dal luogo in cui nascono, da qui in avanti siano oggetto delle cure più attente.

Money

Much has been said about Tetra Pak's healthily unconventional view of expenditure and investment. It has been demonstrated in a variety of contexts, such as technological development, factory construction, and the setting-up of sales offices, to mention but a few. No formula summarises the basic attitude better than Hans Rausing's own words: *"Money is really a raw material among others in the industrial process."* Just as stainless steel, paper, and plastic products are necessary to Tetra Pak, so is capital. It is a simple and pragmatic point of view. As is the case with other raw materials, money must be put to the best possible uses, and unnecessary waste must be avoided. In other words, there have to be good reasons for a payment or investment to be made.

The building of Tetra Pak's factories has been one of the most substantial commitments, and here it was vital for the management to stand up to the urgent demands of the market and move with circumspection. During a Board Meeting in the late 1960s, in the course of which the problem of insufficient capacity had been discussed at length, Ruben Rausing found the issue *"highly satisfactory, experience having shown that a strained situation always ends in people's finding that capacity was greater than expected."*

In addition, it must be said that the dividends paid to owners over the years have been modest; by far the largest amounts were reinvested in the business. After the difficult years, from the early 1970s, self-financing of operations has been the rule, even during periods of powerful expansion. As a natural consequence, the management has had great freedom of action in all situations and was always able to move fast. It might be objected that such freedom is apt to degenerate into capriciousness and rash decisions which, in their turn, lead on to misguided investments. Unlucky investments have been made, of course; but they were mostly related to advanced technological projects whose prospects were hard to assess, and in respect of which long-drawn-out preliminaries would not have yielded better decisions. Conversely, a number of fortunate decisions would probably not have had enough stamina to work their way through all the stages of a conventional decision-making process. If they had been blocked by customary preparatory procedures, highly successful developments would never have materialised. Long-term investment policies of the kind conducted at Tetra Pak would have been impossible if financial markets, quick profits, and expectant shareholders had played prominent parts in the life of the company.

The people working within Tetra Pak were always happily liberated from the customary view that money equals power. The Rausings never refer to money except in direct relation to company business. Matters of private economy have been handled separately, by a small group of employees whom the family trusted implicitly. From the early years onwards, Maja Sjöström-Hamilton has been a key personage; later Lennart Ohlsson and his close associate Felix Seiler have held similar positions of trust. Among Tetra Pak employees, the Rausing family fortune was never an interesting topic of conversation, whereas the world at large likes to talk about it, not least the people who write for publications in the fields of finance and business. Year after year, headlines proclaim that *"The Rausings are high up on the list of the richest people in the world."* Public opinion seems undisturbed by the fact that such claims rest on a rather indiscriminative confusion of private assets on the one hand and capital tied to extensive industrial undertakings on the other. Nor does anybody seem particularly anxious to point out that operations as a whole belong within the framework of a trust.

Finally, a word about the alleged prodigality of Tetra Pak. More than once, the company has been said to *"spend money like water, especially the sales and marketing people"*. The statement is not entirely without foundation, but it cries out for modification. As severe and restrained as the company's attitude to unnecessary expenditure in other directions has always been, as generous are its views on the right way to treat customers. The sales and marketing divisions always had a great deal of freedom when it came to spending money – in the proper manner. Generosity has been the watchword, not ostentation. The difference between those two words is a matter not so much of the actual sums involved, but rather of the ways in which they are spent. There has been no uncontrolled, automatic lavishness; here, as so often, it has been a matter of showing care, commitment, and intuition, being irrational in the right way, possessing the ability – a superior skill – of *"allowing success to bear you along while proving your ability to bear success"*.

Maja Sjöström-Hamilton in Lund and Felix Seiler in Lausanne are two of the people to whom the Rausing family have kept turning for advice on their private finances. Few persons have held such positions of trust over the years.

307

SIGNAR N. BENGTSON

"Towards New Horizons" was the theme of a seminar for customers, organised in June 1991. Distinguished speakers presented their view of the world economy and other interesting topics. The programme also included first-rate entertainment.

VIP'91

TOWARDS
NEW
HORIZONS

In fact, new horizons were opening in a literal sense too, as the seminar took place on board the M/S Sea Princess sailing on the Baltic. Ports of call were Copenhagen, St Petersburg, Helsinki, Gävle, and Stockholm.

Nothing venture ...

Many people at Tetra Pak – and occasional outsiders, too – have heard of the Rausing motto, *"minimise risks by maximising risks"*. Its meaning is not so complicated as it might seem, but the phrase does call for an explanation: by daring to take big chances at a certain stage, concentrating hard on one area, you safeguard your future existence in a long-term perspective. The opposite principle is referred to as the spreading of risks or diversification.

Life at Tetra Pak has to a great extent been characterised by the *nothing venture, nothing have* attitude. The first project, the tetrahedron, was attended by maximal uncertainty for a number of trying years. Insecurity continued with the ensuing developments: asepsis and the Tetra Brik. Technological installations performed badly, delays arose, and finances were under strain. Instead of leaving management and staff disheartened, however, these very difficulties inspired them to new efforts. All the eggs were in one basket; as there were no alternative options, the firm was simply obliged to get on with selling what it had.

The precariousness of the situation became even more apparent when Åkerlund & Rausing was sold to Svenska Tändsticks AB (later Swedish Match) in September 1965. Considerable credits had been drawn from the Å&R Group, primarily from the Östanå papermill. This fact was well known to all Östanå employees and drew a muttered comment from the ranks: *"If it hadn't been for Tetra Pak, I bet we'd all have had better wages!"* At heart, however, the people working in the Å&R Group were proud of its "enfant terrible" and enjoyed contemplating the future prospects of Tetra Pak. For the wayward child, it had been good to feel the underlying security of such a large, solid business company, with a wide product range. And now the child was selling its own parent! To the world at large, both outsiders and employees, the decision seemed incomprehensible. The deal had been triggered by the wish of Holger Crafoord, close associate and partner for many years, to be released from his financial commitment to Å&R at a time when capital was necessary for the further expansion of Tetra Pak. Although Tetra Pak operations were now profitable, investment swallowed all available assets. In view of this, the sale must be regarded as a major gamble on the part of the Rausing family. Today, the decision may appear natural; but in the mid-1960s it was anything but self-evident. Å&R was a flourishing concern at the crest of its development. The business led the field in Scandinavia, was busy

Many resilient "market forces" have graced the staff of Tetra Pak. Ebbe Krook, top, and Tuve Johansson are excellent representatives of the group of managers who walked through fire and water – not to mention milk – to achieve their aims.

creating a sales network in Europe, and owned a factory in Germany: its future looked bright indeed. Conversely, Tetra Pak was struggling against severe liquidity problems, the classic tetrahedron was its sole properly established product, the new systems did not generate any income, and technology and development continued to devour funds at an alarming rate. That was the real situation – and yet!

Clearly, then, the policy of concentration was in evidence from the very beginning, with all the hazards it entailed. For many years, Tetra Pak was mainly concerned with milk and dairy products. It retained its one-product-company image for a long time, although a certain broadening of its range did take place. New segments, primarily juices, were slow to manifest themselves. These days, a number of other foodstuffs are packaged as well: table wine, mineral water, soups, cooking oil, and so on. Today, the element of risk exposure is of course much smaller than during previous periods in the company history. Firm rootedness in the world market, including solid progress in non-European countries, contributes to this position of strength; so does the acquisition of the Alfa-Laval Group in 1991.

The willingness to take risks is, as we all know, the hallmark of an entrepreneur: without stout hearts there would be no industrial development, or indeed any development at all. With hindsight, though, one may say that the Tetra Pak venture went far beyond what was really acceptable. The Rausing family would probably not have had the courage to stand the course if they had been able to foresee the full extent of the troubles ahead. At the same time, the atmosphere of scarcity, the obligation to live dangerously, has had a decisive influence on the fighting spirit of the company. Everybody, from the top management and down into the ranks, has been affected by this conviction for decades – *"we've just got to make it!"* There was no way back and no ways out, only the way ahead. The determination which grew out of dire necessity proved literally capable of moving mountains.

Ebbe Krook and Tuve Johannesson are excellent representatives of the group of marketing staff who acted in the international arena and were able to combine audacity with the stamina required for living with hazards. Trained in the classic *nothing venture, nothing have* philosophy, they both – at different times and in different contexts – made major contributions, both as Managing Directors of local marketing companies and as members of contemporary group-management teams. Ebbe Krook devoted much labour to Eastern Europe and South America; for instance, he managed the Mexican company for several years. Tuve Johannesson was the senior executive in charge in South Africa and Australia before being summoned home to Sweden in the early 1980s and asked to take over responsibility for Swedish activities. From 1983 to 1987, he was Deputy Managing Director (Vice President) in the Tetra Pak Group management, stationed in Lausanne.

Naturally, concentration – operating on a narrow base – has coloured Tetra Pak's attitude to competition: it was always essential to be one step ahead, trying to be number one in the limited area which the company has chosen. Everybody has been quick to respond to any threats, and executives in affiliated companies have had plenty of scope for action. Strategies and tactics have varied from one country to the next; the purpose was what mattered: using every ounce of power and energy to fight for the market and try to conquer it. Another Rausing contention: *"Competition is a fine thing, as long as you're able to stay on top of it!"*

Recruitment – past and present

At some point in the early years at Åkerlund & Rausing, Ruben Rausing is said to have issued a memo to the following effect: *"When hiring staff, ensure that even a messenger boy has the makings of a managing director."* This may be a slight exaggeration, but the alleged exhortation codifies an ambition which became conspicuous at Tetra Pak: that of selecting young people with great care, giving them adequate employment, allowing them to mature and develop under the company's wing, and then looking inside the business when recruiting staff for higher positions. There was a time when all managers in the company had been appointed before they were even 30. This attitude amounts to an expression of respect for youth, a belief in the ability of young people to make sterling contributions if given freedom and responsibility. School certificates, employers' references, and CVs played a part, of course; but the most important thing was to make sure that talent had a chance. There was never any talk of keeping newcomers on a leash for long periods. This is not to say that the Rausing family or the company management showed little or no interest in their employees, leaving them to their fate. On the contrary, the people at the top were keen to provide guidance for those

Maybe a future manager? The principle of giving swift promotion to ambitious young people was a company policy from the start.

311

working close to them. Only, there should be no pointers. The basic contention was that a pattern would emerge and that good examples would ensure that it proliferated throughout the organisation.

In the early days, recruitment methods could be unorthodox to say the least, intuition being allowed plenty of scope. This was how Lars Leander, later Marketing Director and Deputy Managing Director (Vice President) for many years, came to join the company. One day in the early spring of 1957, there was a typewritten piece of paper on the Academic Association notice-board, with the heading *"Wanted: A Language Genius"*. A few brief lines explained that the Tetra Pak publicity division required a young person, trained as a linguist, to take care of the printed matter about to be produced in the big international languages. Leander plucked up his courage, made a telephone call, and pointed out that he might be the sought-for language genius. He was asked to report to Publicity Manager Sixten Nilsson. After some conversation, he was also introduced to the Managing Director, Hans Rausing.

The introduction was followed by a rapid interview which took a highly unexpected turn. The following exchange is a reasonably accurate representation of it:

– *Right, so what do you think we should talk about?*
– *Well, I could begin by telling you something about myself …*
– *But talking about oneself is something everyone can do. I understand you're a good linguist?*
– *That's right, I do speak a couple of languages.*
– *Then tell me about this paperknife, in as many languages as you can!*

Having said that, Hans Rausing threw the paperknife he had been toying with across to the interviewee, who tried to describe the object in short, pithy sentences in German, English, French, and Italian. The entire audience took some ten minutes. A nervous wait ensued, and then the Publicity Manager asked Leander to see Mr Boris Carlsson, Chief Accountant, about the terms of his employment.

A few weeks later, the 26-year-old publicity assistant began working at Tetra Pak. After about a year he was transferred to the sales division; in 1963 he took charge of European sales; and from 1968 to 1983 he was responsible for international marketing in its entirety. In the early 1980s, powerful expansion led to yet another geographical reorganisation of the market. At that point, stationed in Lausanne, Leander returned as head of the European region. He left his line position in 1988, but retained his

membership of the management and group executive board until the autumn of 1992. Having completed various special assignments, he retired towards the end of 1995.

Linguistic skills and a liberal-arts – not an economic – background and education became the platform from which Lars Leander operated throughout his years at Tetra Pak. In addition to his marketing responsibilities, his disposition and interests led to his taking on the function of "company cultural ideologist", a position which became more and more accentuated in later years. Thus, for instance, Leander was in charge of the planning of a number of international customer events. He also provided the impetus for the regularly recurring market conferences, which gradually became a significant component in Tetra Pak's endeavour to bridge gaps and smooth out differences within the Group. During these conferences, people of widely diverging nationalities, with dissimilar experiences, opportunities, and cultural backgrounds, have been able to get together for a couple of intensely active days in the course of which they discussed common problems and spent time together in an unrestrained and informal atmosphere, forming acquaintances and friendships across national boundaries. On these occasions, social arrangements would usually be located in unconventional settings, far away from the swimming-pool, discotheque, and night-club of the traditional conference hotel. In the search for unusual settings for these meetings, in conditions – sometimes somewhat Spartan – that brought participants close to Nature, no pains were spared. The constant ambition was to encourage the company *esprit de corps*, a sense of "we're in this together", according to the best traditions at Tetra Pak.

It must be pointed out that the interview described above was an exception. In fact, few big business companies have invested so much time and thought in recruitment as Tetra Pak, even when very young people were taken on. This carefulness has been especially apparent in connection with the employment of sales and marketing staff, often regarded as possible future M.D.s in foreign subsidiaries. The main features of the distinctive Tetra Pak recruitment policy were drawn up by Torsten Lundberg, Staff Manager during an intense and turbulent period of expansion, 1963–83. Selection would always take place in close collaboration with the Marketing Director, who was actively involved in the process for a number of years. As time went by, the routines employed in the recruiting of marketing trainees came to form a very accurate instrument which has also been adopted by other companies in

In recent years, market conferences have assumed a more relaxed style. Marco '87 took place in the form of a floating seminar on board the M/S Funchal. A practical all-in-one arrangement, during which the classic "Tetra spirit" was emphasised by simple and effective means. All hands on deck!

Mixco '93

Göran Grosskopf, Chairman of the Board, supplying information about the new Tetra Laval Group during Mixco '93. This, too, was an arrangement with a difference, located on the Tetra Pak factory premises in the province of Värmland in central Sweden. As the name suggests, this was a mixed conference including participants from other divisions: development, services technology, finance, and staff management.

MARCO 89

Among the many market conferences arranged within the Tetra Pak Group, Marco '89 is surely the most memorable one. Over 200 participants spent five unforgettable days in tents on a spectacularly beautiful island off the coast of northern Norway. The programme was mostly concerned with environmental issues, discussed while sea-eagles were wheeling in the skies above keeping watchful eyes on the camp.

315

Torsten Lundberg, who headed the staff division from 1963 to 1983, exercised a decisive influence on the forms of recruitment and selection that prevail within the Group.

the group. Modified forms of the model have been applied in other divisions as well.

A recapitulation of the standard procedure, such as it was applied from the mid-1960s and over the next 25 years, may be of interest. At the end of January every year, an advertisement would appear in the Swedish dailies. Applications were invited before 1 March. Depending on the current economic climate, varying numbers of answers would come in – a couple of hundred in the early years, gradually increasing to about 1,000 around 1990. The staff division then perused all applications within a month. Afterwards all applicants received replies, either a "no" or an invitation to a brief meeting, but not to a regular interview.

The first weeding-out took place, perforce, on the basis of qualifications recorded on paper. However, the concrete outcome of the "explosion" in higher education became increasingly obvious: applicants would have better marks, satisfactory testimonials regarding practical work, years of study abroad, more and better language training, and so on. Quite simply, it became increasingly difficult to choose the right individuals on the basis of the growing piles of applications. Soon the people in charge of recruitment decided to solve the problem by seeing as many candidates as possible face to face; after all, every one of those letters of application might conceal a nugget of gold. In recent years, as many as 100–150 people have been invited to "contact talks" during which both the Staff Manager and the Marketing Director have been present. Each candidate was given 30 minutes, no more, no less. Consequently, some twenty people were seen during a long working day, which means that this stage in the proceedings could take up to a week. The idea was not to hit on the right person straight away; but even the briefest presentation would yield a general feeling, sufficient for a "no" or "perhaps". Even if, as sometimes happened, it was soon obvious that a candidate was not suitable for Tetra Pak, the conversation would always take the full 30 minutes. Nobody would be informed of the outcome immediately; everyone was told a few days later, in writing.

Following these quick but invaluable meetings, some 15–20 people would be invited to a whole day at Tetra Pak, usually in Lund, where factories and manufacturing could be inspected as well. They were then put through a comprehensive programme of interviews and tests in the presence of additional company executives. The components in the programme were usually tailor-made for Tetra Pak. Impressions from the second stage of the process would be digested internally during the evening of that same day, whereupon a group of six to eight persons were called to a final interview. There were no more tests on that occasion, only meetings with members of the company management. It was not always possible for all of them to come, although these "final days" were regarded as sacred. Nevertheless, several management representatives would be present, Hans or Gad Rausing usually among them. Quite a turnout, in other words, in view of the fact that most of the interviewees were young academics aged around 25.

The last phase was an internal voting procedure which had to be unanimous. If even a single vote out of five or six was cast against a candidate, he or she could no longer be considered. There was the odd occasion during all these years when none of the finalists was found to be up to standard, which meant that nobody was taken on. Generally, the outcome was that three or four young marketing employees started working for the company, but without any clear idea of where they would end up – in fact, nobody would know. The recruitment procedure was not undertaken in order to fill vacancies, but to create reserves for the future. Opportunities would turn up soon enough. This highly deliberate way of investing in young people made it possible to maintain the principle of in-house promotion.

And what about all those people who were summoned to Lund for an initial interview, maybe involving hours of tedious travel, just for half an hour's chat? Did they not feel frustrated on receiving a negative reply a couple of days later? A follow-up survey showed that these persons – without exception – appreciated having had a chance to be heard, to speak up for themselves, however briefly. In the long run, this routine has even engendered goodwill for the company.

Many people might feel that taking such pains over hiring staff amounts to overshooting the mark. Why not pass the entire process on to the staff division, together with some consulting firm, and request a couple of "heads on a plate"? Such a policy was not felt to be acceptable; Tetra Pak wanted to take the trouble and see things through from beginning to end. All the hard work soon yielded abundant rewards. In a few decades, a number of exceedingly able co-workers were drawn into the group, thereby securing the management teams of today and to-morrow. That said, it must be pointed out that rapid expansion sometimes made it necessary to sidestep the principle of internal recruit-ment. From time to time, "head-hunters" have been consulted, par-ticularly over high executive posts. In addition, the merger with

Alfa-Laval created increased opportunities for internal mobility at the management level within the new, large Group.

By way of conclusion, here is a telling but extraordinary example of what Tetra Pak recruitment according to the described formula could mean to a young person's career: In January 1974 Gunnar Brock, aged only 23 and a very new B.Sc.(Econ.) from the Stockholm School of Economics and Business Administration, replied to the annual newspaper advertisement. Despite Tetra Pak's favourable attitude to youth, this candidate was thought to be a little bit *too* young and was therefore relegated to the group of reserves. A last-minute cancellation made a gap in the interviewing programme. Brock was rung up one late afternoon, happened to be at home, and appeared for a preliminary contact talk that same evening – and three months later he was a company employee. After a couple of years on assistant posts in the international marketing division in Lund, Brock occupied a number of M.D. chairs in rapid succession – Belgium, Hong Kong, Australia, and Britain. In 1988, he was

Numbers have grown, times have changed. The picture of this small group of salesmen, taken during the first European meeting in 1957, has an unmistakeable "50s flavour".

The M.D. group of 1994 works in a different environment, one characterised by high efficiency and computer technology. Behind these impeccable exteriors, however, the traditional "Tetra Pak soul" is still alive and well.

The Swedish Navy trained Gunnar Brock as an underwater demolition man, but his activities at Tetra Pak have been of a very different character and taken him off in the opposite direction. A meteoric career has led him to the post of President of the expansive Tetra Pak Group.

asked to join the then head office in Lausanne as Vice Group President in charge of international marketing. When the Tetra Laval Group took concrete shape in the early days of 1993, he was offered the post of M.D. of Alfa Laval, the second-biggest unit in the Group. Since September 1994, he has been back at Tetra Pak, now as its Group President. His competence, experience, good judgement, and well-balanced personality ensure that the company traditions are carried along into a bright future in a world that is often dark and complicated enough. Gunnar Brock has described atmosphere and philosophy in the Tetra Pak Group in a few succinct phrases; some of them are reproduced here:

– *The flexibility and freedom of action you find in this privately-owned company are unique.*
– *No other business company gives so much freedom and responsibility to people who are so young.*
– *Leading a Tetra Pak company is the closest you get to being in charge of your own business while remaining an employee.*
– *Tetra Pak doesn't just have an identity; this company has a soul.*

That Gunnar Brock is putting his own life and soul into the management of Tetra Pak is obvious to everyone.

Lights and shadows

No portrait can be painted in light colours only; shades and sombre patches are necessary for a clear picture to emerge. This portrait of the soul of Tetra Pak has its dark brush-strokes, too; but spells of universal gloom have been rare in the history of the company. Whenever dusky hues manifested themselves, they were mostly related to problems of a tangible, practical nature; the preceding chapters have illustrated a number of such difficulties.

At the personal level, it would of course be possible to find the occasional individual who felt dissatisfied, passed over, or unfairly treated; and some people may well have found themselves in trying situations through no fault of their own and resented it. In a fast-growing, and these days very big, group of companies it is inevitable for critical voices to be raised from time to time. Nevertheless, intrigue and power struggles always seemed alien to Tetra Pak staff. Why is that? Maybe the simple answer is that there was never much time or opportunity to devote to wire-pulling operations. The great undertakings of the company, the purposes shared by all, were what mattered. The organisation has always been carried along by a well-nigh inexplicable faith and missionary spirit.

There is a danger that outsiders might regard this narrative as an idealised account. Those who lived in and with everyday realities at Tetra Pak will, however, be able to testify that light colours did indeed prevail.

Models and backgrounds are constantly changing, but all that a picture can do is to convey an impression of a certain moment, time, or epoch. Nor is it possible to keep adapting and retouching a portrait; the paints must be allowed to dry. With all its faults, the canvas must at some point be relinquished to whatever posterity makes of it. Not many painters will be as privileged in the matter of self-confidence as Picasso who, looking at his works, exclaimed *"I don't seek, I find!"*

In this case, the painter can draw some comfort from the feeling that he has – after a good deal of seeking – done his best to apply his own colour range to depicting that exciting adventure which is the history of Tetra Pak. It is time to clean the brushes and put the easel aside. If the spectator finds the picture appealing, that will be felt as a great reward.

Epilogue – Quo Vadis?

Who can fail to remember the Beatles hit from the 1960s, with its wistful refrain, "I believe in yesterday"? When our thoughts dwell on what has been, it is easy to lapse into nostalgic strains. Everything is going so well; let us stay with the familiar things! The wind of change is blowing, and it is not to everybody's taste. Nevertheless, it is when times are good that changes must be implemented: once they have become necessities, it is usually too late. The question in the heading has to be repeated, time and again: Quo vadis – where are you, or in this case we, going?

If nobody inquires and calls into question, there can hardly be any answers.

This book has told the story, in a somewhat rhapsodic manner, of Tetra Pak's evolution from the very first tentative steps in the mid-1940s up to the present time. The company has passed through a number of crises on its way towards the stars. Not least the financial situation was often a source of deep concern; here it is really appropriate to speak of a "Dance of Debt". To new generations of employees, it is almost impossible to grasp that there were times when the business literally did not have enough food around to see it through the day. Later developments, however, from the mid-1970s onwards, provide a picture of unbroken success, a picture with few counterparts in Swedish industrial enterprise.

The tale of Tetra Pak as an independent group of companies is a document related to a definite period of time: it is a story which, properly speaking, ends with the realisation of the merger with Alfa-Laval, in the summer of 1991. A brief concluding look at subsequent developments seems in order at this point, though.

The development of Tetra Pak as it had come to be known culminated in the purchase of the Alfa-Laval Group. There had been discussions concerning the co-ordination of capital before, and on more than one occasion; but not until now were concrete results attained. The driving force behind the implementation of the deal was – besides Hans and Gad Rausing – the then Group President of Tetra Pak, Bertil Hagman. All preparations were made under conditions of absolute discretion, and on Monday 28 January 1991 the news was broadcast far and wide: Tetra Pak had made a bid for Alfa-Laval. It was the biggest business transaction that had ever taken place in Sweden. It was confirmed in the late summer of that same year, when all affected agencies and authorities, including the EC Commission in Brussels, had granted their approval. At that point, a new era began in the history of both companies.

Many eyebrows rose when the news was published. Now what was to become of Tetra Pak, this singular, successful family business which had gone in for packaging milk and juices with such mulish persistency? And where would Alfa-Laval be going with its 20,000 employees and its proud traditions? Would it disappear from the stock exchange, pass into private ownership, head towards an uncertain fate in the mists of anonymity? There was much speculation and talk of cultural clashes. In the early days, a large number of people were feeling lost and confused.

We still do not have all the answers – time has been too short. Still, the years which have passed since the Tetra Laval Group began to function in practice do allow for some cautious conclusions. A structure has emerged which makes use of special competence and knowledge on both sides but which also, by virtue of integrating units that logically belong together, reinforces efficiency and vigour. Everybody appears to have gained from the transaction, particularly the market and customers. The units of the Group have become stronger, better equipped for taking on toughening competition and harder times in a long-term perspective beyond the ever-faster fluctuations in global economic conditions.

So what, in concrete terms, has happened since the merger? On the basis of analyses made in advance, the two companies Tetra Pak and Alfa-Laval were recast – and partly renamed, too. The Group was given the logical name Tetra Laval, and it started operations in January 1993, primarily concentrating on systems for the production and distribution of foodstuffs. It comprises four autonomous industrial groups. Each has its own distinctive competence and leads the market in its particular field. Overall responsibility for each unit rests with a Managing Director

The Alfa sign inserted into the well-known Tetra Pak triangle became the symbol of the new Tetra Laval Group. Göran Grosskopf is Chairman of the Board of the entire Group.

(or President) who works independently and reports directly to the Board of Tetra Laval, which is chaired by Professor Göran Grosskopf. A summary presentation of the Tetra Laval Group includes the following components (1995):

Tetra Pak develops, manufactures, and markets systems for the processing, packaging, and distribution of liquid foods. Now that process technology has been integrated in operations, the company's ability to assist the foodstuffs industry is even greater than it used to be. Today, Tetra Pak is the only company in its line of business which is capable of offering customers complete programmes, comprising both process lines and solutions to problems of packaging and distribution. In order to be able to respond adequately to the demands of the market, new systems are constantly being incorporated in the Tetra Pak range. From 1994 onwards, for instance, Tetra Pak has been able to deliver a number of interesting and competitive alternatives in the all-plastic area as well, by way of complements to paper-based packages.

Tetra Laval Food provides systems for the processing and packaging of solid and viscous foods. Its customers are found in many segments of the foodstuffs industry, primarily those of fast-food and convenience dishes, vegetable oils and margarine, and ice-cream.

Alfa Laval develops, manufactures, and markets process equipment and systems for separation, heat-exchanging, transport of fluids, and process control. Its products and systems are used in the foodstuffs, chemical, petroleum, and gas industries, as well as in the contexts of water purification and effective utilisation of energy.

Alfa Laval Agri is a total-service company for milk-producing agricultural units. The company markets equipment and complete systems for milk production and livestock management. Services form an essential element in operations, and so does the sale of a wide range of fixtures and fittings.

Clearly, then, most of Tetra Laval's customers are in the foodstuffs business. As ambitions in the Group expand, a whole new universe of opportunities is opening up. We are all painfully aware of what is usually referred to as global overpopulation, of scant resources, malnutrition, and famine. But the biggest problem is not the insufficient production of food *per se*; it is the enormous wastage and destruction of raw materials that are taking place due to deficiencies in the chain of handling: process technology, packaging, storage, distribution. Many countries in which conditions are particularly desperate urgently require the concerted expertise which the new Group is now in a position to provide. Being able to contribute to lowering the percentage of loss for a few vital foods from the present level of 30–40 per cent – sometimes higher – down to, say, 10 per cent is a target which should not only be dreamt of, but actively and concretely worked for. At the same time, developments in the leading markets must not lose momentum; that is, after all, where resources and means are generated which make it possible to realise long-term investment policies in less favoured markets. Conditions in the Tetra Laval Group – its organisation, market expertise, technology, and product knowledge – are ideal for the implementation of such a programme, however comprehensive and demanding it may appear. That it will require much time and effort from people in the Group goes without saying.

Tetra Laval is a privately-owned industrial group with 36,500 employees (1994) in a total of approx. 500 companies. It is not listed on the stock exchange. Its profile has certainly changed: the "small family business in southern Sweden", in which the personal commitment of the Rausing family used to dominate, has turned into a big industrial group with an annual turnover of SEK 65 billion (1994). By and large, the family themselves have settled for exercising their influence in a limited way, through the Board. A pity, say some; inevitable, say others. Still, the Rausings are determined not to interfere in day-to-day work. Operative responsibility has been entrusted to experienced and competent management teams. Today, Tetra Laval activities have a scope and complexity which call for the top-level performance of specialists in a variety of fields. Having made sure that the best possible conditions were established for happy future coexistence in the new Group, Hans and Gad Rausing took the consequences – and retired from management. They also relinquished their positions on the Board in mid-1993, with the title of "Honorary Chairman".

Many years ago, Ruben Rausing's visionary idea was born under the sign of uncertainty. Since those days, an unshakeable faith in the future has seen Tetra Pak through all its troubles, towards the goal and the reality we know.

For Tetra Laval, too, the main direction has been clearly articulated. But success has no automatic component; it has to be regenerated every day. If the Group's aims are to be achieved, its employees must keep asking questions, and flexibility and mobility must be in evidence every-where. The very concept of success is opposed to the idea of standing still; the word derives from the Latin *cedere*, "to go". And that is just what the people at Tetra Laval are able to do: go forward, with enthusiasm and a sense of purpose, to meet the new century – and a new millennium.

329

Ruben Rausing, 1895–1983,
a visionary and pioneer
who became one of Sweden's
leading industrialists
in the twentieth century.

6

A Vision Becomes Reality
"Visions are like the rainbow ..."
Summer skies after rain in Lund, the towers of the Cathedral in the background.

8

The Man from Raus
The fishing hamlet of Råå on the west coast of southern Sweden, Ruben Rausing's birthplace. Picture from the turn of the century.

12

Ideas Take Shape
The prism reflects the shape of the tetrahedron. Tetra Pak was created, like diamonds, under pressure.

24

A Chain Reaction
Red Cross aid leaving for a Continent ravaged by war. Tetra Pak's machine concept was born after the war years.

38

'Mission Impossible'
How are we finally going to solve the problem of materials? Gad Rausing invested much thought and effort in the cracking of this nut.

46

The Starting Shot
Emil Zatopek, triple Gold Medallist and winner of the marathon at the Olympic Games in Helsinki, in 1952.

58

A Swedish Prophecy
"St Lucy, her carol, and her crown of fire", traditionally celebrated in Sweden on 13 December. From the Stockholm ceremony in 1992.

66

Open Sesame
Manual telephone exchange from the early 1950s. Now was the time to send the message flying across the globe.

80

Long Live Milk
Asepsis abolishes time and space. Milk becomes a "boundless" product, even when conditions impede distribution.

92

A Square Deal
Baptism of fire for the new Tetra Brik! Åke Gustafson watches Hans Rausing being served milk by Erik Torudd.

104

A Brick Becomes a Corner-Stone
The friezes of the Acropolis are supported by columns with capitals. The Tetra Brik became the corner-stone of a more modern construction.

112

A House of Want
"If Winter comes, can Spring be far behind?" It took until the 1970s for Tetra Pak to overcome the economic hardships of the early years.

122

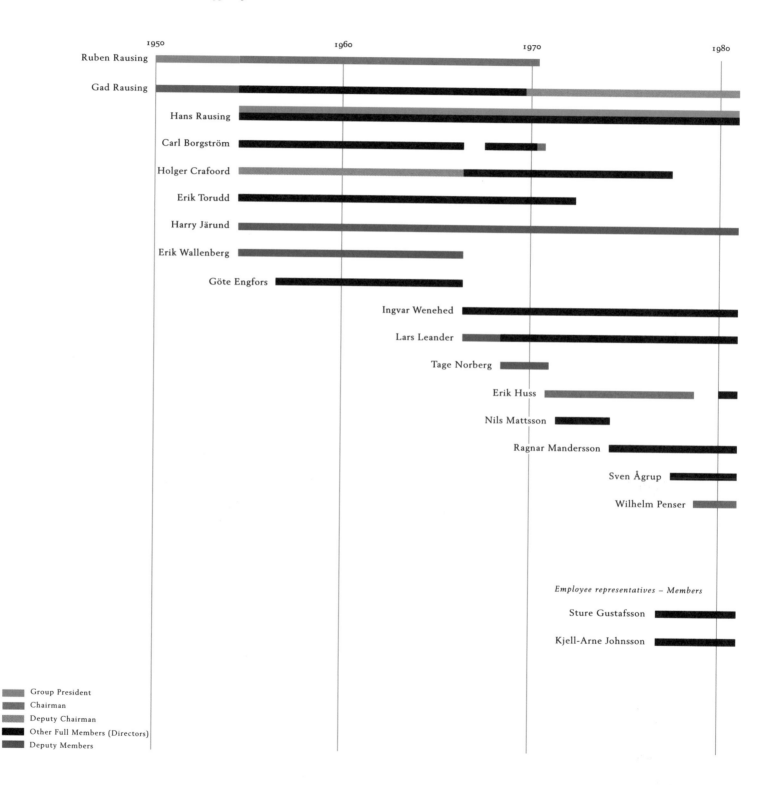

BOARD OF TETRA PAK 1950–1981

III

	Group President
	Chairman
	Deputy Chairman
	Other Full Members (Directors)
	Deputy Members

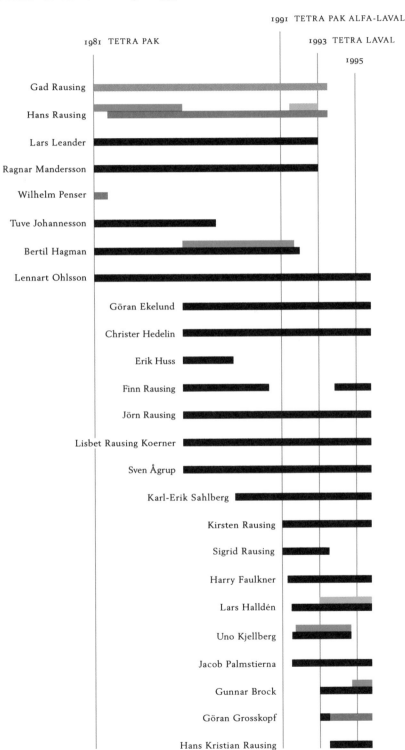

IV

For practical reasons, the presentation of the Directors on the Board of the Group has been divided into two periods, 1950–1981 and 1981–1995. As new organisational structures were introduced over the years, official designations changed. The present compilation refers to the chief Board of Tetra Pak up to June 1991, followed first by the Board of Tetra Pak Alfa-Laval until December 1992 and then by the Board of the Tetra Laval Group from January 1993 onwards.

FIGURES

V

There are many possible ways of telling a company's story. This book has assumed the comparatively easily digested mode of the narrative. Hence, the text has not been encumbered with a lot of figures.

However, the occasional reader might find readily comprehensible compilations of statistical data serviceable, which is why these simple charts have been provided. For many years, Cai Lewin and Stig Olofsson were the leading experts in this field, and both have been very helpful in this matter.

The charts, which refer to Tetra Pak activities only, supply a general picture of developments and constitute useful measurements of the Group's expansion.

Even so, it is impossible to present materials which will satisfy every wish. For example, there are no balance sheets and no data on profits and losses, capital structures, dividends, investments, and so on. As Tetra Pak was – and the entire Tetra Laval Group remains – privately owned, these kinds of figures are not usually published in consolidated form.

In addition, the reader will remember that this publication does not claim to present a financial analysis of the company.

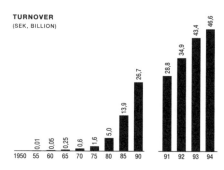

TURNOVER
(SEK, BILLION)

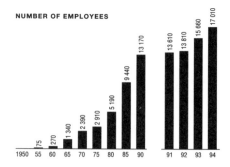

NUMBER OF EMPLOYEES

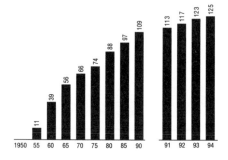

NUMBER OF MARKETS

MARKETING COMPANIES

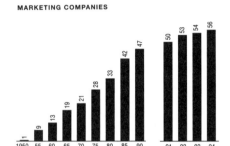

1950	55	60	65	70	75	80	85	90		91	92	93	94
1	9	13	19	21	28	33	42	47		50	53	54	56

FACTORIES FOR PACKAGING MATERIALS

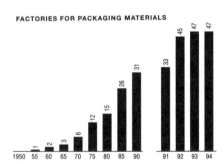

1950	55	60	65	70	75	80	85	90		91	92	93	94
	1	2	3	6	12	15	26	31		33	45	47	47

NUMBER OF INSTALLED PACKAGING MACHINES

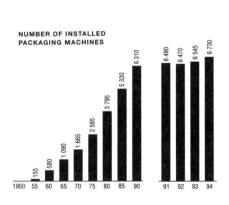

1950	55	60	65	70	75	80	85	90		91	92	93	94
	155	580	1 090	1 665	2 565	3 795	5 330	6 310		6 480	6 470	6 545	6 730

RAW MATERIALS
(TONS, THOUSAND)

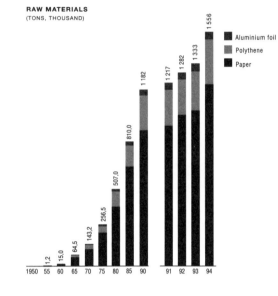

- Aluminium foil
- Polythene
- Paper

1950	55	60	65	70	75	80	85	90		91	92	93	94
1,2	15,0	64,5	143,2	256,5	507,0	810,0	1 182			1 217	1 282	1 333	1 556

TYPES OF PACKAGE
(UNITS, BILLION)

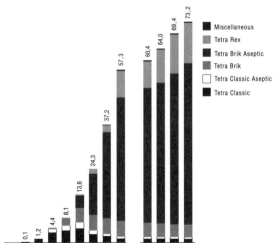

- Miscellaneous
- Tetra Rex
- Tetra Brik Aseptic
- Tetra Brik
- Tetra Classic Aseptic
- Tetra Classic

1950	55	60	65	70	75	80	85	90		91	92	93	94
0,1	1,2	4,4	8,1	13,6	24,3	37,2	57,3			60,4	64,0	69,4	73,2

PACKAGED PRODUCTS
(UNITS, BILLION)

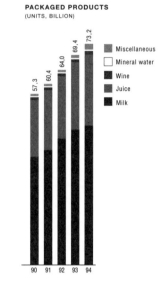

- Miscellaneous
- Mineral water
- Wine
- Juice
- Milk

90	91	92	93	94
57,3	60,4	64,0	69,4	73,2

REGIONS OF SALE
(UNITS, BILLION)

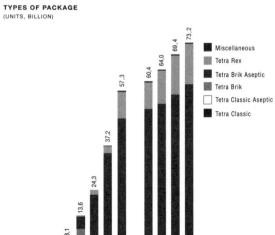

- North, Central and South America
- Far East/Oceania
- Middle East, Central Asia, and Africa
- Europe

90	91	92	93	94
57,3	60,4	64,0	69,4	73,2

VI

The story told in this book has not adhered to a strict chronological outline; it was planned around themes rather than dates. In order to make developments easier to follow from year to year, some of the most important milestones in the company's history are presented below. It was necessary to make a selection, and the years and events referred to were chosen as being the ones most likely to interest the reader. In most cases, corresponding references are found in the current text or in the descriptions that accompany the pictorial material.

VII

1895

The year of Ruben Rausing's birth in the parish of Raus, south of Helsingborg on the west coast of southern Sweden.

1929

Creation of the packaging company Åkerlund & Rausing. Manufacturing located in Malmö for the first ten years.

1939

The company leaves Malmö and moves to newly-built premises in Lund, in the southern industrial area of that city.

1944

Years of trying to develop a milk package lead to the invention of the tetrahedron for this purpose. Decision made to proceed with the tetrahedron. First patent application in March. The principle of continuous filling is fixed.

1945

Several different machine designs are tested as experimental ideas. At the same time, systematic work begins on developing suitable packaging material.

1946

An initial experimental machine for the continuous manufacture of tetrahedron packages is demonstrated in September. The machine concept is subjected to further development, and the search for suitable packaging material continues.

1950

The new project has assumed a clearer outline. In June it receives its name, Tetra Pak. Somewhat later, in December, the limited company Tetra Pak is registered.

1951

Decision made to register the brand name of Tetra Pak in some 60 countries. First-ever public demonstration of the machine system at a press conference in Lund on 18 May. Still no appropriate packaging material; development work intensified.

1952

In December, the first machine for one-decilitre cream packages starts operation in the Lund Dairy Association.

1953

The Stockholm Milk Centre installs its first machine, also intended for one-decilitre cream. Polythene introduced for the coating of packaging material.

1954

Hans Rausing appointed Managing Director and Gad Rausing Deputy M.D. of the company. A new machine model for half-litre packages is completed. Deliveries made to the Swedish market. The first machine outside Sweden is installed in Germany, and export orders are recorded, to France among other countries.

1955

Satisfactory solutions to the problems with materials gradually established. Polythene has replaced other materials, and extruder laminating has been introduced.

1956

Tetra Pak's Lund plant completed; operations move away from Åkerlund & Rausing. Manufacturing of materials begins under the company's own roof. The office is located within the factory. Development work begins on the creation of an aseptic, bacteria-free, package.

1957

The manufacture of machine models for several new package sizes has begun. The first one-litre machine is installed in Linköping.

1958

The project of developing a sterile system for the packaging of long-life milk takes shape in earnest. Systematic experiments on the chemical-thermal sterilisation of the paper flow begin. Plain office premises are erected beside the factory building in Lund. The packaging of still drinks and fruit juices assumes larger dimensions.

1959

An aseptic prototype machine is completed. The first contract is signed with the Soviet Union regarding the delivery of tetrahedron machines for pasteurised milk. Licence agreements for the manufacture of Tetra Pak paper exist in eight countries. The number of packages sold during the current year passes the 1000-million mark. Development work on a machine for square packages begins.

1960

Manufacturing capacity in Lund extended to meet increasing demands. Larger office premises completed.

1961

The aseptic tetrahedron system presented at a press conference in Switzerland. Internal evaluation of an experimental machine for rectangular packages begins. Delivery of the first order to the Soviet Union effected; it comprises some ten tetrahedron machines and a line for the manufacturing of materials.

1962

The aseptic package evaluated commercially; the trial market is Berne in Switzerland. Co-operation introduced with Milliken Corporation regarding the marketing of Tetra Pak in the United States. Milliken erects a conversion plant for Tetra Pak materials.

1963

World première of the Tetra Brik, first in Motala, then in Stockholm. Factory premises and offices extended in Lund. Serial deliveries of aseptic machines to the European market begin.

1964

A faster Tetra Brik machine is completed; it works on the principle of continuous filling. Aseptic tetrahedron machines installed outside Europe.

1965

Tetra Pak's first factory on foreign soil starts in Rubiera, Italy. Åkerlund & Rausing sold to Svenska Tändsticks Aktiebolaget (later Swedish Match). The deal supplies capital for the further expansion of Tetra Pak.

1966

The Tetra Rex packaging system is introduced in Sweden, on the basis of a licence agreement with interested parties in the U.S.

1967

Premières for the Tetra Brik outside Sweden, in Europe and Japan. Manufacture of Tetra Rex cartons begins in Lund.

1968

The Rigello bottle for carbonated drinks presented to international journals. Field tests with a prototype machine of the Tetra Brik Aseptic model in Switzerland. The Soviet Union confirms a big order for aseptic tetrahedron machines and equipment for the local manufacture of materials.

1969

Serial deliveries of Tetra Brik Aseptic begin, chiefly to the European market. A factory for the manufacture of materials is completed in Limburg, Germany. The mug package Tetra Cup, made of expanded polystyrene, is tested in the market.

1971

Packaging materials "made in France" begin to be delivered from the Dijon plant. The Gotemba factory in Japan completed. Total production in the Group exceeds 10,000 million packages.

1972

Tetra Pak participates in the Peking Trade Fair in the People's Republic of China. First contract for Tetra Brik machines with the Soviet dairy industry.

1973

Second Italian factory ready to start operations in Latina, south of Rome.

1974

Juice concentrate in two-decilitre Tetra Brik packages is a great success.

1975

The Romont plant in Switzerland goes into production.

1976

The Tetra King, made of expanded polystyrene, field-tested in Sweden. Large delivery of Tetra Brik machines to one of the Moscow dairies.

1977

Brik Pak Inc. registered in the U.S., and the rectangular package is launched in the American market.

1978

A new method presented for the manufacture of lactose-reduced milk. In Europe, Tetra King machines are installed for the packaging of cream in Germany and table wine in France.

1979

The first Tetra Brik Aseptic machine delivered to China.

1980

A new, higher-performing generation of aseptic Tetra Brik machines begins to be delivered. Total Group production of packages: some 25,000 million units.

1981

Head office set up in Lausanne, Switzerland; Group executive staff move there. The Food and Drug Administration (FDA) approves the aseptic Tetra Brik system for the American market. Two new factories start production, in Berlin and in Seishin, Japan.

1983

Dr Ruben Rausing dies, aged 88. The new office building in Lausanne is opened. The Rigello project is discontinued.

1984

A factory in Denton, Texas, becomes Tetra Pak's first own manufacturing unit in the U.S.

1985

Bertil Hagman appointed Group President, succeeding Hans Rausing who remains the Group Chairman of the Board.

1986

The new Tetra Top packaging system, evaluated in Belgium, is introduced in Spain.

1987

A licence factory for the manufacture of materials is opened in Beijing, PRC. Tetra Pak is now present in 100 markets all over the world. Table wine in the Tetra Brik is a notable success, especially in the Argentine market.

1988

A joint-venture agreement concerning the manufacture of materials is signed in the Ukraine.

1989

Total annual output exceeds 50,000 million packages.

1990

Tetra Pak participates in a Russo-Brazilian project for juice manufacturing in Lipetsk, Russia. A co-operation agreement is signed regarding the installation of packaging machines and the setting-up of a service station and training centre in Podolsk, near Moscow.

1991

Tetra Pak acquires Alfa-Laval; the deal is concluded in August. Hans Rausing steps in again as President of the new Tetra Pak Alfa-Laval Group while maintaining the position of Group Chairman. Uno Kjellberg appointed President of the Tetra Pak Group. A second materials factory is opened in Foshan, China.

1992

The Group head office is moved to Lund. At the same time, Tetra Pak activities are divided into three operative units with regional head offices in Lausanne, Atlanta, and Singapore. For the first time, Tetra Pak and Alfa-Laval conduct a joint exhibition of their products and services at the DLG exhibition in Frankfurt. Theme: "Creating the Future". In Kiev, Ukraine, and Kuban, Russia, factories are taken into operation for the manufacture of Tetra Pak materials.

1993

The new Tetra Laval Group is established, comprising four industrial components: Tetra Pak; Tetra Laval Food; Alfa Laval; and Alfa Laval Agri. A fifth unit, Tetra Laval Holdings & Finance, serves as an over-arching finance company. Hans and Gad Rausing leave the Group Board. Göran Grosskopf appointed Chairman.

1994

Yet another regional head office is set up in Istanbul. Gunnar Brock appointed President of the Tetra Pak Group. Annual production approaches 75,000 million packages.

1995

Jubilee year due to the centenary of Dr Ruben Rausing's birth.

A FINAL WORD

Many people have lent valuable assistance during the writing of this company history. Unable to list all their names, I wish to express my warm gratitude to every one of them here. Their powerful commitment ensured that collaborative efforts were enjoyable as well as invigorating.

However, a few people must be mentioned by name. My former colleague and co-worker Eric Rasmusson kept up with the developing project with much helpful interest, and several sections rely on materials supplied by him.

My assistant for many years, Helena Myhrman, was a tower of cohesive strength. She undertook the work of documentation and study of original sources with impeccable judgement and unfailing stamina. In addition, she contributed perceptive textual criticism. More of the latter was provided by Pia Ohlsson, whose collaborative efforts included the efficient administration of contacts with translators as well as production planning. Sigvard Westergren invested much labour in the compilation of internal pictorial materials, ably and willingly aided by Britt Kristensson. Berit Schannong supplied practical assistance, too.

My wife Annik was an invaluable partner in numerous discussions, keen, sensitive, observant, and encouraging – thanks!

In the capacity of external adviser, Prof. Ulf Ohlsson, Professor of Economic History at the University of Gothenburg, provided very helpful points of view.

Finally – and above all – I wish to thank all members of the Rausing family for entrusting me with the responsibility for the task which has now been completed. It has brought me great pleasure.

X

LARS LEANDER

For a couple of years, work on collecting and processing source materials deemed to be of significance for posterity's view of Tetra Pak has been in progress. No selective filing activities geared to such a purpose had been undertaken before.

Minutes from board meetings and other documents of fundamental interest have constituted an important source. The materials perused extend from 1946 to the present.

Interviews were made with a number of key persons. Results in the form of recapitulatory notes exist, as well as, in a few cases, video-taped conversations. Many of the people who worked for Tetra Pak during the pioneering years – marketing staff, technicians, and others – have also contributed written statements which are of value in the context of company history.

Local subsidiaries were asked to supply brief compilations of historical data as well as summary descriptions of conditions in each market.

Due to the general character of this publication, only a small proportion of the available information appears in print. Other factual materials, comprising a wealth of interesting details, have been stored for future use.

It seemed essential to document the development of Tetra Pak while there was still time. A memorable motto inscribed by the entrance to the Nordic Museum in Stockholm offers an appropriate conclusion to these remarks:

"A day may come when no gold of ours will suffice to acquire a living image of days gone by."

XI

Idea and text
Lars Leander

Cover
C-O Hultén

Production
Tecknargården, Landskrona, Sweden

Graphic design
Tony Manhart

Translation
Marianne Thormählen

Language consultant
John Condliffe

Artwork
Stefan Risberg

Illustrations
Anders Adolvsson, Tilde Manhart

Editors – photographic material
Jytte Rigby, Sigvard Westergren (material on file)

Sources of photographic material
AIR/CURCHOD, Arbetet Nyheterna, Arla, Bildhuset, Billedhuset,
Ulf Cronberg, Hagbloms Foto, T Hartman, IBL, IMS Bildbyrå,
Gerry Johansson, KW Gullers/The Nordic Museum, Ola Lager,
Kenneth M Linton, G Mangold/Bildagentur Anne Hamann,
The Museum of Cultural History in Lund, MIRA Bildarkiv,
Ingrid Morejohn/Bildbruket Picture Works, NASA/Hasselblad,
Nestec SA, Leif O Pehrson, Pressens Bild, private archives of
the Rausing family, Red Box SA, Reportagebild, Råå museum,
the picture library of the Swedish Employers' Confederation (SAF),
Scandia Photopress, Stellan Stebe, Lars Strandberg, Studio Gullers,
Studio Owe Hallin, Studio Toivo Steen, The Swedish Broadcasting
Corporation Picture Library (Sveriges Television Bildarkivet), Tessa
Traeger Studio, Tetra Pak, Elisabeth Zeilon and Helena Åkesson

Printer
Fälths Tryckeri, Värnamo, Sweden

Bookbinder
Sambok, Farsta, Sweden

Typefaces
Berling and Neue Helvetica

Paper
Scandia 2000, 150 g and Transparent, 73 g

XII